P9-BYA-079

Expert Advice From The Home Depot®

Decorating Projects 1-2-3®

Decorating Projects 1-2-3®
Editor: Paula Marshall
Contributing Editor: Catherine M. Staub, Lexicon Consulting, Inc.
Contributing Associate Editor: Julie Collins, Lexicon Consulting, Inc.,
Contributing Project Designers: Sue Banker, Wade Scherrer
Contributing Stylists: Cathy Kramer, Cathy Long
Contributing Assistants: Randall Noblet, Holly Reynolds, Emma Sarran, Lexicon Consulting, Inc.
Contributing Graphic Designer: Shelton Design Studios
Copy Chief: Terri Fredrickson
Publishing Operations Manager: Karen Schirm
Senior Editor, Asset and Information Manager: Phillip Morgan
Edit and Design Coordinator: Mary Lee Gavin
Editorial and Design Assistant: Renee E. McAtee
Book Production Managers: Pam Kvitne, Marjorie J. Schenkelberg, Rick von Holdt, Mark Weaver
Contributing Copy Editor: Kelly Roberson
Contributing Proofreaders: Heidi Johnson, Sue Fetters, Nancy Ruhling
Contributing Indexer: Stephanie Reymann

Meredith® Books
Executive Director, Editorial: Gregory H. Kayko
Executive Director, Design: Matt Strelecki
Managing Editor: Amy Tincher-Durik
Executive Editor/Group Manager: Benjamin W. Allen
Senior Associate Design Director: Tom Wegner
Marketing Product Manager: Brent Wiersma
National Marketing Manager—Home Depot: Suzy Johnson

Publisher and Editor in Chief: James D. Blume
Editorial Director: Linda Raglan Cunningham
Executive Director, New Business Development: Todd M. Davis
Director, Sales—Home Depot: Robb Morris
Executive Director, Sales: Ken Zagor
Director, Operations: George A. Susral
Director, Production: Douglas M. Johnston
Director, Marketing: Amy Nichols
Business Director: Jim Leonard
Vice President and General Manager: Douglas J. Guendel

Meredith Publishing Group
President: Jack Griffin
Executive Vice President: Karla Jeffries

Meredith Corporation
Chairman of the Board: William T. Kerr
President and Chief Executive Officer: Stephen M. Lacy
In Memoriam: E.T. Meredith III (1933–2003)

The Home Depot®
Marketing Manager: Tom Sattler

First Edition.

Printed in the United States of America.
Library of Congress Control Number: 2006930018
ISBN-13: 978-0-696-23042-4

Note to the Reader: Due to differing conditions, tools and individual skills, Meredith Corporation and The Home Depot® assume no responsibility for any damages, injuries suffered, or losses incurred as a result of following the information published in this book. Before beginning any project, review the instructions carefully, and, if any doubts or questions remain, consult local experts or authorities. Because codes and regulations vary greatly, you should always check with authorities to ensure that your project complies with all applicable local codes and regulations. Always read and observe all of the safety precautions provided by any tool or equipment manufacturer, and follow all accepted safety procedures.

We are dedicated to providing inspiring, accurate and helpful do-it-yourself information. We welcome your comments about improving this book and ideas for other books we might offer to home improvement enthusiasts.

Contact us by any of these methods:
Leave a voice message at: 800/678-2093
Write to: Meredith Books, Home Depot Books
1716 Locust St.
Des Moines, IA 50309-3023
Send e-mail to: hi123@mdp.com.

How to use this book

his book begins with **Sense of Style**, an introduction to design principles, understanding color, and popular decorating styles. Most interior designs are eclectic—a mixture of styles and themes that reflect and express personal taste. To make smart choices about how decorative elements work together, you need to know a little about the common styles. We break the first chapter into explanations of several of the most popular decorating styles—traditional, country, contemporary, casual, eclectic, Victorian, and world influence—and illustrate recent trends with each style.

Color is key to your home's personality, and combining new colors will make your home come alive. This chapter also defines terms you'll need to know and offers information for how to use the color wheel to select and combine colors.

Understanding color and the essence of home interior style will give you a starting point, as well as ideas about what decorating direction to go. Throughout the book you'll find style-specific photographs that will inspire you and spark your thinking as you develop your plans.

Tool Time

The right tools and materials make all the difference for any project. Though a variety of unique tools and materials are required for each project in the book, the **Tools and Materials** chapter introduces several handy tools for a basic home tool kit. You'll also find step-by-step instructions for the most common miter and coping techniques to install trimwork and complete other wood projects.

Decorative Projects

Once you have a good idea of where you're going, it's time to get started with specific projects. The rest of the book gives you inspiration and ideas with beautiful and richly detailed photographs and it provides clear and easy-to-follow step-by-step instructions to make decorating projects a reality. You'll also find all the necessary project materials in Stuff You'll Need. In addition to all the step-by-step instructions the pages are filled with tips from the experts that will help you get the projects right the first time. Read through the material list, all of the instructions, plus the tips before beginning any project. Gather all of the tools and materials you'll need and clear enough space to work. Step-by-step projects are divided into the following chapters:

Walls, Ceilings, and Floors provides the foundation for every room. This chapter has your home covered from top to bottom. Projects range from installing a ceiling medallion to adding molding and trim to stenciling wood floors and laying floor tiles.

Windows and Doors shows you how to put up blinds and shutters, select and install window coverings, and install trim and molding.

Lighting plays an integral role in decorating from its effect on color to how lamps accessorize a room. Successful room lighting begins with a lighting plan. Then learn how to embellish a chandelier, install trapeze lights, and make a custom table lamp.

Furnishings helps you make your furniture compliment the rest of the room. It includes directions for painted and stained finishes, customizing existing furnishings such as cabinets and bookcases, and building custom pieces such as display shelves and a side table.

Decorating Projects 1-2-3®
Table of contents

Chapter 1
Sense of Style 6

Chapter 2
Tools and Materials 26

Chapter 3
Walls, Ceilings, and Floors 34

Chapter 4 Windows and Doors 118

Chapter 5 lighting 134

Chapter 6 Furnishings 150

Sense of style

You know it when you see it, either in other people's houses or in books and magazines: cohesive, appealing rooms with a stylish mix of furnishings, fabrics, colors, and accessories. Yet you may be unsure how to achieve a similar look in your home. To develop your own interior design scheme, you need to understand how to pull together all of the elements, including color and decorating styles.

Where to begin

Start by looking at the rooms featured in this chapter. They highlight many of the latest trends and interpretations of classic decorating styles including traditional, contemporary, and fresh country. Because decorating is highly personal, you'll also find design approaches such as eclectic and casual that emphasize individual tastes and lifestyles. Thanks to a global economy, more design is influenced by travels and family heritage, so you'll also discover world design influence as well.

Chapter 1 highlights

Put it all together

Most of this book is devoted to step-by-step instructions for decorative projects to enhance your home. This chapter illustrates how a series of potential projects such as installing trimwork, embellishing a chandelier, arranging artwork, and lighting a room combine to create a beautiful finished space. As you appreciate the finished rooms highlighted in this chapter, also notice the individual elements that combine to create a pleasing decorating scheme.

Beginning the design process

A wise interior designer once said there are three rules for decorating a home. It's just that nobody is quite sure what they are. He was joking of course, but it's easy to understand when you consider the array of decorating and design choices and volumes of information available. How do you bring together home decorating elements to truly express and reflect your personality? How do you decide on the right color for the dining room walls, the right molding and trim for the study, the curtains for the windows in the bedroom, or the perfect floor covering in your living room? After you've put all the pieces together, how can you be sure you'll like living in what you've worked so hard to create?

By asking yourself these questions, you're doing what designers or decorators do as they begin to formulate a plan for a client. Decorating pros know following a rigid set of rules doesn't work; the key lies combining decorative elements and styles best suited for the setting and the homeowner's preferences.

Most decorating schemes are a mix of styles. Few of us are interested in decorating our homes strictly according to the dictates of a particular look. Yet it's still important to know the basic elements of each style—as well as the keys to selecting appropriate color—so you can begin creating a design that reflects your personal taste and makes good use of the objects you love.

Intensity and style

Intense hues are found in every style. Strong colors on Colonial walls define spaces from room to room. Contemporary walls are often punched up with bursts of full-intensity primary colors. Complex colors and combinations tend to be more visually interesting, demanding focus. Muted hues create more neutral backgrounds and draw attention to accessories, furniture, and window treatments. The goal is to choose colors that harmonize and complement the design elements in the room.

Creating a design strategy that works

Homes are creative works in progress that rarely come together overnight. Although decorating is, above all else, an exercise in creativity, it pays to follow a few key steps as you begin your decorating journey.

1. Familiarize yourself with your room. Note what's working and what's not and determine which architectural features, furnishings, and artwork you want to emphasize and which elements you would rather camouflage or get rid of.

2. Consider color and pattern. The decorating process often begins with color, yet the sheer number of hues available and the variety of options for selecting the right scheme can be daunting. You may choose to pull a color from patterned upholstery, a rug, or a large piece of artwork that's already in your space. Or you may decide to decorate with favorite colors that appear in other areas of your life, such as your wardrobe. Then again you may wish to follow the tried-and-true rules of the color wheel to create the perfect combinations. Regardless of how you come to your color conclusions, remember the key is to follow your personal style. Turn the page for more help with choosing color.

3. Identify a style or theme. You need not stay within the rigid constraints of a specific period style, such as Colonial or Victorian, or a sense of location, such as Southwestern or Asian. But identifying the overarching theme for your spaces early on—whether they're country, traditional, contemporary, or something in between—ensures a unity within your design scheme.

▲ Each element in this living room—from the comfortably upholstered furnishings to the painted walls—contributes to its soft modern design.

▲ A pale wash of colors and fabrics creates a relaxed design scheme ideal for making guests feel at home.

▲ Texture plays a role in decorating. Here sleek metal teams with smooth fabric, textured flooring, and rough beams for visual interest.

Understanding color

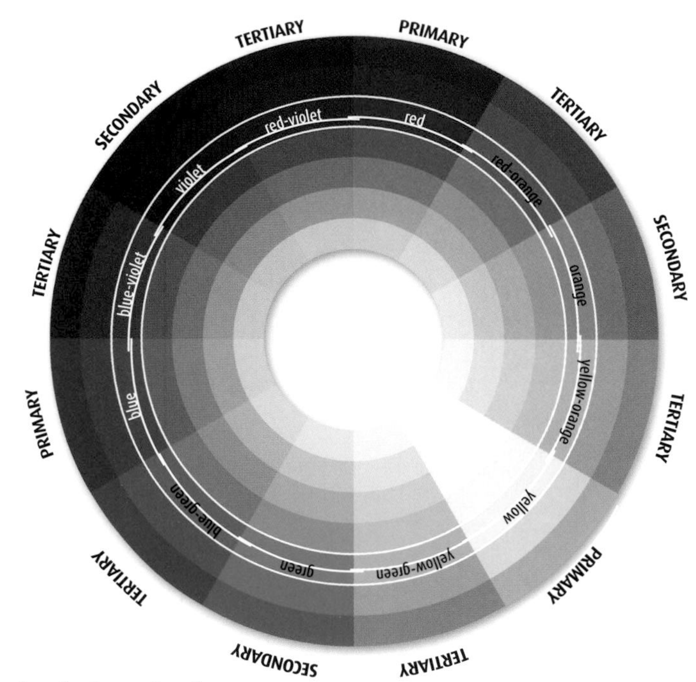

A color wheel organizes the visible spectrum of colors and shows the relationships between them.

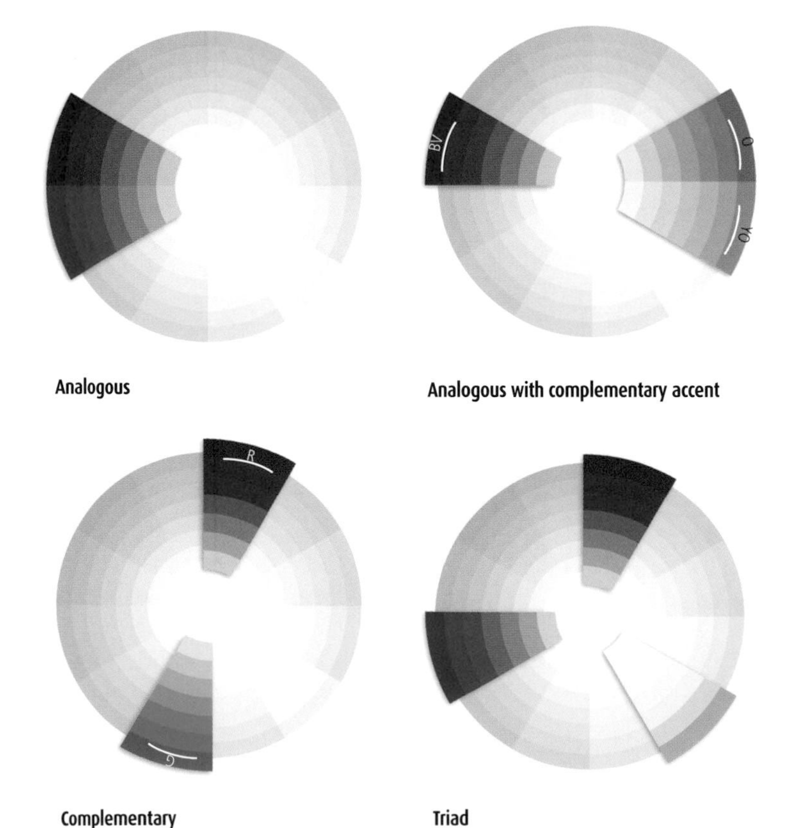

Analogous

Analogous with complementary accent

Complementary

Triad

Whether you're adventurous and ready to splash the walls with bold colors or you prefer the low-risk look of neutral tones, the basics of selecting colors for walls, furnishings, and accessories are the same. Begin by finding the best color scheme for your tastes, your rooms, and your life.

Select colors that appeal to you. What colors catch your eye when you are shopping, selecting clothing from your closet, or looking at decorating magazines? Chances are your favorite colors are also the ones you're most comfortable with, which means they're great options for your home. Of course just because you wear a lot of blue doesn't mean you can slap a coat of bright blue paint on the wall. But once you've identified a favorite color, you can begin building color schemes and finding compatible accents.

Consider mood. Some palettes infuse spaces and, by extension, their occupants with energy. Others calm or soothe. Why? Different colors look differently—active, passive, or neutral—and create varying responses in people. On the warm side of the color wheel, active colors such as yellow, red, and orange tend to wake up a room and create an inspiring venue full of energy, which may be ideal for offices or kitchens. Passive, or cool, colors include blue, green, and purple. Ideal for bedrooms or creative retreats, these colors create a calming backdrop. Neutral colors, such as browns, beiges, grays, taupes, whites, and blacks, neither energize nor pacify. They're terrific for bringing rooms together, creating a natural palette that mimics hues found in nature, or toning down other colors.

Change your room. Every room has certain features that can't be overlooked, from wood flooring to wainscoting on the walls and even the size of the room. Rather than working against these features, consider how you can work with and even enhance them with color. For instance cool colors tend to recede visually, which helps small spaces seem larger, while warmer colors seem to make a large room appear warmer and more intimate. Use white paint on a ceiling to increase the impression of height or on architectural details such as elaborate trimwork to make them pop.

Look beyond paint. Remember that a room's color scheme involves more than the paint on the walls. The shades and patterns of rugs, fabrics, furnishings, artwork, and accessories impact whether your color scheme comes off as masterfully integrated or a messy combination of disparate elements. Most importantly make certain must-have items such as furnishings support the color scheme. Complementary accessories can come later, once the basics are in place.

▲ **Bright, tropical-inspired colors throughout this home are offset with crisp white trim and natural-stained wood floors.**

Use the color wheel

Painting a room white is easy. But so is tackling a more ambitious color scheme—once you understand how colors work together. The color wheel, opposite, organizes colors to help you make choices. The **primary** colors—red, blue, and yellow—are always the same distance apart and in the same order on the wheel. Mix two primary colors to create a **secondary** color—red and yellow make orange; blue and red create violet. **Tertiary** colors occur when a primary color is combined with any secondary color adjacent to it on the wheel—red and violet make red-violet; green and yellow make yellow-green.

How do you pick a color scheme? By combining colors on the wheel. Start with your favorite color—say it's blue—and build possible schemes around it. The basic choice is various shades and tints of blue—a **monochromatic** color scheme. Or you can combine blue with its opposite on the wheel—orange—for a **complementary** scheme. When you bring the other primary colors into the scheme, you create a **triad**, because all three are equidistant from each other. Blue also goes well with blue-violet and blue-green, the **analogous** colors on either side of it. Add a color from the opposite side, such as orange, and you have a **complementary** accent.

Understanding color *(continued)*

▲ **This well-dressed room features a neutral palette enhanced with subtle touches of red in the throw, display box, and area rug.**

Hue, tone, and intensity

When designers begin to pick a color scheme, they consider three color variables—hue, tone, and intensity. Subtle changes in one or more of these variables create big impact throughout a room.

Hue. A simple way to describe color is hue. The three primary hues of red, yellow, and blue are enhanced by the secondary hues of green, orange, and violet. These six hues can be mixed to produce an infinite number of tertiary shades.

Tone. A tint or shade of a color is commonly referred to as its tone. Decorating with colors within the same tonal range is common. Because colors that appear wildly different may have the same tone, tonal unity isn't boring—it allows you to be adventurous. As with any color rule, however, remember that too much may be bad. If the tone in a room is too much the same, the overall effect may be heavy or bland.

Intensity. Intensity refers to the saturation of a color and specifies clearness or brightness. Pure, primary hues are neutralized or softened by adding white; one or more secondary hues can be added to heighten the effect. Add a darker hue to intensify color.

▲ A delicate variety of cool green colors combines in this soothing bedroom. Bright white and dark wood accents ensure the scheme is lively.

Decorating styles

Well-decorated rooms don't necessarily fit into a strict interpretation of style—they are individual and eclectic, combining the best styles, periods, patterns, and colors to create a look that's right for an individual or family's changing tastes and lifestyle. Yet decorating elements—everything from wall treatments to floor coverings, furniture to windows—often are categorized and defined to a large degree by a specific style, locale, or era. Rather than focusing on strict period re-creations, this chapter showcases current stylish interpretations and trends that are common among decorating professionals and homeowners. Draw on them for inspiration and ideas, using them as a resource and starting point. The only rule: Don't be bound to a certain style at the expense of your personal vision. Be open. Be flexible. Remember that your distinctive look constantly will evolve.

New traditional

Traditional style is a decorator's elegant catchall, largely referencing timeless design influenced by the furnishings and accessories of the 18th and 19th centuries. Traditional style is a link with the past that blends popular trends, adjusting and softening highly decorative and elaborately visual concepts to create comfortable and timeless interior designs. The aim is not to reproduce historic looks but to rethink or reinvent those ideals for the modern home.

Architectural details. Traditional-style rooms often are airy and open, with high ceilings and large windows that, although heavily curtained, admit lots of light. Extensive use of wood moldings and decorative trim is common, and such woodwork is often painted to match walls and ceilings.

Window treatments. Elegant and complex window treatments—such as valances and layered swags—are still common, but updated simple and subdued window fabric panels allow other features in the room to take center stage.

Furnishings and fabrics. Traditional furniture features interesting shapes, such as camelback and rolled-arm sofas and chairs with turned legs. Comfortably upholstered furniture may boast rich-looking patterned fabrics.

Color. New Traditional style is less heavy-handed than past interpretations. This is particularly true in regard to color, which appears lighter. Most New Traditional designs avoid an overabundance of the previously popular patterned wallpapers and painted mural backgrounds and are based more on personal taste than rigid style constraints.

Accessories. Objects such as paintings, patterned rugs, and collections complete a new traditional room.

Mastering the floor plan

Successfully arranging a room involves determining how your furnishings and accessories work together and relate in your overall space. The easiest way to begin is to **find a focal point**—it's the cornerstone of your arrangement. A fireplace or spectacular view may be all you need. In rooms without a natural focus, group furnishings around a painting, artfully displayed collectibles, or a tall piece of furniture, such as a bookshelf or armoire. Consider whether you need to **add or remove furnishings**. You may decide that deleting some pieces opens up floor space. Likewise adding more furniture and dividing the space into activity centers may make a room more livable. To customize your space allow yourself to **bend the rules**. A sofa need not be flanked by end tables, and a dining table can be positioned off-center in the room. Play with floor plans to find the arrangement that's most comfortable and convenient for you.

▶ **Painted wood moldings and decorative trim match the color scheme of this luxurious traditional bedroom. Gold tones in the rich bed linens, window treatments, and upholstery unite the space.**

◀ Unlike in the past, when large windows were heavily curtained, this room's spacious versions are left unadorned to allow in plenty of natural light. Floor-to-ceiling bookshelves offer display space for books and collectibles behind an arrangement of furnishings outfitted in a subdued mix of fabrics and patterns.

▼ Warm beige-painted walls and neutral-tone window treatments provide a backdrop for a subdued living room. The focal point fireplace boasts a custom-made mantel with the intricate detailing often found in traditional spaces. Red antique Chinese lacquerware on the mantel and gold-framed paintings add decorative touches to the space.

Fresh country

Fresh country style has evolved from the very rustic furniture and folk art of Early American style to a broader interpretation of country that's more relaxed, comfortable, and easy to live with. The touchstone of fresh country is simplicity and practicality—collections are still pivotal to country style, but rooms boast a cleaner, simpler aesthetic. Often a decorating scheme in a fresh country room works around a favorite fabric, furnishing, or collection.

Architectural details. Pale, honey-tone woods are popular for floors, trimwork, and furnishings. Wainscoting and chair rails are common, and moldings have a simple profile.

Furnishings and fabrics. Select comfortable major furnishings to anchor a room—avoid pieces that are overly fragile. Whitewashed, white, and beige furnishings with finishes that are worn or aged to create a timeworn look create a simple foundation for Fresh Country spaces. Fabrics and upholstery are often cotton, although vintage fabrics may be used to add character.

Accessories. Displaying treasures is key in fresh country decorating—but avoid going overboard. Let efficiency generate good decorating ideas by hanging braided garlic from the ceiling, lining china along a plate rail, or leaving cupboards open to display pottery or bowls. Look for collectibles that can be used daily rather than stored away.

Variations. A more traditional interpretation of country style still has a place. Floors may be bare wide-plank wood or stone. Upholstered pieces are limited to a sofa and a few chairs, and functional pieces such as baskets are typical accessories. For a more rustic look, glean inspiration from the countryside by incorporating elements created from twigs, sticks, barn boards, and logs. Or emulate cottage style by visiting flea markets, antiques shows, and tag sales for unique items. A soft color palette and a mix of fabrics with a variety of patterns add further cottage touches.

▲ **Sleek, functional appliances contrast with timeless country elements—including a grooved ceiling reminiscent of beaded board and an island fashioned from a mercantile cabinet topped with marble—in this fresh and spacious kitchen. Farmhouse touches, such as a wood floor and wicker chairs, add classic country flavor.**

▲ **Fresh country style pares rich antiques and collections to the bare essentials. In this space white-painted furniture creates a cottage feel and ties together adjoining rooms.**

▲ Once a strict period interpretation of American style, today's country designs value ease, comfort, and casualness. In this bedroom a handmade quilt adorns an antique bed that was bought, along with the nearby dresser, at an auction. Shutters on the lower half of the window serve as curtain substitutes.

Mixing in character

A few aged pieces found at antiques shops, flea markets, or even garage sales create unrivaled personality in your rooms. Whether you scout secondhand stores, online auctions, or local dealers for antiques, vintage handcrafted pieces, and quirky finds, **find a reputable dealer**. A piece is more valuable if it has a known maker and date, fine design, original hardware, and little or no damage or repairs. Be sure to **know the market**. It helps to have an idea of what you want—whether it's Shaker, Louis XV, or midcentury modern—before you go. Study up on history, construction, and recent auction and retail prices. If you find a piece you like, **check the condition**. Wood frames should be sound with no sign of structural damage. Wobbly legs, marred finishes, or worn upholstery cost money to fix, so factor repairs into the cost before you buy.

▲ This rustic country-style kitchen boasts 6-inch-wide pine boards on the floor and an old-style stove with a patent date of 1926. The antique blue-gray table beneath the window may be moved around the kitchen for extra workspace.

Contemporary

Contemporary style embraces several waves of interior design, including Art Nouveau and Art Deco, in which architects and designers pared away centuries' worth of accessories and ornamentation and created a functional minimalism. Today's contemporary spaces are no longer as stark and cold as the style dictated in the past, however; spaces are more personal, livable, and warm, although simplicity and clean lines still rule.

Architectural details. Materials and design elements in contemporary homes are unadorned. Molding may be absent along the floors and around doors and windows. Large windows feature plate glass without muntins to blur the line between indoors and out. Open floor plans call attention to architecture, emphasizing the relationship between rooms and between the home and the environment. Walls may stop short of the ceilings or make use of cutouts and skylights to alleviate boxed-in spaces.

Window treatments. Opt for sheer curtain panels or, if you dispense with curtains, add narrow horizontal blinds or wood slat blinds for privacy.

Furnishings. Furnishings provide sculptural value and utility and are often clean-lined, mixing leather and metals with light, tight-grained woods and soft accent pieces. Some homes draw on the high-tech look, with commercial fixtures and furniture and metal shelving. To soften contemporary rooms, mix friendly '50s-style furniture with even more modern pieces.

Color. Many contemporary rooms have neutral wall colorings and furniture, with selective use of bold color—such as a single painted wall or bright splashes of color in patterned rugs and accessories—thrown in for good measure. For even more soothing, simplistic spaces, quiet colors are used throughout.

Lighting. In contemporary settings lighting, such as small fixtures suspended from wires, is high-tech and concealed. Lighting may be tucked into the ceiling or hidden behind soffits; lamps are sleek and sculptural.

Accessories. Contemporary interiors are absent of clutter and typically serve as settings to highlight a few prized art or antique pieces. Minimal objects play a role in the overall look.

▲ **This modern take on contemporary design successfully bucks the rules with dark earth tones, substantial white-painted molding, and a multitude of lighting styles. Splashes of color in the painted end tables, the sleek shape of the bed, and the room's absence of clutter are more common contemporary attributes.**

Creating scale and balance

To obtain the right proportions, you'll have to work out furniture relationships and **choose and arrange pieces** so they appear compatible in scale. Start with your largest piece of furniture—usually the sofa. Then add other furnishings that visually fit around it. If the overall effect is still off, check your equilibrium. **Create formal symmetry** by placing objects that mirror each other on opposite sides of an imaginary line running down the middle of a space. The objects need not be identical, but if they're close in size and shape they'll look like a match. Or **try asymmetrical arrangements**, which distribute visual weight in an informally balanced way. For instance five smaller objects grouped on one side of a room may balance a single massive piece on the other.

▲ **Sculptural pendent lights, white walls, and smooth light-wood cabinetry keep this contemporary kitchen bright despite the minimal natural light. The dishware stacked on simple glass shelves is functional and decorative.**

▲ White walls showcase works of art in contemporary settings. With uncluttered walls tables and mantels act as neutral spaces for display.

Casual

Casual style, a relaxed approach to decorating, ensures rooms accommodate and welcome everyone from children and pets to weekend guests. Furnishings set against a backdrop of light wood and subdued tones are comfortable and made for relaxing. When it comes to decorating a casual space, nothing is overly fragile, and simplicity and comfort are key.

Window treatments. Outfit windows with shutters, blinds, or shades for light control. Simple fabric valances add decorative touches.

Fabrics and furnishings. Casual furnishings—often outfitted with washable slipcovers—are soft and comfortable. Durable fabrics on furniture and pillows, including cotton, linen, and soft leather, are usually textured rather than shiny. Furnishings and accessories that encourage relaxing—particularly ottomans and piles of pillows—are a must.

Color. Neutral colors such as tan, gray, beige, or off-white rule, but this doesn't mean casual spaces are boring. Soft pastels convey a peaceful feeling, while dark accent shades such as navy, rust, olive or forest green, wine, and cranberry add a punch of color.

Accessories. Collections of treasured or found items are common. Beach memorabilia, such as shells, sea glass, and sand, is popular. Other spaces may include antique tin, pottery, wood beads, or antique bottles. Artwork tends to focus on country or casual themes.

Adding texture

Although texture isn't as dramatic as bold color or lively pattern, it is a design element that makes the difference between a ho-hum room and one that is inviting and comfortable. An interplay of contrasting textures—weathered wood beside a fuzzy throw or wrought iron against smooth leather—delights the senses of sight and touch. Forget matching and **mix things up** by pairing opposite textures, such as a smooth glass-top table with rugged wooden chairs. Select textures to **set the mood** you want. Soft, fine patterns convey a romantic atmosphere, while rugged, hard surfaces may be more masculine. Floors and walls benefit from variances too, so **texture the background** by placing a shaggy rug on smooth hardwood or contrasting a rough stone wall with a shiny mirror.

▲ These sunny spaces are made for relaxing. Light wood floors, warm yellow walls, and white trim and wainscoting set the casual style of three adjoining spaces filled with a mix of durable slipcovered and wicker chairs and wooden tables.

▲ Bright white tones dominate this comfortable bedroom. A funky rice paper lampshade, pink throw pillows, and photographs suspended above the bed add personal style. Corralling personal belongings in baskets is a creative way of storing items out of sight.

▲ Collections of baskets, pottery, and glassware are displayed on freestanding and built-in shelves in this intimate dining area. The rustic table is perfect for eating family meals or creating kids' crafts.

Eclectic

Eclectic style is just as its name says—eclectic. Composed of elements drawn from various decorating influences and eras, eclectic rooms feature a combination of favorite furnishings and accessories that don't fit the confines of a specific style. These spaces are all about imagination and unexpected contrasts but are not completely random—an underlying theme helps pull a room or house together. Before you tackle this decorating style, be sure to decide what atmosphere you want to create (calm or energetic, sophisticated or hip) and look for a piece of art, a rug, or a furnishing to inspire the room.

Color. Create surefire cohesion in an eclectic space with color. Avoid white walls in favor of hues that can be repeated throughout the room. Pick a few colors and showcase them in a variety of items from fabrics and paint to art and accessories.

Fabrics and furnishings. Look for fabric and rug patterns to anchor your room. Introduce texture by including furnishings pulled from different periods, styles, and cultures. For variety combine furnishings constructed from several materials. Remember that rooms incorporating pieces from too many different styles may appear fragmented, so be sure to create some consistency in color, shape, or texture to pull the room together.

Accessories. Allow yourself to play with quirky accents and funky collections in an eclectic room. The key is not to go overboard. To ensure collections and displayed pieces aren't overwhelming, group similar items in odd numbers, avoid too many similar shapes, and try not to display everything at the same height.

▲ **The bright squares of color in this large area rug help bring seemingly disparate elements together, including a large red Asian armoire, a single striped pendent light, and brown sofa.**

▲ **Similar yet distinct woodtones combine in this dining room, where the table is situated directly below a sculptural chandelier. For visual variety the sideboard is topped with marble. The large contemporary painting adds color.**

▲ **Although the walls of this room are white, an assortment of patterns, woodtones, and textures ensures the space is far from mundane. Limiting the color palette pulls the look together. A seating area situated in front of a focal point fireplace includes a white wicker chair upholstered in pale plaid fabric and two elegant dark-wood chairs with animal-print upholstery. Potted plants and a variety of white sculptures add personality.**

Victorian

The Victorian Era was characterized by numerous styles and color schemes—many of which were done on a grand scale and accompanied by a plethora of embellishments and displayed objects. Although today's version of this style is toned down a bit from the past, it's still characterized by rich materials and tones and boasts a formality that other modern-day decorating styles lack.

Architectural details. During the Victorian Era large scale often ruled. In modern rooms this translates into coffered ceilings, ornate moldings, and carved, darkly stained woodwork. Floors and woodwork most often boast natural finishes with elaborate inlays.

Window treatments. Originally windows were elegantly dressed in layers of draperies. For a subdued appearance try lace curtains, sheers, or scarves.

Furnishings and fabrics. When used selectively rich brocades and velvets on furniture, walls, and window dressings are elegant reminders of a time when excess was everything. Lace and fringe often complement Victorian furnishings, which are often formal pieces with rigidly tall chair backs and ornate carvings.

Accessories. The past's heavy ornamentation has been toned down, but Victorian rooms still incorporate knickknacks. Paintings with romantic themes, photographs, and mirrors often are displayed in ornate, heavily embellished frames.

▲ **The rich patterns of this room's window treatments, upholstery, and rug are characteristic of Victorian styling. Ornate gold frames—fitting with the warm color scheme—accompany traditional paintings on the walls.**

Adding accessories

Imagine a room without accessories—no tabletop treasures or books to explore, no art directing your eye to the walls. It doesn't feel right, does it? Accessories infuse a room with personality, but the key to decorating with them lies in ensuring the perfect balance. **Find a focal point** such as a mantel, built-in bookcase, or empty wall on which to begin adding personal touches. As you move on to adding accessories to other parts of the room, **apply the tenets of scale and visual weight** to everything from tabletop and shelf vignettes to the room as a whole. Remember that you need not accessorize every surface—**vary the pace** by mixing uncluttered zones with high-drama areas. Most importantly **know when to stop**. Rather than displaying everything you love at once, rotate your treasures so you can showcase your favorite things without creating too much clutter.

▲ **This room's update of Victorian decorating features subdued color on the walls and a restrained use of patterns on furnishings and fabrics. Heavily embellished gold frames and a plethora of accessories, including collections of bronze candelabra and crystal decanters, are true to the period style.**

World influence

Decorating today is becoming more influenced by personal experiences, travel, or family heritage than ever before. A global economy has made it easier to find furnishings, art, and accessories from all over the world. As such, designs from countries and regions far and wide are influencing decorating styles. Some of the most popular influences include:

Southwestern. This United States style brings to mind images of the desert, the bold natural colors of the sunset, and Native American accents. Organic materials such as iron, adobe, wood, and smooth rocks are often used. Look for rustic, often oversized furnishings, boldly patterned handwoven rugs or blankets, stylized regional art, religious icons, Pueblo pottery, and colors such as burgundy, purple, and bright turquoise.

Asian. Contemporary homes are often influenced by Asian design, which ranges from the minimalist interiors and natural hues commonly found in Japanese decorating to the bright colors and figures of Chinese style. Asian homes are designed with serenity and calm in mind. The minimalist approach and use of colors and objects found in nature makes Japanese design a popular choice for spalike bathrooms and serene bedrooms. Chinese style, with bold colors such as red and mustard yellow, figurines of mythical creatures, dark-toned furnishings, and fabrics such as silk, tends to be more energetic.

Latin flair. Folk art, framed artwork inspired by the likes of Diego Rivera and Frida Kahlo, and bold colors fill rooms decorated with Latin flair, which focuses on creating inviting spaces for uniting families. Keep furnishings simple to draw attention to focal point objects. Walls may be painted two different colors to contrast with the furniture.

Moroccan. You'll find vibrant colors such as the reds, greens, and blues of the sea and golds, yellows, and silvers of the desert in Moroccan-style homes. The tropical atmosphere may include textured walls and terra cotta tiles. Look for layers of rugs and pillows, ornately carved accents, and colorful paintings. Fabrics may be draped on the walls and ceilings, and collections include colorful bottles, large woven baskets, and even exotic plants.

Decorating with patterns

Selecting one pattern you love is easy enough—the tough part comes when deciding how to use it in your room and finding others to mix with it. To avoid overwhelming your decorating scheme with patterns, **maintain balance** by distributing pattern easily around a room. If you place it in one part of a room, balance that cluster with weighty furnishings or architectural features elsewhere. For a pleasing harmony **stay within a color family**. Patterns don't have to be the same color, but a thread of color continuity can pull a look together. It's generally best to **create a casual or formal attitude**—avoid mixing a formal silk damask with country gingham, for instance. Still not sure about patterns to choose? You may wish to use premixed collections sold by wall-covering stores, fabrics centers, and interior designers, which take the guesswork out of picking the perfect patterns.

▲ Surrounded by square and circular windows and teak paneling reminiscent of a Japanese bathhouse, a whirlpool offers a tranquil spot for relaxation. A few minimalist details, such as a vase holding bamboo and other plants, ensures the space remains serene and uncluttered.

▲ The walls, columns, and fireplace of this Southwestern home are constructed from stucco to emulate the look of thick adobe walls. Colorful pillows and blankets accent white couches in the space.

▲ This seating area boasts dramatic style with details culled from India and Morocco. Rich red hues adorn everything from the painted arch on the wall to the throw pillows on the sofa. A swing chair, elaborately carved coffee table, and a plethora of candles complete the opulent look.

DEWALT

Chapter 2 highlights

Tools and materials

Start with the right tools and materials and you are likely to get the most enjoyment from home decorative projects. These two elements make your work go more smoothly and result in a finished project that is better and more professional looking.

The decorative projects in this book require a variety of tools and materials. You'll find a list of specific items you need with each project. This chapter contains information about the most basic tools—hammers, drills, levels, miter boxes, and saws. These tools are commonly used in most home projects and are worth purchasing for a basic tool kit.

Some techniques are also fairly common. This chapter includes instructions for the most common miter and coping techniques used for installing trimwork and completing other wood projects. Finally, no matter the project, safety is critical. In this chapter you'll find basic recommendations for working safely on projects large and small.

Safety

Project safety starts by taking care of yourself. The most critical element is to stay focused. Most mishaps occur because of small mental mistakes. Remove distractions, particularly when working with power tools. Keep small children away from work areas. You won't be able to pay attention to them while trying to attend to the task. Most children are intrigued with tools and could hurt themselves. Keep your work area tidy and organized. It will be easier to find the tools and materials you need, and it will lessen the chance of a mishap with a misplaced screwdriver or stray nail. Choose the right tool for the job and use it safely. Turn off the power at the circuit breaker when you're drilling a hole in a wall. Live wires can cause serious injury. Take your time. Read the directions carefully, look at each step for each project, and imagine where you might have troubles and how to prevent them.

Use protective clothing and equipment

Wear the proper safety gear including recommended gloves and clothing, safety glasses, and ear protection when working with power tools. Keep these points of protection in mind:

Eyes. When you are scraping, nailing, sawing, hammering, spray painting, or working with other power tools, wear plastic safety glasses or goggles to protect your eyes from flying particles. If you get something in your eye, rinse it out immediately with fresh water.

Ears. Power tools can generate a lot of noise. Wear hearing protection when operating power equipment. Earplugs have foam inserts to protect hearing. Earmuffs cover the ear. Both are designed to protect hearing by reducing the high-frequency and high-decibel noise of power tools and machinery.

Hands. Many liquids associated with home projects are toxic or harmful to your skin. When handling them wear appropriate gloves: latex for latex paints and stains and neoprene for most solvents. Wear leather work gloves when handling sharp-edge metal or when sanding or scraping. Do not wear gloves when working with power saws. The glove could catch on a moving blade.

Feet. Tools are heavy and most fasteners are sharp. Protect your feet by wearing sturdy shoes with thick soles.

Lungs. Many home projects generate solids and solvents; it's important to keep them out of your lungs. Sanding and sawing produce a fine powder, which is difficult to avoid breathing. Wear a tight-fitting, dust-resistant mask when sanding. When you smell a solvent, stain, or paint, you are breathing it. Wear a respirator recommended for the product and make sure the workspace is adequately ventilated whenever you are working indoors.

Clothing. Whenever you will be using power tools, wear a close-fitting shirt with short or rolled-up sleeves to avoid catching fabric on moving parts.

Ask questions

Professionals, hobbyists, and serious do-it-yourselfers ask questions and share information all the time. This book is a great resource and provides detailed step-by-step instructions. But you may have additional questions. Don't hesitate to ask the experts at The Home Depot for information about the best techniques, the right tools, material selection, and anything else that will help you work safely.

SMART & SAFE

LEAD PAINT ALERT

If you are sanding or removing paint, especially if it is a light color and was applied before 1978 (it may be hidden beneath one or more top coats), have it tested for lead by a professional (or use a household lead test kit from The Home Depot). Do not attempt to remove lead-base paint either by sanding or with a heat gun. Contact the Environmental Protection Agency (EPA) at 800-424-LEAD or go to www.epa.gov/lead for guidance.

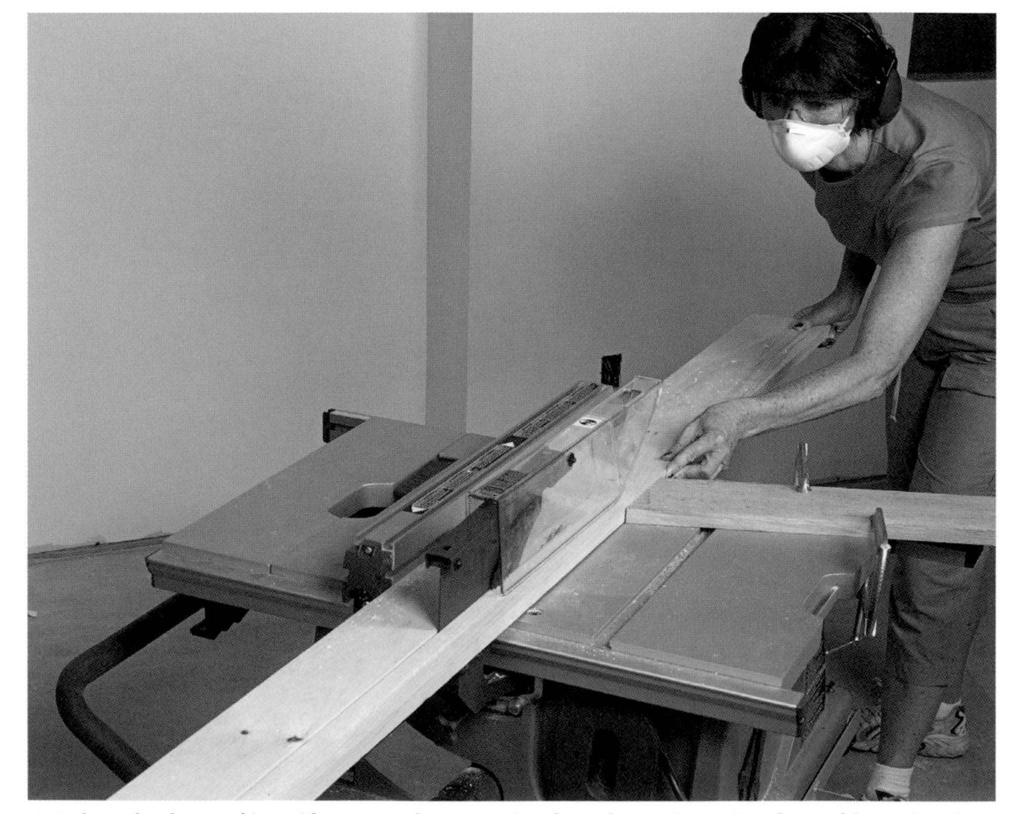

▲ **Being safe when working with power tools means using the tool properly, staying alert and focused, and wearing the appropriate safety gear and clothing.**

Home project tool kit

Good-quality tools are one of the most important investments you'll make as you become more involved with home decorating projects. When you're preparing for a specific project, fill your toolbox with the best products you can afford. Good tools save you time and effort. If cared for properly, quality tools will last a long time and will make your projects easier. While each job will have its own requirements, the tools on this page will help you start a basic home kit.

Hammer

When you buy a hammer, consider three things: the weight, the shape of the head, and the handle. For the projects in this book, you'll want a 16-ounce finishing hammer with a claw for pulling stray nails. Many carpenters prefer wooden handles because they transmit less shock to the arm and elbow. Other materials—fiberglass, graphite, and steel—are somewhat lighter or stronger, and have grips to protect you from the shock. Take a few practice swings in the store to see what hammer feels most comfortable to you.

Level

You want every project you install to be level (flat with no slope) and plumb (straight up and down). A carpenter's level is the best tool for checking level and plumb for small projects. An object is plumb if you butt the level against it and the bubble centers between the lines in the end vial. Set the level flat on an object to tell if it's level. Make slight adjustments to your project until it is level and plumb.

Drill

If you plan to do lots of projects throughout the house where grounded outlets aren't handy, a cordless drill is convenient. Cordless drills come in 9-, 12-, 14.4-, 15.6-, 18-, and 24-volt models. The higher the voltage, the more powerful—and heavy—the drill. As with other tools hold a drill in the store as if you're using it to determine which model is the most comfortable. Plug-in, reversible, variable-speed drills offer continuous, consistent power.

▲ **Choose a finishing hammer similar to one from this group. On the left is a wood 10-ounce finishing hammer used primarily for cabinetmaking. Next to it are four 16-ounce claw hammers—the best choice for the decorative projects in this book—in wood, fiberglass, graphite, and steel.**

▲ **Cordless drills go anywhere. Lower-voltage cordless drills are lighter but won't have the power of a higher-voltage model.**

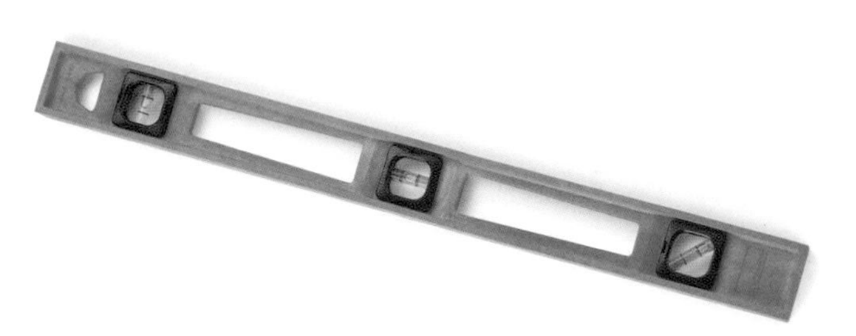

▲ **A carpenter's level is a straightedge with leveling bubbles used to determine horizontal or vertical planes. Choose from several lengths according to the type of work you'll do.**

▲ **A reversible, variable-speed drill that takes bits up to ⅜ inch is the standard for home projects. A trigger that adjusts speed gradually is easier to drive screws with than one that jumps quickly to its highest speed.**

Miter boxes and chop saws

Next to a straight cross cut, a miter cut is the most common cut in decorative home projects. Most moldings have joints that are mitered at inside and outside corners. The angle of cut on each piece is one-half the angle of the corner. On a typical 90-degree corner, the moldings are each cut at 45 degrees. Miter cuts are also used to build display shelves using molding. If you're adept at using a handsaw, lay out the angle with an adjustable square and cut the miters by hand. You'll get better results, however, with a miter box.

Three types of miter boxes are available. The best one depends on how much molding you have to cut, how many angles you need to cut, and how much money you want to spend.

▲ Fixed-angle miter box and backsaw
The entry-level miter box is either a solid maple box or molded plastic and has slots at 90 degrees for straight cross cuts and 45 degrees for miters. The best saw to use with the miter box is a backsaw; it has a long rectangular blade with a solid bar of steel or brass along the back edge.

This simple miter box works well for cutting small moldings. It can't handle large moldings—they won't fit in the box. You're also limited to 45- and 90-degree cuts. With time and use the slots in the miter box get wider and the cuts become less accurate. To trim only a window or door or install a room of small base molding, this setup works well.

▲ Power mitersaw or "chop" saw
These saws typically carry a 10-inch blade that pivots down into work held on a small table with a built-in fence. They are often called chop saws because of pivoting action. Professional finish carpenters work with power mitersaws. Equipped with a good carbide blade, these saws effortlessly cut through any wood molding. The blade locks at any angle between 45 and 90 degrees to either the left or right. Unlike manual saws, power mitersaws allow you to trim just a sliver at a time from a cut to get a perfectly tight joint.

The blade on a compound mitersaw tilts in two planes for more advanced cuts. Sliding mitersaws, on which the blade pivots into the workpiece and slides along rails, are akin to radial-arm saws and can cut stock up to 12 inches wide precisely.

Power mitersaws are as potentially dangerous as they are powerful and precise. Use caution: A careless cut or a misplaced finger can be instantly disastrous. Protect your eyes and ears too. Chop saws throw dust and occasionally a large piece of wood. Wear safety goggles. Wear hearing protectors to counter the noise of the chop saw.

▲ Adjustable mitersaw
This saw looks like a hacksaw mounted in a rigid metal frame that rotates on a stand. The saw blade locks at the desired angle between 45 and 90 degrees to either the left or right of center. There's no side-to-side play in the saw as there is in a fixed miter box, so the cuts are smooth and clean. A downside to these mitersaws is that you have to supply muscle power. Unless you plan to install trim throughout your entire house, this is an efficient and accurate tool for any molding project.

Mitering for outside corners

Mitering outside corners—such as those that go around a chimney or cabinet that juts into a room—is simpler than coping inside corners. An outside corner is a true miter; the key is to position the molding correctly in the saw. Put the molding in the saw so the top of the molding is against the floor of the saw. Then lean the molding back so that the bottom of the molding is against the fence. Putting the top of the molding against the floor of the saw may seem backward, but the opposite way creates a gap in the joint. Mark the bottom of the molding with a piece of tape for proper orientation. Follow these steps to make molding cuts for a chimney that juts into the room. The directions begin with the left side, work across the front, and finish on the right side.

1 **MITER THE MOLDING FOR THE LEFT SIDE.** Start with a piece of molding longer than you need and put it in the mitersaw, as shown. The bottom of the molding is against the fence, and the top of the molding is against the floor of the saw. The piece leans back; only two surfaces touch the saw, and there is a triangular gap between the rest of the molding and the saw. Set the saw handle 45 degrees to the left and slide the molding so that the scrap will be to the left of the blade. Cut through the molding to create the miter. Set the saw to make a square cut and cut the piece to length from the other end.

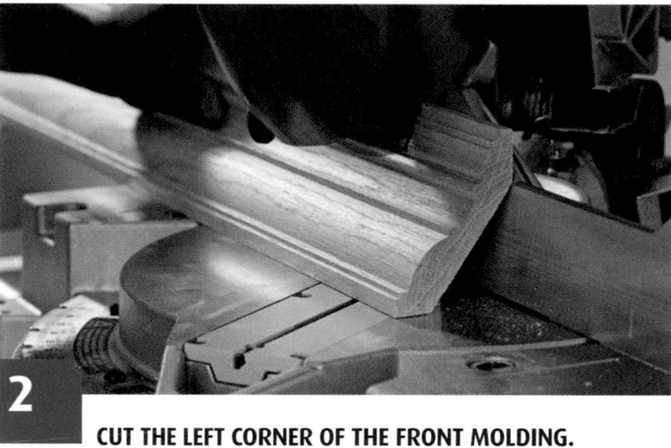

2 **CUT THE LEFT CORNER OF THE FRONT MOLDING.** Set the saw handle 45 degrees to the right and put the molding in place so the scrap piece will be to the right of the blade. Cut a piece about 6 inches longer than you need. Once you make the cut, you should have two parts of a corner. Set them in place on the wall to see how they fit and have a helper draw a line marking where the bottom of the untrimmed molding meets the wall.

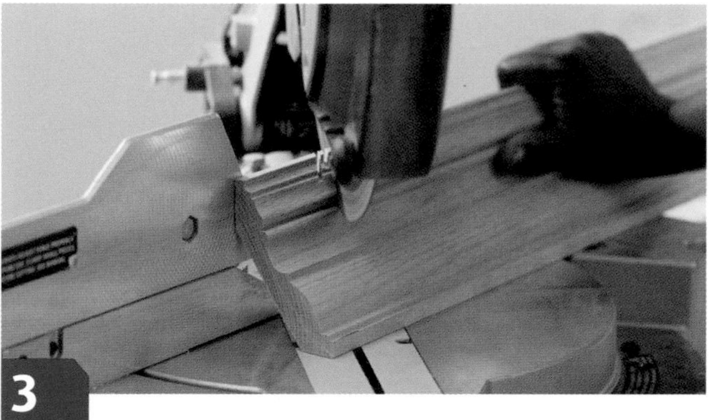

3 **CUT THE RIGHT CORNER OF THE FRONT MOLDING.** Set the saw handle to the left, positioning what will be the scrap to the left of the blade. Carpenters like to sneak up on this cut to make sure they don't cut the piece too short. Here's how to do it: Position the molding so that it's obvious that the piece you cut will be too long. Make a cut that just touches the molding so that you can see where the blade will hit it and how far that is from the layout line. Slide the molding toward the blade, enough to get close to the mark. Take another trial cut. Keep cutting and sliding until the trial cut is at the layout line and then cut the piece to length.

4 **CUT THE MOLDING FOR THE RIGHT SIDE.** Put a new piece of molding in the saw; set the saw handle to the right, positioning what will be the scrap to the right of the blade. Miter the stock, then set the blade square, and cut it to length from the other end.

Coping crown molding

Because crown molding slopes between the ceiling and the wall, coping it is different from coping a flat molding, such as a chair rail. The purpose is the same, however—to create nesting joints that mimic a miter but that won't be affected by wall irregularities.

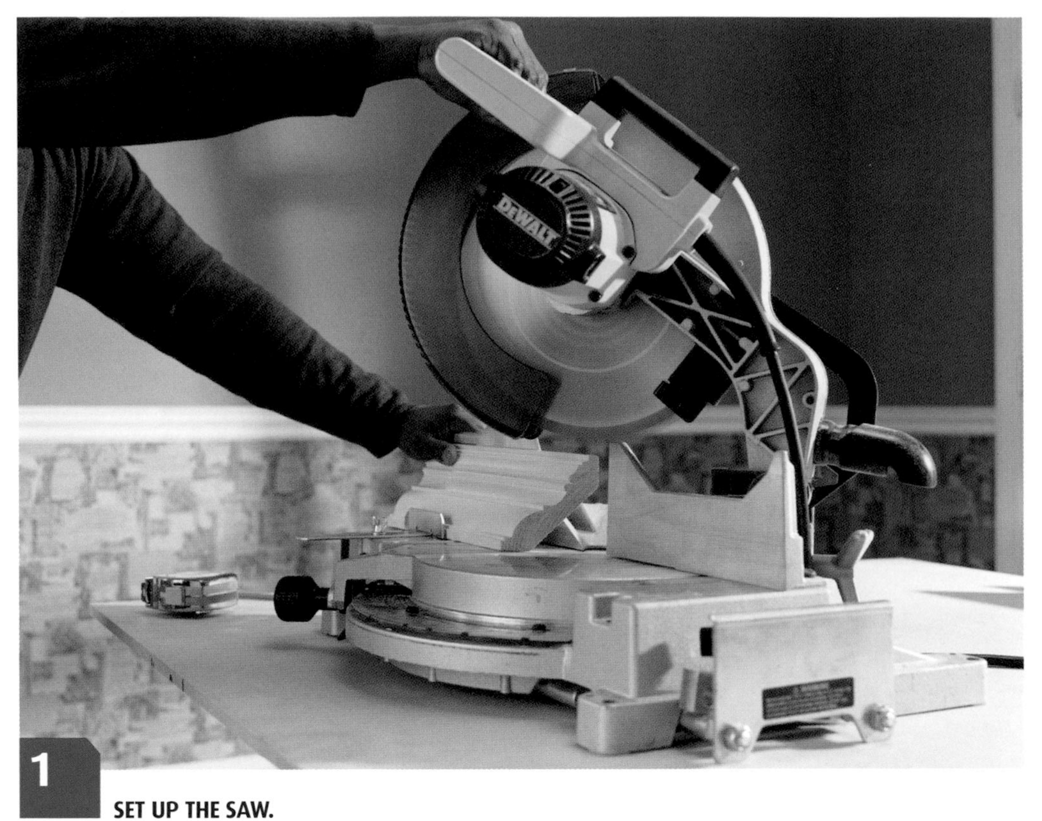

1 **SET UP THE SAW.**
Part of the challenge of coping is orienting the molding in the miter box. Mark the bottom edge of the molding with tape to avoid confusion. Then rest the top of the molding on the bottom of the miter box. Lean the molding back so the bottom is against the back fence of the miter box. Set the saw to cut at 45 degrees and miter as if cutting a miter for a regular inside corner. Set the piece so that the top is flush with the saw fence.

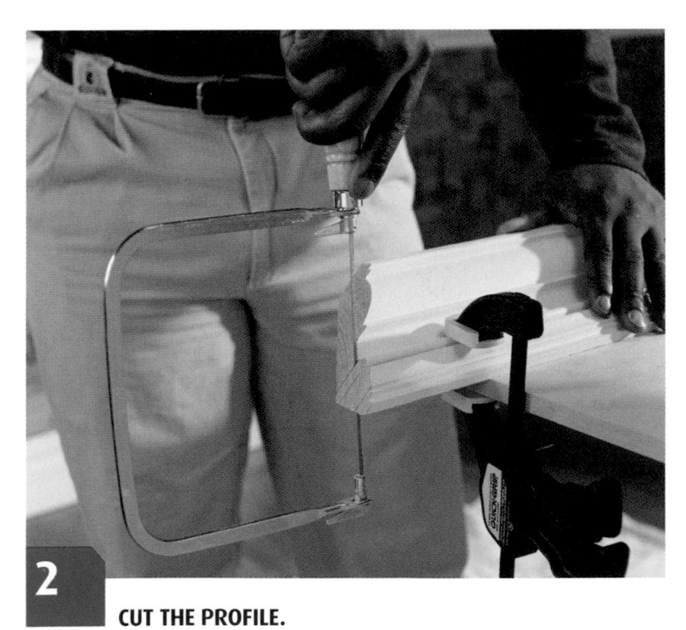

2 **CUT THE PROFILE.**
When you look at the face of the molding, you'll see that the miter cut exposed the profile of the molding. Cutting along the profile creates a joint that will nest against a similar piece of molding.

3 **TEST FIT THE CUT.**
The coped piece should nest tightly against the molding on the adjoining wall, as shown. If it doesn't, file high spots with a rat-tail file.

Coping a chair rail

When miters work, they're great, but when they're bad, they're horrid. If the room is out of square, if there is a buildup of drywall compound in the corners, or if the moldings are slightly different thicknesses, putty will not fix the gap. Learning how to cope a joint, which is trimming a profile in one piece of molding so that it will butt against its mate without needing an angled joint, will save you many headaches.

1 MITER WITH THE PIECE FLAT ON THE MITER BOX.
This is a normal mitering operation, with the miter cut as it would be for an inside corner. In the next step, however, part of the stock will be cut away, so a longer piece than the finished length is needed. Miter the piece so it's longer than needed by at least the thickness of the stock. If you cope both ends, the stock should be longer by at least twice the thickness.

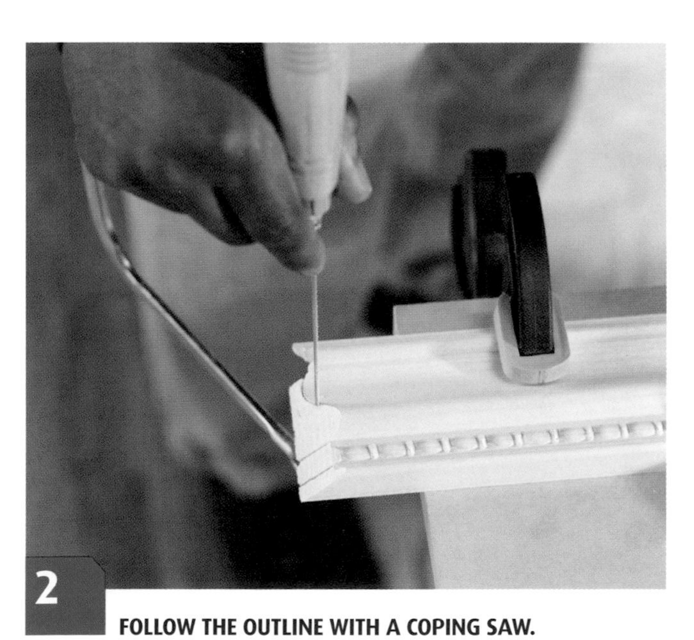

2 FOLLOW THE OUTLINE WITH A COPING SAW.
The miter reveals a crisp profile of the molding. Cut along the profile, creating a socket that fits over the face of a similar piece of molding. Angle the saw as you cut, creating a gentle point that will be the only part of the joint to touch the neighboring molding.

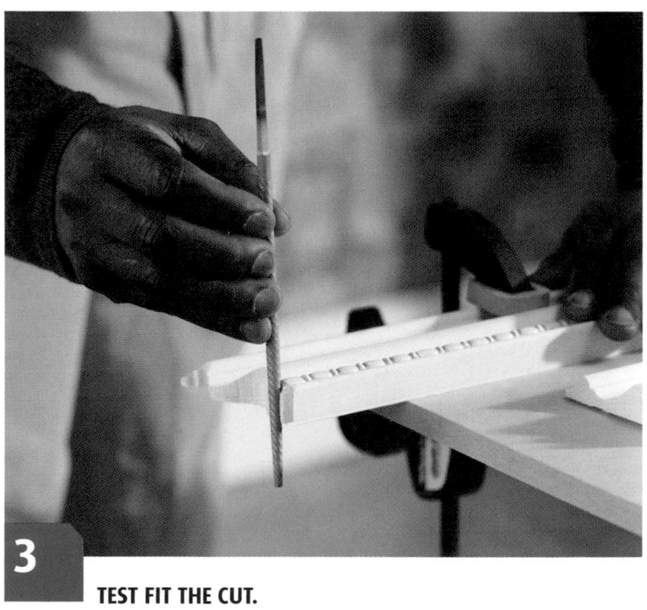

3 TEST FIT THE CUT.
Check the joint by fitting it against a cutoff. Don't be surprised or dismayed if the fit is less than perfect. Even experienced carpenters fine-tune joints. Sand and file to get a good fit.

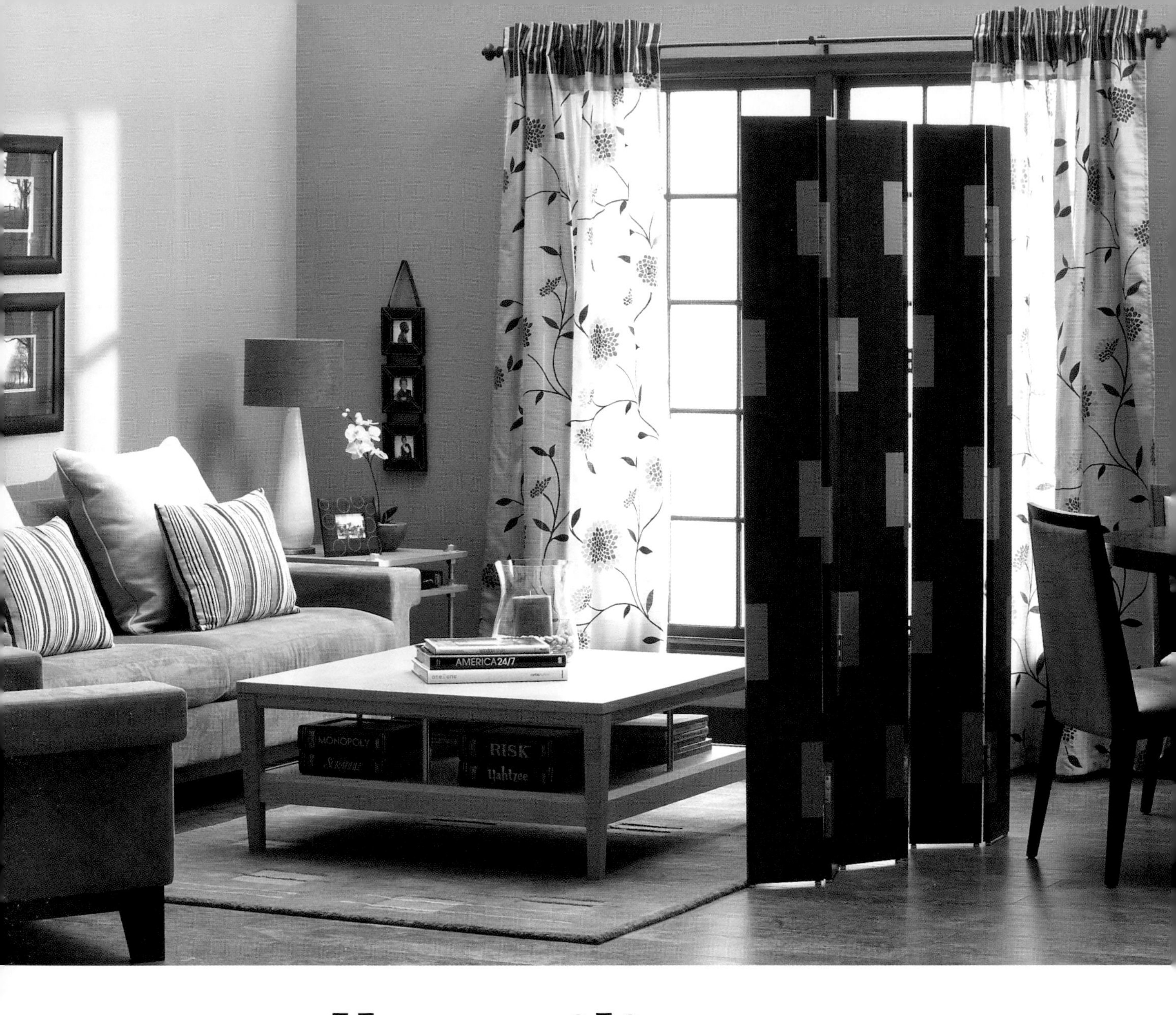

Walls, ceilings, and floors

Every room requires the proper backdrop—and nothing creates tone, mood, and style quite like walls, ceilings, and floors.

Walls in particular are key for setting the stage and may convey a specific design depending on the combination of paint, decorative treatments, and architectural accents. What's affixed to your walls—whether it's a tile backsplash, beaded-board wainscoting, or even a mirror or framed photo hung on the wall—is important too.

Ceilings deserve attention as well. Proper ceiling treatments can make a room seem taller or close in a space that feels too large. Moldings, medallions, and fans are some simple items that add detail to an otherwise ho-hum ceiling.

Remember that what's on the floor makes a statement. Install a wood floor inlay or carpet tiles in a decorative pattern. Stencil patterns in the shape of a rug on the floor. Painting a sisal area rug is another easy, quick update that can be switched out as your tastes change.

Chapter 3 highlights

Chair and picture rails

PROJECT DETAILS

SKILLS: Painting, measuring, marking, cutting, nailing

TIME TO COMPLETE

EXPERIENCED: 8 hrs.
HANDY: 12 hrs.
NOVICE: 16 hrs.

STUFF YOU'LL NEED

TOOLS: Paintbrush, tape measure, level, power mitersaw or miter box and backsaw, stud finder, electric drill, hammer, nail set, sandpaper
MATERIALS: Chair or picture rail, primer or varnish, finishing nails, wood putty

▲ **Moldings transform a room. Here the chair rail marks a change from wallpaper to paint. This picture rail is both functional and decorative, but in many homes it is purely decorative.**

Chair and picture rails dress up a room and help define period and style. Originally used to protect plaster walls from damage, chair and picture rails also establish a border between two different wall treatments, such as a wallpapered lower section and a painted upper section. Chair rails also provide a transition between lower paneling and upper paint or wallpaper.

Even if a chair rail isn't intended to be functional, it should still be placed at a height that will protect the wall from damage from chair backs. Depending on the chairs in a room, the rail should be placed 30 and 40 inches from the floor. Adjust the height as necessary to avoid awkward meetings with the bottom of window frames, as well as to suit rooms with ceilings that are unusually high or low.

Picture rails are usually installed from 10 to 16 inches below the ceiling line, depending on the height of the wall. Follow the same procedures for installing picture rails as you do for chair rails. Picture rails should be mounted securely to the wall whether they are intended to carry the weight of hanging objects or to be used as purely decorative elements.

GOOD IDEA

BEGIN WITH LONGER WALLS
When installing molding around a room, always start with the longest wall and work in the direction of the shorter ones if possible. If you make an error and cut a piece slightly short, you can still use it for shorter lengths of wall.

1 **PRIME THE RAIL.**
To prevent warping, paint or varnish both sides of the molding before installing it. If you plan to finish the trim after it is nailed on, apply a coat of finish to the back now.

2 **DRAW A LAYOUT LINE.**
Determine the height of the chair rail. Mark the wall at that height and use a level to extend a horizontal line for the top edge of the rail.

Check for level to make sure the layout line on one wall is even with the layout line on the other. Near a corner put the level on the line of each adjoining wall. If you get a level reading, the lines are level.

GOOD IDEA

HIDE THE NAILS
Make finishing nails less conspicuous. Drive them at an angle into a crevice in the profile.

GOOD IDEA

BUY A BUNDLE
Buy molding from the same bundle to make sure the pieces are as identical as possible. The molding profile changes as the cutters wear down.

CLOSER LOOK

SCARF JOINTS
If you don't have a piece of molding long enough to span the wall, you can splice two pieces together. The joint that is made by making opposing miter cuts on the pieces to be joined is called a scarf joint. If you measure and cut precisely, the scarf joint will become almost invisible. That's because the miter cut emphasizes the profile of the molding, making it blend more effectively, especially if the molding is to be painted.

Chair and picture rails *(continued)*

3 MAKE MITER CUTS AT CORNERS.
Moldings with simple profiles can meet at 45-degree miter joints for inside and outside corners. Complex moldings meet better at inside corners if joints are coped.

4 MAKE SQUARE CUTS AT DOOR AND WINDOW CASINGS.
At doors and windows end the molding with a square cut. If the molding is thicker than the casings, make a transition by cutting a bevel on the portion of the rail that protrudes. Along walls that can't be spanned with a single length of rail, scarf two or more pieces.

5 NAIL THE CHAIR RAIL.
Locate the studs with a stud finder or by tapping a nail through the wall in a spot where the holes will be concealed by the trim. Studs are almost always spaced every 16 inches on center. Hold the chair rail in place and transfer the stud locations to the rail. Drill pilot holes at each mark and attach the molding with finishing nails. Countersink the nails, putty the holes, and smooth outside corners by sanding the exposed edges.

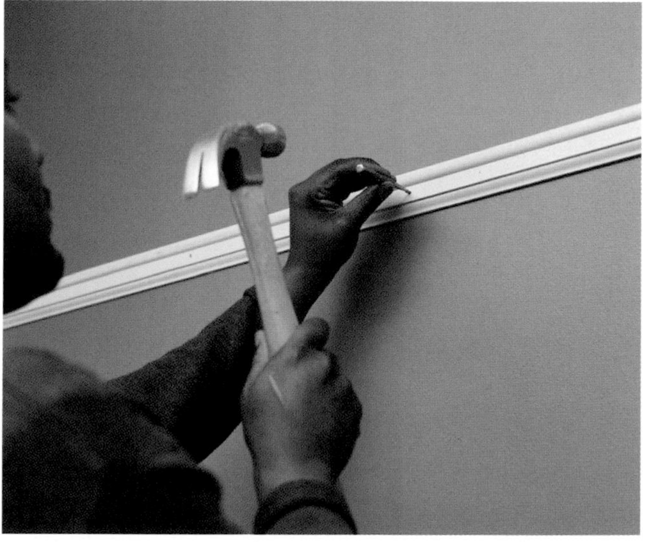

Installing picture rails

Picture rails are installed the same way as chair rails; they have a cove along the top edge to hold specialized hardware from which pairs of wires descend to support pictures. If the trim is decorative, it can be nailed in place. If the trim will be used to hang pictures, screw it to the studs, countersinking the screws and covering them with wood putty.

Crown molding

PROJECT DETAILS

SKILLS: Painting, measuring, marking, drilling, cutting, nailing, caulking

TIME TO COMPLETE

EXPERIENCED: 8 hrs.
HANDY: 12 hrs.
NOVICE: 16 hrs.

STUFF YOU'LL NEED

TOOLS: Paintbrush, tape measure, stepladder, 4-foot level, stud finder, power mitersaw, coping saw, clamps, electric drill, hammer, nail set, caulk gun
MATERIALS: Crown molding, primer or varnish, finishing nails, wood putty, caulk

GOOD IDEA

COMBINE MOLDING
You can combine two moldings to make a third molding. One of the easiest combinations starts with nailing a baseboard to the wall along the ceiling. Nail it upside down so that the decorative edge faces the floor. (Baseboards with a bead along the edge work well.) Then attach a crown molding to the baseboard, positioning it to expose the decorative edge.

DESIGNER TIP

SUIT ROOM SIZE
Size the molding to suit the room. Wide molding can lower the ceiling too much in a small room, and narrow molding disappears in spaces with high ceilings.

▲ Crown molding enhances almost any decor—from elegant Colonial to this rustic Southwestern look.

Although carpet, paint, and furnishings receive more attention, crown molding sets the tone for formality and grace in traditional spaces by highlighting and finishing the upper areas of a room.

Why bother with crown molding? Aside from its beauty it artfully conceals gaps that can open up between wall and ceiling. Crown molding is also a visual transition from one surface to another. Not every house requires this treatment—crown molding might simply clutter a contemporary design. But it's an asset in homes that draw on traditional styles, adding a touch of refinement and formality.

Installing crown molding requires cutting some coped and mitered joints, and you may want to ask a helper to hold long pieces in place. You can hire a carpenter for the installation or—if you want to do the job yourself but can't cope with coping—buy no miter/no cope molding that uses plinth blocks in the corners.

Before shopping for molding decide whether to use a clear finish on natural wood or to save money with finger-jointed stock or medium-density fiberboard (MDF) that you paint. As you walk the aisles, look for ways to build an impressive molding by combining common types of stock; store personnel can help suggest combinations.

Don't have a stud finder? Drive a nail into the wall a couple of inches from the corner. Work high enough so the trim covers the holes but stay at least 2½ inches from the ceiling. Drive nails at 1-inch intervals until you hit something solid. The next one should be 16 inches away.

Crown molding *(continued)*

GOOD IDEA

LEAVE ROOM FOR ERROR
When you cut pieces that are square on one end and coped on the other, cut the piece long and then cut it to length after you're happy with the coped joint. By initially cutting the pieces long, you have the luxury of botching one or two coping attempts without having to throw out the molding.

Carpenter's secret

To match existing molding, ask to see a store copy of the Wood Moulding & Millwork Producers Association's wood molding booklet. If your molding isn't in the booklet, order custom-made molding from a cabinetmaker or architectural mill house. Be prepared to place a large minimum order.

Painter's secret

Nervous about cutting tight joints? For first-timers plan to paint the crown molding. You'll be able to caulk and paint any gaps.

1 PRIME THE MOLDING.
Molding will be less likely to warp if it is finished front and back. Either completely apply finish before installing the trim or at least brush a coat of primer or varnish on the back.

2 MEASURE THE ROOM AND MARK THE STUD LOCATIONS. The molding will be nailed into the wall studs. Find them with a stud finder, and make faint pencil marks high on the wall (where they won't be covered by molding) to guide the nailing. Draw a pencil line along the wall to lay out the bottom edge of the molding.

3 MAKE SCARF JOINTS FOR LONG RUNS.
Where you need two or more strips of molding to span a wall, have them meet at an angled scarf joint cut. Because the strips overlap, the combined length must be greater than that of the wall width. Mark the strips for 45-degree cuts that will position the joint over a stud. Make the cuts with a mitersaw.

4 DRILL PILOT HOLES.
To prevent molding from splitting, drill pilot holes the diameter of the finishing nails you'll use. Mark the locations of pilot holes by holding the molding in place and transferring the wall stud marks onto the molding. Drill holes at the angled ends of scarfed pieces too.

5 **MAKE COPING CUTS AT INSIDE CORNERS.** Crown molding isn't mitered at inside corners. It's coped—the end of one piece is cut to nestle into the profile of another. For this to work cut and install the molding in this sequence: In a room with four walls, the first wall's molding is square at both ends. Cut and install it now. On the second wall the molding is square at one end and coped at the other. The third wall is treated the same way. The molding on the fourth wall is coped at each end.

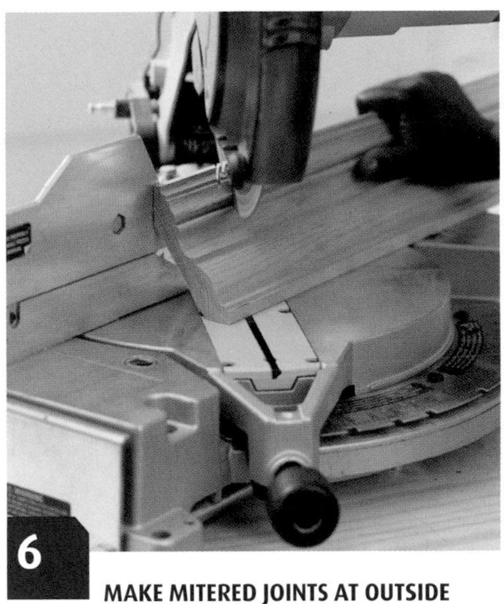

6 **MAKE MITERED JOINTS AT OUTSIDE CORNERS.** If there are outside corners, the moldings meet at 45-degree miter joints. Mitering, like coping, requires you to put the molding in the saw with the top edge on the floor of the box. Mitering is explained on page 31.

7 **NAIL THE MOLDING.**
Hold the strips in place and nail them in place. Once the molding is up, drive the heads below the surface with a nail set and fill the holes with putty. If you will apply a clear finish over stain, use a putty that matches the stain or that will take stain. If you will paint the molding, fill the holes with glazing compound—the putty that's used around windows. It dries quickly and paints well.

8 **CAULK THE SEAMS.**
Dark, gaping seams can become obvious if you paint the molding a light color. Fill gaps between the molding and the ceiling and between the molding and the wall with paintable caulk or one that matches the stain you use. Apply the caulk with a caulk gun and smooth out the surface with a moist finger. If you paint the molding, caulk gaps in the joints.

Carpenter's secret

When nailing crown molding nail the bottom edge into the wall studs. On the two walls perpendicular to the ceiling joists, nail the top edge of the molding into the joists. On the other two walls, there's nothing in the ceiling to nail into. On these walls cut 2×4s to make triangular nailing blocks. Nail the blocks into the studs and into the plate at the top of the wall. When you install the molding, nail it to the nailing block.

DESIGNER TIP

CONSIDER COLOR
When choosing paint for crown molding, remember that a dramatic color can cause the ceiling to look low or make the molding look too ornate.

Custom molding

PROJECT DETAILS

SKILLS: Measuring, marking, cutting, nailing, painting

TIME TO COMPLETE

EXPERIENCED: 8 hrs.
HANDY: 12 hrs.
NOVICE: 16 hrs.

STUFF YOU'LL NEED

TOOLS: 4-foot level, saw, hammer, nail set, power mitersaw or miter box and backsaw, pencil, paintbrush
MATERIALS: 1×3 pine (twice room perimeter plus 8 feet), 11⁄16×2⅝-inch chair rail (WM390, room perimeter plus 8 feet), 11⁄16×2½-inch chair rail (WM298, room perimeter plus 8 feet), 11⁄16×1 1⁄16-inch cove molding (WM100, twice room perimeter plus 16 feet), #4 finishing nails, #6 and #8 finishing nails, screws, masking tape, wood putty, paint or stain, wood

Carpenter's secret

PIECING MOLDING
Although walls may be 12 or more feet long, moldings are available only in 8- or 10-foot lengths. No problem. Just splice or scarf a shorter length onto the long one to complete the wall. Make a splice joint by mitering the endpieces and overlapping them. The angle is not crucial (although 35 to 45 degrees is best). Cut the first piece with the molding on one side of the miter box. Put the second piece of molding against the other side of the box when you cut it. Overlap both pieces.

▲ **Molding combinations are limited only by your imagination. This design made of stock pieces found in most lumber stores creates an intricate and interesting double chair rail.**

Home centers and lumberyards carry large selections of wood moldings. Look closely and you'll notice that there are usually two or three choices with slight variations—mostly the same profiles in different widths. If it's variety you want, create custom molding yourself. Complex moldings and trim usually are built from several pieces. Traditional baseboard is a good example. The main piece is often 1× stock. The top profile is a separate base cap molding. A quarter-round shoe molding sits against the floor. When painted it looks like one piece.

This chair rail is a combination of simple profiles found on the sample boards at home centers. Each molding is identified in "Stuff You'll Need" by a number assigned by the Wood Moulding & Millwork Producers Association. The upper rail, for example, is based on an 11⁄16×2⅝-inch chair rail called WM390. The lower rail is built around WM298, an 11⁄16×2½-inch chair rail. The rest of the stock is either 1× or cove molding.

If all this molding talk seems like a foreign language, ask an associate at The Home Depot to take you on a tour of the molding and trim area.

When you make a cut in a miter box, never try to cut right along the line on the first try. Make a cut that you know leaves the piece a bit long and then edge the piece over to make another cut.

1 MAKE A SAMPLE PROFILE. Determine which molding you want to create. Sketch the molding and then make a full-size drawing to take to the store. Purchase samples—you may be able to buy 1-foot lengths of the moldings—and use these to create short sample assemblies. Before you purchase the molding, hold a sample in place in the room to get a sense of the scale and fit.

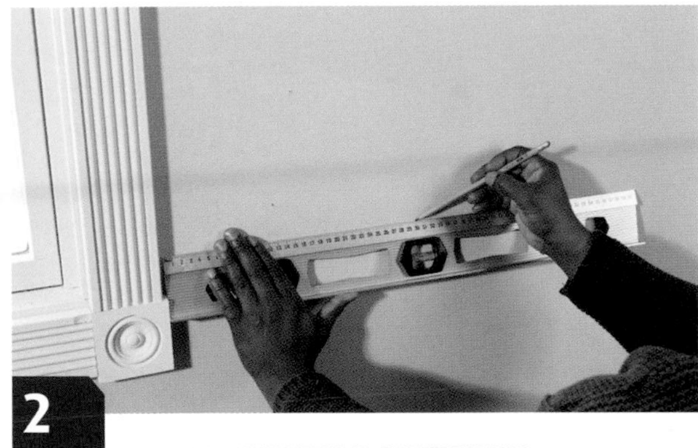

2 DRAW A LAYOUT LINE ON THE WALL.

The foundation of the double chair rail molding is a pair of 1×3s. Determine the height of the chair rail; 30 to 40 inches from the floor is the typical range. For a true chair rail that protects the walls from chair backs, place the bottom molding at the same height as the chair backs. Draw a level line where the bottom edge of the lower 1×3 will be. You need only this line. You will position the top 1×3 by placing a spacer against the lower one.

3 CUT THE LOWER 1×3 TO LENGTH.

Butt the 1×3s at the inside corners and miter the outside corners. Nail the 1×3 to the wall, driving #6 or #8 finishing nails into the studs. Or use screws because most of the surface will be covered by molding.

4 USE A SPACER TO POSITION THE SECOND 1×3.

Cut a short length of 1×3 and rest it on top of the piece nailed to the wall. Position the second 1×3 on top of the scrap and nail it to the wall. Use the scrap as a spacer to keep the second 1×3 parallel with the first. If the boards are short, cut the top piece to stagger the joints.

5 NAIL ON THE ADDITIONAL MOLDINGS.

Before you nail the top trim in place, bevel the edges where the molding will fit window or door frames. This will provide a cleaner look. Nail moldings to the face and edges of the two 1×3s.

MITER MOLDING AT INSIDE AND OUTSIDE CORNERS. Use a chop saw or miter box and backsaw to cut the inside and outside corners. You may have to piece moldings together for the right lengths. (See "Carpenter's Secret," *opposite*). Wherever possible miter the end of the first piece and nail it in place. Hold the second piece in place and mark it to meet the first piece. Miter at the mark, and put the molding in place. It's faster and more reliable than measuring. If you're in doubt about the length, err on the side of cutting the piece long and trim it to fit.

7 PRIME AND PAINT THE MOLDING.

Mask the wall at the top and bottom edges of the molding. Set the nails and fill the holes with latex wood putty. Prime and paint the new molding. An alternative to painting between the moldings is to run a strip of wallpaper that matches the room's decor.

No miter/No cope baseboard

PROJECT DETAILS

SKILLS: Measuring, cutting, nailing, drilling, caulking, finishing

TIME TO COMPLETE

EXPERIENCED: 6 hrs.
HANDY: 8 hrs.
NOVICE: 12 hrs.

STUFF YOU'LL NEED

TOOLS: Clamp, miter box and backsaw, hammer, drill, nail set, caulk gun, 150-grit sandpaper
MATERIALS: Inside and outside corner blocks, baseboard molding, #6 and #8 finishing nails, wood shims, base molding, caulk, latex wood putty, paint or wood stain and finish

WORK SMARTER

FINISH FIRST
Paint or stain the molding before you install it if you have the room. If you lack the space, carefully mask off the surrounding areas and apply finish after installation.

▲ No miter/no cope baseboard is easy to install. The corner blocks eliminate having to cut angles for potentially complex joints and make it easier to deal with corners that are out of square. The look above is Victorian.

Cutting miters and coping joints are two jobs that discourage homeowners from installing molding and trim. Walls often are out of square, so there's a need to work around the angle of the miter cut, the position of the molding, or both. If the angle of the cut is off, the joint won't fit—it's that simple and that frustrating.

If you're serious about carpentry, mitering and coping are skills to add to your repertoire. However, a no miter/no cope alternative eliminates miter and cope joints altogether. Instead of running the molding around the corners, install precut corner blocks that fit the inside and outside corners. Nail the blocks in place and make square cuts at each end of the molding to fit between them. These cuts are easily made with a fixed-angle miter box and backsaw or a power mitersaw. The blocks come in several sizes and styles to fit the look of your room.

TOOL SAVVY

FINDING STUDS
To find studs the high-tech way, you can buy a stud finder—a handheld device with lights that glow when the finder is over a stud. But sometimes the old way is just as good. A few inches out from the corner, drive a nail into the wall. If the nail hits something solid, it's a stud; if not move over an inch and try again. Repeat as often as necessary until the nail hits a stud. Plan to position holes where they will be covered by molding and work at least 3 inches above the floor to avoid hitting framing that runs along the floor.

1 CUT THE CORNER BLOCKS IF NEEDED.
If the corner blocks are higher than the base molding, cut them down. Position a corner block and straight molding to judge how much to trim (*above right*). Clamp a stop inside the miter box and cut the blocks to length with a backsaw at the same time.

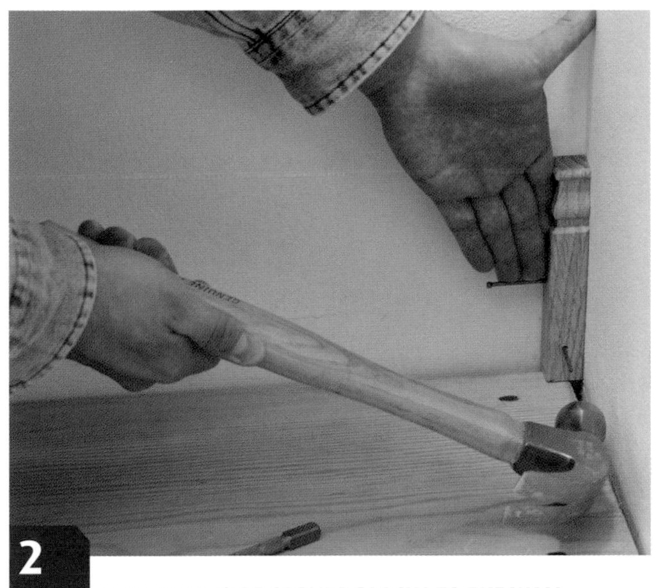

2 NAIL THE INSIDE CORNER BLOCKS TO THE WALL.
Nail into one face of the inside corner blocks with #6 finishing nails, angling the nails toward the corner to draw it in. Keep the nails at least 1 inch from the top and bottom of the blocks and predrill the holes to prevent splitting. If the corner is not perfectly square, gaps will be present on either side. Fill gaps with caulk after installation.

3 PREDRILL THE OUTSIDE CORNER BLOCKS.
Outside corner blocks are difficult because they need to be nailed diagonally through the corner of the block. Predrill the holes from the inside out—it's easier to start the drill bit on the inside ledge. Clamp the block to a bench with a scrap of wood underneath and drill through. Position the corner block and drill through into the corner of the wall to break through the metal corner bead.

No miter/No cope baseboard *(continued)*

4 NAIL ON OUTSIDE CORNER BLOCKS.
Drive nails through the predrilled holes into the corner of the wall.

5 CHECK CORNERS FOR SQUARE; SCRIBE AS NEEDED.
The corner blocks follow the prevailing contour of the walls, which usually means at least one of the joints with the base molding will be slightly out of square. This is easy to gauge before you cut the molding. Take a length of molding—a 3-foot length works well—and make a square cut on both ends. Hold this piece in position against the corner blocks to gauge whether the end cut on the molding will be square. If it's not hold the molding in position and draw a mark from the corner block onto the face of the molding. A metal rule, shown, is reliable, and a compass also will work. Cut the end of the molding to the scribed line. If both ends of a piece need to be scribed, repeat the process on the second end.

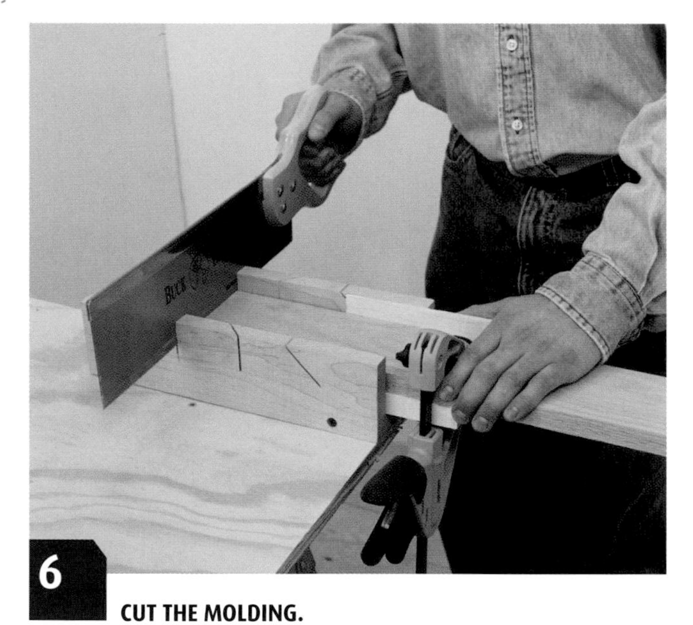

6 CUT THE MOLDING.
Use a miter box and backsaw to cut the molding. Clamp the wood firmly in the box. To make a cut that is slightly off square in a fixed-angle miter box, position the molding under the saw so the scribed mark lines up with the saw. Place a shim between the molding and the edge of the miter box to keep the molding from shifting. Hold the molding and make the cut.

7 NAIL THE MOLDING TO THE WALL BETWEEN CORNER BLOCKS. Use #6 finishing nails. Locate the nails about 1 inch from the floor to catch the bottom plate of the wall. Nails higher than 1½ inches from the floor need to hit a stud. Studs are typically spaced 16 inches on center starting from the inside corners of the room. Drive the nails, then set them below the surface of the wood with a nail set.

Don't let molding names limit your selection. For example, moldings labeled "casing" work perfectly well as chair rails, and vice versa. If the shape looks right for how you want to use it, then it probably is.

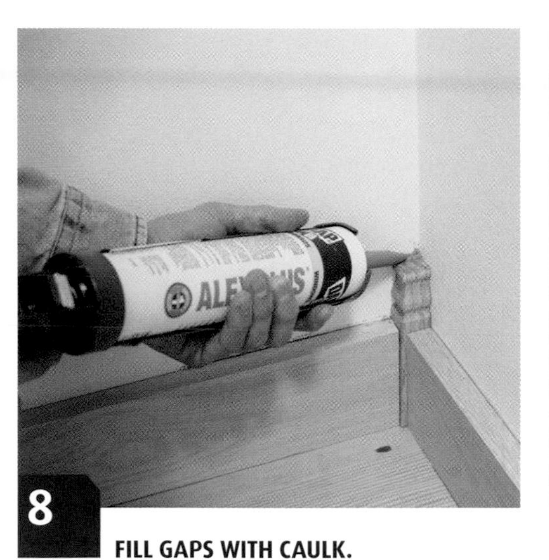

8

FILL GAPS WITH CAULK.
Gaps are inevitable around the top of the corner blocks. Fill the gaps with woodtone caulk before you stain the base molding. Use plain white latex caulk if you plan to paint.

TOOL SAVVY

DRILLING PILOT HOLES
Hardwoods may split if you don't drill pilot holes for the nails. Carpenters use a nail as a drill bit. Tighten the nail in the chuck as if it were a drill, and drill a hole with it wherever you will drive a nail. Because the nail pushes the fibers out of the way rather than severing them like a drill does, some of the fibers spring back, leaving a perfect pilot hole slightly smaller than the nail.

9

FINISH THE BASE MOLDING.
To stain, mask off the wall and floor before application. Follow up with a clear top coat of polyurethane. Fill the nail holes with latex wood putty, then sand with 150-grit sandpaper. To paint, apply a primer and then the top coat.

▲ **Corner blocks sit on the floor at outside and inside corners to provide a finished return with no miter/no cope molding.**

When molding flexes away from the wall at a point with no framing to nail into, drive a nail at an angle through the molding and into the wall. Move over an inch and drive another nail through the molding and into the wall at the opposite angle.

Gallery of molding ideas

Trimwork and molding are some of the finishing touches that help define the style of your home. Properly integrated trimwork impacts the look and feel of a room. The right baseboard, chair rail, window trim, or crown molding unifies a space and provides visual focus.

One of the biggest challenges regarding trimwork is choosing from the hundreds of different molding products available. Start with your decorating style and then consider what molding profiles and applications best enhance your approach to interior design. The rooms here offer a sampling of the styles and finished looks you can achieve.

Crown molding

The elegant trim along the ceiling in a home with Colonial or traditional decor is what often comes to mind when crown molding is mentioned. While crown molding is a decorative element, it has a practical purpose as well. It masks the line between the ceiling and the wall, which is a prime candidate for cracking. As a result many decorating styles embrace crown molding. To help you decide on the right look for your rooms, bring home some molding samples from The Home Depot and see how they look on the wall in your room.

▲ **This chair rail doubles as a shelf to display slender items. Combined with simple door trim and a display shelf above the door, the room feels cozy.**

▲ **Growing interest in design and decor has produced an appreciation for more complex molding and trim on the walls and ceilings.**

▲ **Crown molding creates a transitional element between a papered wall and a painted ceiling.**

◀ A lightweight crown rail can complement a picture rail, creating a wide composition with a graceful feeling.

◀ No matter the style, crown molding adds focus and dimension to a room. Here the crown molding coordinates with the trim on the cabinetry above the built-in seating.

Tin tile backsplash

PROJECT DETAILS

SKILLS: Measuring, cutting, nailing

TIME TO COMPLETE

EXPERIENCED: 8 hrs.
HANDY: 10 hrs.
NOVICE: 12 hrs.

STUFF YOU'LL NEED

TOOLS: Tape measure, pencil, handsaw, hammer, heavy gloves, tin snips or large heavy scissors, drill
MATERIALS: Furring strips, tin tile, finishing nails, copper nails, epoxy glue

▲ **Tin tiles in a copper finish add interest and character to this kitchen backsplash.**

Although a backsplash—as the name implies—is subject to splashes from cooking and cleaning, it's one element in the kitchen that needn't be as durable as countertops, floors, and appliances. This means the backsplash area is a great spot for adding color, texture, and personality to the room. For a finished look suitable for country or casual kitchens, install a tin tile backsplash. Tin tile is available in a number of colors and patterns to fit your decorating scheme. This version, which reaches from the top of the countertop to the bottom of the upper cabinets, was affixed to the wall with copper-finish nails that blend into the color of the backsplash.

1 **MEASURE BACKSPLASH HEIGHT.**
Measure from the counter to the base of the upper cabinets for the backsplash height. Continue measuring around the trim pieces and cupboards.

2 **MARK FURRING STRIPS.**
Furring strips are attached to the wall along the perimeter of the tiles. The tiles are nailed onto them. Transfer the backsplash height and other measurements to the furring strips.

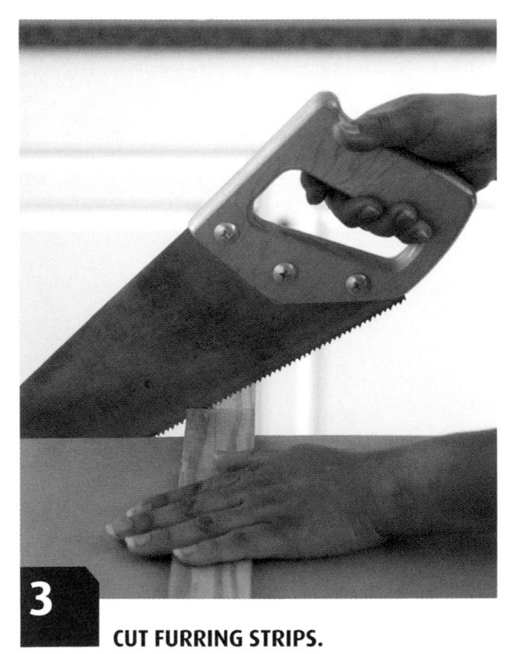

3 **CUT FURRING STRIPS.**
Using a handsaw cut the longest furring strips first. Wait to cut the remaining pieces until you have attached some of them to the wall and have checked measurements for the remaining pieces.

4 **INSTALL FURRING STRIPS.**
Beginning with the longest pieces, nail the furring strips to the wall along the perimeter of the backsplash area. The position of the furring strips doesn't have to be exact because the tin tile will cover them.

WORK SMARTER

SEAMLESS TILES
For a completely flush overlay where the copper tiles will overlap one another, apply epoxy glue between the tiles. The glue will minimize the gap between the tiles. Ask your Home Depot associate for the proper glue to use on the tiles.

DESIGNER TIP

SWITCH STYLE
Thanks to new options wall outlets and switches can be a stylish accent to your backsplash. One manufacturer offers a line that simulates the look of wood finishes and natural stone. Other options are sleeker and more contemporary than standard models. After choosing your backsplash material and color, look for switches and outlets in coordinating finishes.

Tin tile backsplash *(continued)*

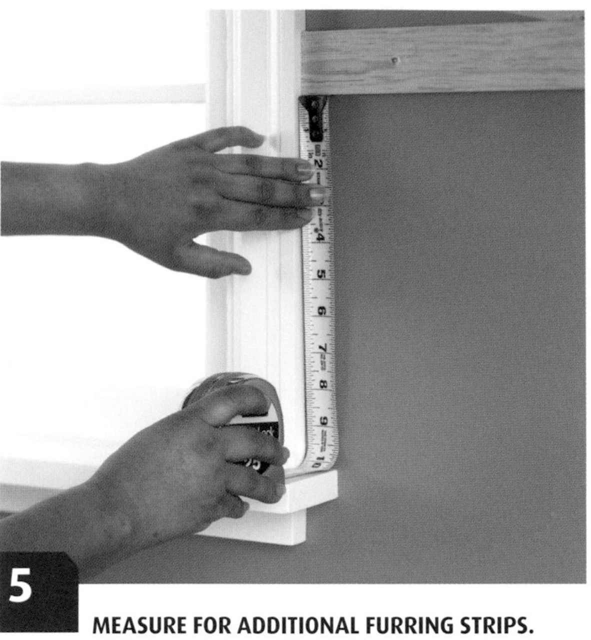

5 **MEASURE FOR ADDITIONAL FURRING STRIPS.**
Take new measurements for the remaining furring strips. Mark and cut the pieces.

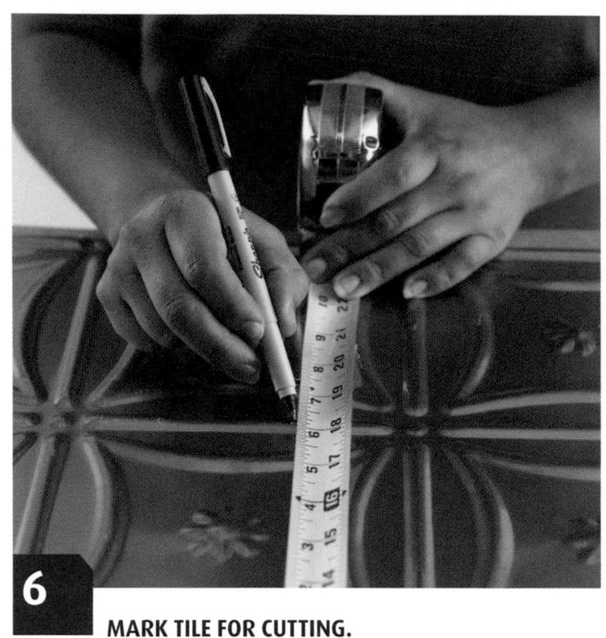

6 **MARK TILE FOR CUTTING.**
Before cutting any tin tile, check the measurements you made for the furring strips. Measurements need to be accurate to avoid gaps between the tin tiles and adjoining surfaces. Before transferring the measurements to the tile, plan how cuts will interrupt the tile pattern. Overlap any connecting pieces so the pattern matches for a seamless look. Transfer cutting marks to the tile using a marker.

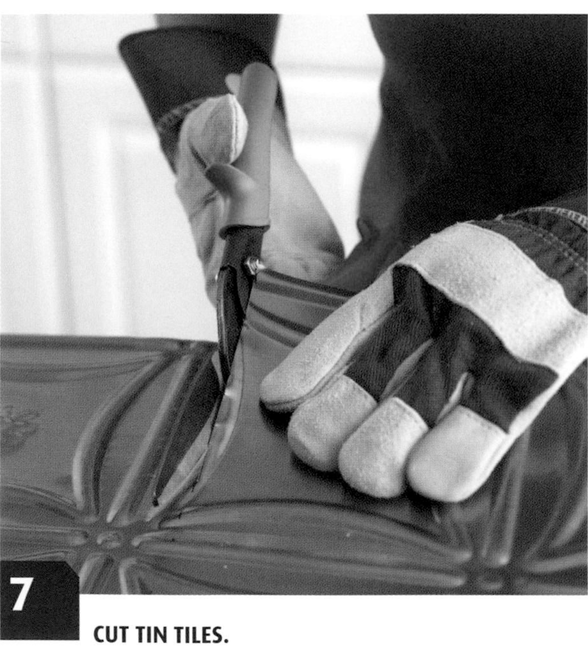

7 **CUT TIN TILES.**
Wearing heavy gloves and using tin snips, cut the tin tile along the marks. Take care to cut accurately to avoid gaps and uneven edges once you install the tiles.

8 **MARK FOR CUTOUTS.**
Measure and mark the location of outlets, switches, and other obstructions in the backsplash area. Transfer the measurements to the tile.

9

DRILL PILOT HOLE.

Drill a pilot hole anywhere inside the area to be cut out. Make the pilot hole large enough so you can get part of the tin snips into it. If you don't have a large enough bit, you can drill more than one hole to create a larger space for the tin snips.

10

CUT HOLE IN TILE.

Insert one blade of the tin snips into the pilot hole and cut out the area for the outlet or other obstruction. Don't worry if the edges aren't perfect. The switchplate or outlet cover will hide uneven cuts.

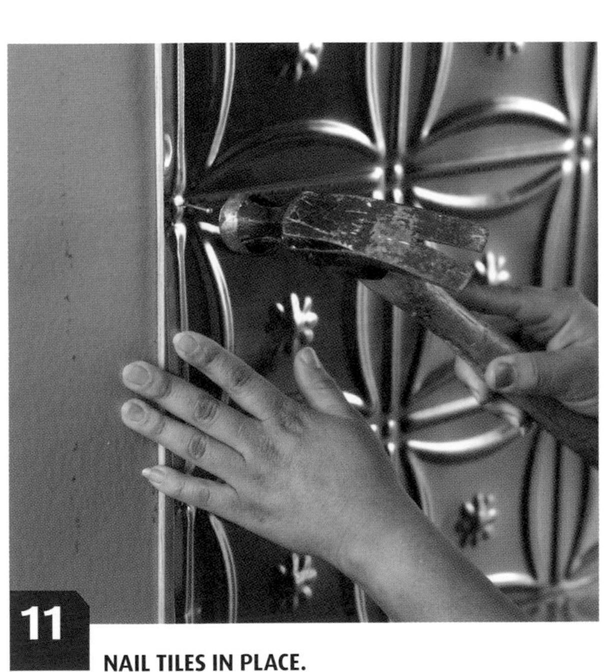

11

NAIL TILES IN PLACE.

Nail tin tiles into place with matching nails. Drive nails along the edges of the tiles into the furring strips. Overlap adjoining tiles to line up the pattern for a seamless look and to avoid gaps between tiles.

BUYER'S GUIDE

DON'T BUY TOO MUCH

Partial boxes of tile probably can't be returned so measure your backsplash area carefully before buying tiles. Purchase enough tiles to completely cover the area and allow for overlapping of seams.

DESIGNER TIP

TILE SELECTION

Tin tiles are available in a number of colors and patterns. Look at a variety before making your selection so you choose a tile that best complements your kitchen design scheme. If you can't decide buy one of each of your favorite tiles. Place each sample in your kitchen to test it just as you would a paint color swatch.

Magnetic chalkboard

PROJECT DETAILS

SKILLS: Painting

TIME TO COMPLETE

EXPERIENCED: 4 hrs.
HANDY: 6 hrs.
NOVICE: 8 hrs.

STUFF YOU'LL NEED

TOOLS: Ruler, black marking pen, scissors, small paint roller cage, roller cover with ¼-inch nap, small paint trays, ¾-inch round dowel

MATERIALS: Newspaper, 3-inch-wide painter's tape, magnetic latex primer, chalkboard latex paint, semigloss paint in border color

▲ **Adding a decorative border enables you to coordinate the magnetic chalkboard with the design of the room.**

Magnetic primer teamed with chalkboard paint can transform virtually any surface into a play and display space or a hardworking family organization area. The magnetic primer is applied first using a mini roller applicator. The more coats you apply, the stronger the magnetic hold. Apply chalkboard paint over the top for a writing and drawing surface that can be erased easily. Use newspaper to trace a template for letters such as these, which are ideal for a child's room. Trace around the template and then use low-tack painter's tape to mask off the pattern. Remove the painter's tape while the paint is wet. Follow manufacturer's instructions to season the chalkboard finish.

1 **MASK OFF PATTERN.**
After tracing the template in the desired position, tape off the pattern for the magnetic chalkboard using low-tack painter's tape. Press down firmly on the inner edges of the tape. Also tape inside open areas such as the inside triangle on the letter A.

2 **APPLY THE MAGNETIC PRIMER.**
Pour magnetic primer into the paint tray. Following the manufacturer's directions roll the primer over the open areas of the design. Allow the primer to dry. Use a magnet to check magnetic strength. Roll on more coats if desired. Allow primer to dry between coats.

3 **APPLY CHALKBOARD PAINT.**
Pour chalkboard paint into a clean tray. Following the manufacturer's directions roll over the areas painted with magnetic primer. Remove the tape and allow to dry.

4 **ADD A DECORATIVE BORDER.**
Dip the end of a round dowel in paint. Dot the paint on the wall at the edge of each letter to create a border. To prevent the paint from dripping, dab off most of the paint before each stamp. Continue making dots along the edges of the letters. Allow the paint to dry.

GOOD IDEA

FLEXIBLE APPLICATION
You can use magnetic primer on just about any flat surface including drywall, wood, and metal, making it ideal for application on a wall or cabinet. Chalkboard paint can be applied to these same surfaces. Pairing the two increases options for use.

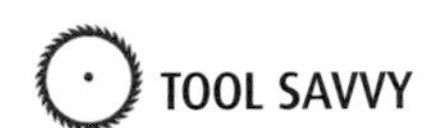

TOOL SAVVY

TOUCHING UP
After removing the painter's tape, use a paintbrush, if necessary, to touch up the rounded corners on the letters. It can be difficult to make perfectly rounded corners with the tape and roller.

Message center

PROJECT DETAILS

SKILLS: Drilling, nailing, cutting, painting

TIME TO COMPLETE

EXPERIENCED: 3 hrs.
HANDY: 5 hrs.
NOVICE: 8 hrs.

STUFF YOU'LL NEED

TOOLS: Drill, saw, hammer, 1-inch paintbrush, mini paint rollers and trays, utility knife
MATERIALS: Two 1×4×72-inch premium white pine boards cut to 65 inches, two 1×2×72-inch premium white pine boards cut to four 35-inch boards, two 1×2×72-inch premium white pine boards cut to $62\frac{1}{2}$ inches, two 1×2×72-inch premium white pine boards cut to four 32-inch boards, four pieces of 1×2-inch premium white pine cut to $2\frac{1}{4}$ inches, 11-foot $\frac{1}{2}$-inch quarter round, 24-foot shoe molding, $1\frac{5}{8}$-inch drywall screws, wood glue, #16 $1\frac{1}{4}$-inch wire brads, $\frac{5}{8}$-inch wire brads, 1 qt. primer, 1 qt. chalkboard paint, $\frac{1}{4}$×24×48-inch tempered hardboard, two acoustic ceiling tiles, cork drawer shelf liner, two-hole seamless eye #3 hangers

▲ **Black paint helps this message center frame blend with its surroundings. The frame can be painted any color that coordinates with your room's decor.**

Hang a message center above a desk area to create a spot for displaying mementos, writing messages, and keeping track of to-do lists. This easy-to-construct version includes a chalkboard flanked by two corkboard sections. The message center is dressed up with a black frame that includes a chalk ledge, so it's functional and stylish. Make the blackboard by priming a piece of tempered hardboard and painting it with chalkboard paint. For a magnetic hold, apply multiple coats of magnetic primer. Create the corkboard sections by cutting a piece of acoustic ceiling tile to size and applying cork shelf liner. Insert and secure the chalkboard and corkboard panels in the frame, hang it on the wall, and your message center is ready for action.

1 ATTACH PART OF THE FRAME.

Mark the 1×4×65-inch boards at 2 inches and 20½ inches from both ends. Set the 1×4×65-inch boards on their long edge to act as the horizontal top and bottom of the frame. Lay the 1×2×35-inch boards on their long edge to act as the vertical supports of the frame, sitting to the outside of the 2-inch and 20½-inch marks on the 1×4×65-inch boards. Drill 3/32-inch pilot holes through the 1×4s and into the ends of the 1×2s. Secure the 1×4s to the 1×2s with 1⅝-inch drywall screws.

2 NAIL THE FRAME TOGETHER.

Cut two 1×2s to 62½ inches. Lay one horizontally with its side across the vertical 1×2s and its narrow edge against the top 1×4. Position the second 62½-inch 1×2 across the vertical 1×2s with its edge against the bottom 1×4. Use glue and #16 1¼-inch wire brads to attach the horizontal 1×2s to the vertical 1×2s.

3 SECURE END CAPS TO THE FRAME.

Position the 1×2×2¼-inch pieces of wood at the four outside corners of the frame where the horizontals and the verticals meet. Glue and nail them to the sides of the frame so they give the illusion that the wood bends around the side of the frame.

4 ATTACH THE FRAME SIDES.

Position two of the 32-inch 1×2s so they rest on the outer vertical 1×2s. The outer edges should be flush with one another so that the inner edge has an overlap of ¾ inch. Glue and nail in place.

DESIGNER TIP

COLOR CHOICE

Black is a classic color choice for this message center frame and could work with designs ranging from traditional to contemporary. Choose a color for the frame, however, based on your decor. If the message center will be placed in a child's room, consider using primary colors. A crisp white paint could be appropriate for a bright kitchen location. Or you may choose to stain the frame rather than painting it.

GOOD IDEA

DOUBLE DUTY

For greater flexibility of use for the message center, apply magnetic primer to the chalkboard area before applying the chalkboard paint. The more coats of magnetic primer you apply, the stronger the magnetic hold will be. Test the strength of the hold before you apply the chalkboard paint and apply additional coats as needed.

5 ATTACH QUARTER-ROUND TRIM. Position two of the 32-inch 1×2s on top of the two inner 1×2 verticals so there is a 3/8-inch overhang on both sides. Secure in place with glue and nails. Cut a piece of quarter round at 64 inches and glue and nail it with 1¼-inch wire brads to the top horizontal 1×4, where it forms a corner with the horizontal 1×2.

6 ATTACH THE CHALK LEDGE. Cut a second quarter round at 64 inches and glue and nail it with 5/8-inch wire brads to the bottom horizontal 1×4 at its front edge, with the round edge facing in and the flat edge flush with the edge of the 1×4. This quarter round helps to form a ledge for the chalk.

7 APPLY PRIMER TO FRAME. Prime the exterior of the frame. This painting can be achieved using a 1-inch paintbrush in the corners and a 1/4-inch-nap roller for broader areas. Allow to dry.

8 APPLY CHALKBOARD PAINT TO FRAME. Paint three coats of chalkboard paint on the frame. Allow to dry.

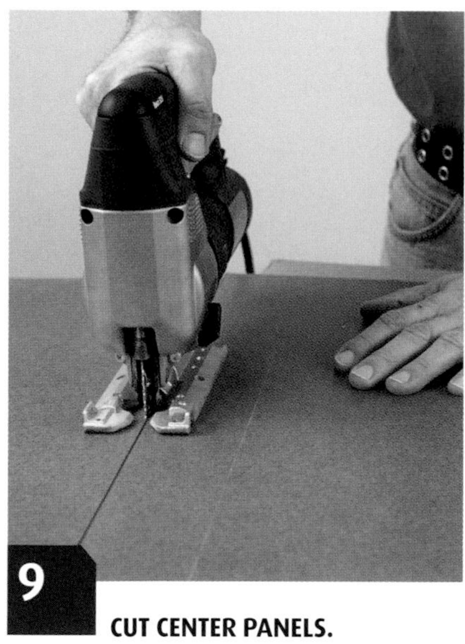

9 CUT CENTER PANELS. Cut the hardboard panel to 24×35 inches to fit the center section of the frame.

10 PRIME AND PAINT CENTER SECTION. Prime the center section and paint it with three coats of chalkboard paint. Allow to dry between coats.

11 **APPLY CORK SHELF LINER.**
Cut two pieces of acoustic ceiling tiles to 17 3/4×35 inches to fit the two outer sections of the frame. Cover one side of the acoustic tiles with cork shelf liner.

12 **REMOVE EXCESS LINER.**
Trim off excess cork shelf liner using a utility knife.

13 **INSERT PANELS.**
Flip the frame on its face and fit the chalkboard panel and the corkboard panels into the frame from the back.

14 **FIX PANELS IN POSITION.**
Secure the chalkboard and corkboards in place with shoe molding anchored with 5/8-inch wire brads.

15 **FASTEN THE HANGERS.**
Attach hangers to the rear edge of the outer vertical 1×2s. When attaching the organizer to the wall, secure fasteners to studs.

GOOD IDEA

ADJUST TO SIZE
The dimensions of this message center can be adjusted to meet your needs and to fit the wall space available to hang it. Before cutting any wood measure wall space and think about how you want to use the board. You may decide to use the same outer frame dimensions but change the sizes of the chalkboard and cork panels.

TOOL SAVVY

SECURE ATTACHMENT
Use a stud finder to locate studs before marking the position for the message center on the wall. A project this substantial needs to be fastened into the studs to remain safely on the wall.

Paint stamps

 PROJECT DETAILS

SKILLS: Painting

 TIME TO COMPLETE

EXPERIENCED: 5 hrs.
HANDY: 7 hrs.
NOVICE: 9 hrs.

 STUFF YOU'LL NEED

TOOLS: Disposable plates, paint applicator (brush or small foam roller), stamping blocks, drop cloth
MATERIALS: Prepared stamping paint or latex paint and glaze

Adding detail

Add detail to your work by painting the stamp with a fine-tip artist's brush. Add shading or highlights to objects or add depth by changing the color as you move from one edge to the other. It's easy, once you get the hang of it. Until you do, practice on a piece of poster board, drywall, or hardboard.

▲ **With stamping you can create any pattern imaginable, from anchors and sails to lilacs and lilies. Stamping goes quickly and allows you to play with design. The anchors on this wall, for example, cover parts of the sail, while each sail faces a different direction.**

Although stamping and stenciling involve painting decorative shapes, they are different techniques. Stenciling is precise, while stamping is freeform and forgiving of mistakes. Stamping allows for variation—no two impressions are identical, and you can break the pattern any way you like. Impressions can face different directions, and the relationship between overlapping patterns can change so that the background stamp becomes the one in the foreground. Though stamping is usually applied to cover an entire wall, that is not a fixed rule. In a child's room stamps may create a path populated by teddy bears; in a family room they may make a border or chair rail.

Make stamps yourself, as was done here, or buy premade stamps. Once you have your stamps and paint, test your technique on poster board or a piece of scrap drywall. If the stamp slides when pressed, you're probably too generous with the paint. When you feel confident begin the project. You need not reapply paint after each impression. Variations in the stamping are part of the effect.

 GOOD IDEA

COMBINE ELEMENTS
For a running border combine two or more elements. Use three blocks to make a grapevine, for example—one for the vine, one for the leaf, and one for the grape. If you are nervous about stamping a border around the walls, practice using the blocks on the back of old wallpaper or a roll of kraft paper cut into several lengthwise strips.

Stamping

1 **PAINT AND APPLY EACH STAMP.** If you don't use a prepared stamping paint, mix your own from half glaze and half latex paint. Place some paint on a plate. Use a brush or foam roller to pick up paint from the plate and distribute it on the face of the block. Here the paint is rolled on one element of the sailboat design. The wall has already been randomly scattered with sail shapes.

2 **OVERLAP DESIGN ELEMENTS.** Parts of a design scheme can be overlapped after the first prints have dried. You don't have to use an opaque paint for the second prints—a translucent glaze helps to blend the colors.

3 **TRACE AROUND STAMPS TO BE PLACED WITH MORE REGULARITY.** Although some stamps can be applied casually, you may want to plot out others, even outlining them for exact placement. Here an anchor is traced then stamped (*inset, above*).

Making your own stamp

Think beyond premade stamps. Any flat object that holds paint can be an interesting pattern for your walls. Flea market vendors may have fabric stamps. Or use the foam from a computer mouse pad, which has the perfect density to hold paint. Trace a pattern and cut it out with a utility knife to create a custom stamp.

1 **FIND A PATTERN AND TRANSFER DESIGN.** Any simple image can become a stamp. Use wallpaper books, pattern books, and children's coloring books to find patterns to photocopy. Cut out the outline of your pattern and put it on the mouse pad. Trace around it with a marker or transfer it to the pad with transfer paper.

2 **CUT OUT THE PATTERN.** Cut out the shapes with scissors or a utility knife. For a handle either run a large safety pin just under the top surface or glue the stamp to a larger scrap of foam.

DESIGNER TIP

VERSATILE STAMPS

To apply patterns around windows, doors, or archways, stamps are more versatile than stencils. If you use stamps such as cats or sheep, for example, you can apply the stamp so that the feet continue to point downward as you move around the opening. In contrast stencil images are repositioned. For example, flowers above a window reach toward the ceiling, while the flowers along the side casing look as if they are lying down. Allow some variation from one print to the next—but not too much.

Plywood accent wall

 PROJECT DETAILS

SKILLS: Measuring, staining, drilling, nailing

 TIME TO COMPLETE

EXPERIENCED: 6 hrs.
HANDY: 8 hrs.
NOVICE: 12 hrs.

 STUFF YOU'LL NEED

TOOLS: Paintbrush, tape measure, pencil, level, drill
MATERIALS: Plywood, tinted outdoor wood stain, screws, metal strips, wall anchors

 TIMESAVER

PRECUT PANELS
Save time and effort by having the panels cut for you at The Home Depot. Take precise measurements with you to the store and ask for the panels to be cut to exact size while you wait.

▲ **Plywood panels stained with a pale blue suit a room that's decorated in fresh country style.**

Stained plywood squares affixed to a wall make a stunning focal point whether they cover the entire wall or only a portion of it. The style such an accent wall conveys depends greatly on the finish applied to the panels. Create a bold checkerboard effect for a child's room by covering the squares with different colors of opaque stain or paint. For a more subdued look, stain the squares one subtle shade that allows the woodgrains to show through. Before you begin attaching the squares to the wall, arrange them on the floor to map out a grid based on how they look next to one another. Once the squares are screwed into the wall, attach a metal strip between them to add visual interest and hide variations in the seams between the panels.

1 APPLY STAIN TO PLYWOOD.
Have plywood sheets precut to size. This grid uses 36×36-inch square panels. Using a foam applicator apply stain to the panels, brushing with the grain. For even coverage use the foam applicator to brush away drips or pools of stain. Allow to dry according to manufacturer's instructions. Repeat the staining process once more. Allow to dry.

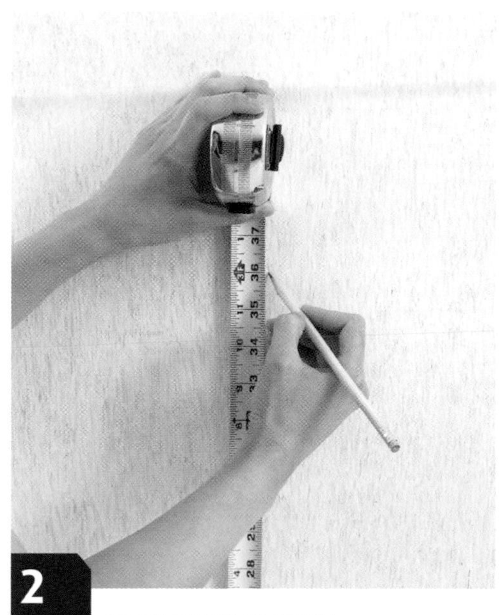

2 MARK THE HORIZONTAL MEASUREMENTS.
The wall panels shown are 36 inches square. While the stain is drying, use a tape measure to make a horizontal mark 3 feet from the top of the baseboard. Make another horizontal line at the 6-foot mark. Use a level and a pencil to draw the horizontal lines. For lower ceilings adjust the sizes of the panels.

CLOSER LOOK

STAINS AND PRIMERS
If you have a little more time to spend with this project and would like a smoother, more even finish on the panels, apply a wood sealer primer to the boards before staining them. The primer will seal the panels so that when you apply the stain it will coat evenly. When you apply stain directly to an unprimed board, how the wood absorbs the stain will vary with the grain.

DESIGNER TIP

CHANGE THE LOOK
Try an opaque stain or paint for a bolder look. Or use two colored stains to create a checkerboard effect.

3 DRAW THE VERTICAL MEASUREMENTS.
Mark the vertical lines with a tape measure. Using a level and a pencil, draw the vertical lines, creating squares across the wall where the accent panels will be attached.

4 DRILL PILOT HOLES.
Drill one pilot hole near each corner of the plywood. To prevent the plywood from splitting, keep the holes ½ inch from the sides of the boards.

Plywood accent wall *(continued)*

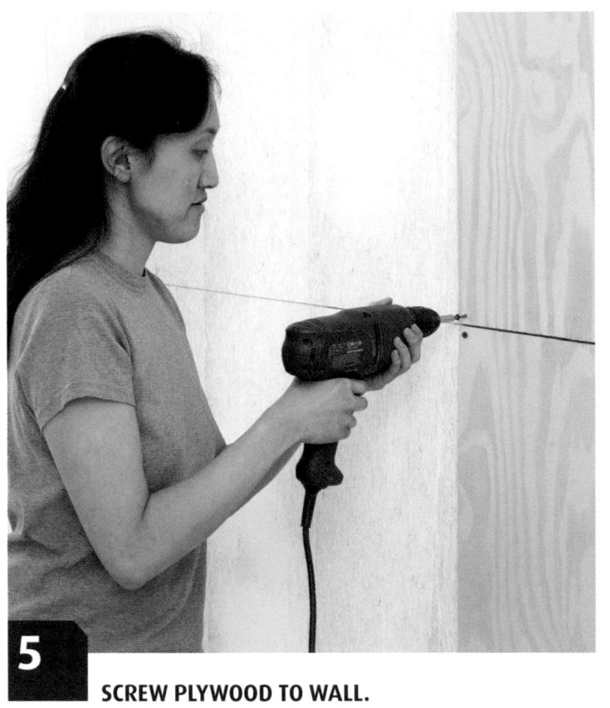

5 SCREW PLYWOOD TO WALL.
Drive the panels into the wall using a bit that fits your drill. Secure all corners of one panel before moving to the next panel.

6 DRILL PILOT HOLES FOR TRIM.
Hold a metal strip over the seam where two plywood pieces abut. Drill a pilot hole through each hole in the metal strip and into the plywood or use a pencil to mark through the holes onto the plywood. Set aside the metal strip.

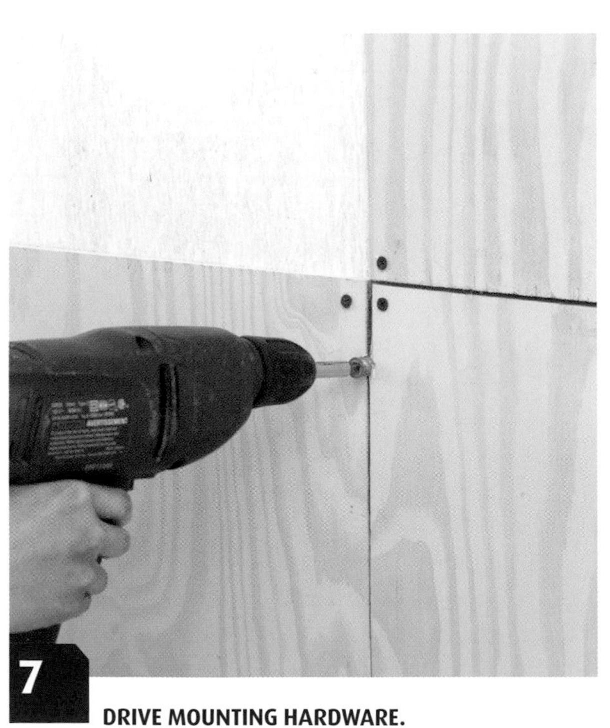

7 DRIVE MOUNTING HARDWARE.
Use a drill to screw mounting anchors into the wall at each of the pilot holes or each pencil mark. Position an anchor at each hole along the metal strip.

8 ATTACH METAL STRIPS TO WALL.
Place the metal strip back over the seams between the plywood panels. Align the holes in the strip with the wall anchors. Drive screws into the wall anchors.

Gallery of wainscoting ideas

Beaded-board wainscoting is appropriate for a casual or country style, while frame-and-panel wainscoting is more suited to traditional rooms. In Colonial homes wainscoting elegantly protects walls from dings, dents, and daily wear. Typically you can choose from solid wood panels or medium-density fiberboard panels. Wood is more traditional, but fiberboard costs less, is more stable, and offers a smooth surface for painting.

■ **Traditional painted panels lighten this room while providing substantial-looking walls.**

■ **Take measurements for a coved chair rail, beaded stiles, and panels that slope to follow the stairs. Stain protects and enhances the grain of natural wood panels.**

Beaded-board wainscoting

PROJECT DETAILS

SKILLS: Measuring, painting, cutting, gluing, installing

TIME TO COMPLETE

EXPERIENCED: 10 hrs.
HANDY: 15 hrs.
NOVICE: 20 hrs.

STUFF YOU'LL NEED

TOOLS: Pry bar, tape measure, level, pencil, stud finder, hammer, paintbrush, power mitersaw or miter box and backsaw, nail set, rubber gloves, notched trowel for adhesive, hand plane (optional), compass, saber saw
MATERIALS: Box extension rings, tongue-and-groove beaded board, cap rail, baseboard (optional), varnish or paint, construction adhesive, #6 and #8 finishing nails, wood putty, paintable caulk

▲ **Typically wainscoting is at the height of a chair rail. Here it reaches almost to the ceiling, with the top rail doubling as a plate shelf.**

Wainscoting—partial paneling used on the lower part of a wall—served for centuries as protection for plaster and added a decorative touch as well.

Wainscoting provides an intimate, traditional feeling in dens, bedrooms, and bathrooms, as well as a somewhat formal look for dining rooms. This partial paneling is used on the lower part of a wall. Installation is typically 32 to 36 inches off the floor, or roughly one-third of the room height. You can also create drama in a dining room by reversing that proportion and making the wainscoting the main feature of the room, as was done here. Whichever proportion you choose raise or lower the top edge to avoid running into windowsills or other trim.

The most common version of wainscoting is the tongue-and-groove beaded-board shown. Home centers sell kits with the pieces—beaded boards or plywood panels, cap rail, and baseboard. You also can special order frame-and-panel wainscoting custom-made to fit a room. The edges between boards are subtly ornamented with a ridge or bead. Wainscoting also can be built from a horizontal series of panels set in frames, similar to a row of traditional cabinet doors. Each board may have a bead running down the center, making a single board look like a pair. Plywood wainscoting sheeting is a modern, easy-to-install alternative.

1 **REMOVE THE BASEBOARD AND OUTLET COVERS.** Coax the baseboard from the wall with a pry bar. Avoid damaging the wood if you plan to reinstall it. You may prefer to use new baseboards with a rabbet to hold the lower ends of the wainscoting boards. The wainscoting will create a well around the outlet covers; install box extension rings, inexpensive metal collars that allow you to bring the outlet to the wainscoting surface.

2 **DRAW A LINE FOR THE TOP EDGE OF THE WAINSCOTING.** Determine the height for the wainscoting, measure up from the floor, and with a level extend a line around the room.

WORK SMARTER

USE A PRY BAR
A pry bar has an enormous wallop. Put a piece of wood between it and the wall to gain leverage, distribute the force, and avoid damaging the wall.

DESIGNER TIP

NO BASEBOARD
In some older homes rooms with wainscoting didn't have baseboard because the beaded boards provided protection for the lower wall. If you opt for baseboard, reuse the existing board if possible. It will match the rest of the baseboard and help to tie the room together.

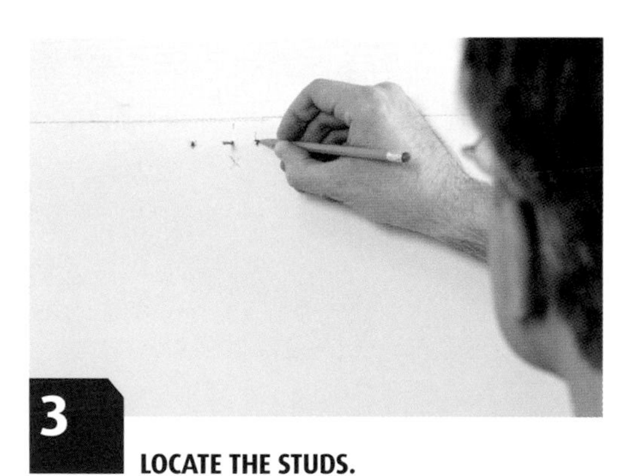

3 **LOCATE THE STUDS.**
The top and the bottom of the wainscoting are held in place by a cap rail and a baseboard that are nailed into the studs. Use a stud finder to locate the studs or use the low-tech method. Begin 16 inches out from an adjacent wall (studs typically are spaced 16 inches apart measured from center to center) and drive a nail into the wall. Make the hole low enough so that it will be concealed by the wainscoting or cap rail and keep it at least 5 inches above the floor—any lower and you may be misled by other framing that doesn't extend to the ceiling. Keep trying until the nail hits something solid: It's a stud. (Don't drive nails near electrical outlets or switches.) Mark the stud at floor level and just above the level line, move 16 inches along the wall, and drive nails to find the next stud.

Frame-and-panel wainscoting

In colonial times installing wainscoting was time-consuming work that required skilled labor.

The frame-and-panel look, without the intensive labor, is available to do-it-yourselfers. Check home centers and home renovation magazines for companies that, based on room measurements, make frame-and-panel walls. The wainscoting usually is shipped unassembled and is installed piece by piece on the wall.

Before placing an order determine whether the panels are solid wood or built over medium-density fiberboard. Wood is traditional, of course, but fiberboard costs less and is more stable. After the panels are on the wall, no one will know the difference.

Do it yourself

Take the measurements for coved chair rail, beaded stiles, and panels that slope to follow the stairs. Have a well-equipped shop build them for you and tackle the installation yourself.

Beaded-board wainscoting *(continued)*

GOOD IDEA

BEGIN WITH THE OBVIOUS
Start installation in the most obvious corner of the room. Little errors will be hidden in less obvious parts of the room.

Cutting for outlets

To accommodate electrical outlets cut rectangular notches in the beaded boards. Lay out the hole by rubbing lipstick or chalk onto the edges of the outlet's electrical box. Position the board on the wall and press it against the box. Put the board on a work surface and drill ½-inch holes just inside each corner. Cut along the line with a saber saw.

4 PREFINISH ALL COMPONENTS.
Finish the back of the wainscoting as well as the front to minimize possible warping. Finish the back while you can still get to it. If you wish, you can finish the front, as well as the cap rail and baseboard, at this time too. Keep in mind that you'll have to fill nail holes at the end of the job, so make sure to have matching putty.

5 DETERMINE YOUR NEXT STEP.
What you do at this point depends on what you're working with. If the baseboard has a rabbet that houses the beaded boards, cut it to length and install it. Nail it to the studs with #6 finishing nails, and countersink the nailheads. When splicing two lengths of baseboard to span a wall, achieve an inconspicuous seam by overlapping them with a scarf joint. If the baseboard isn't rabbeted and it will be nailed on top of the boards, install the beaded board first, as described below.

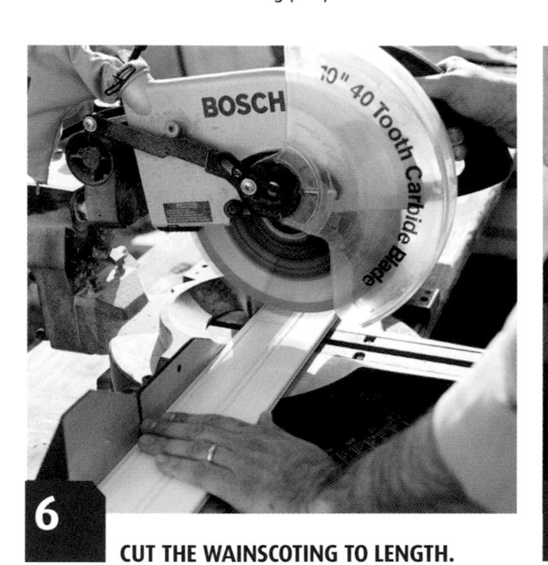

6 CUT THE WAINSCOTING TO LENGTH.
Begin at either end of the wall and measure to determine the length of the wainscot boards. If you have a rabbeted baseboard, measure from the bottom of the rabbet to the line marking the top of the wainscoting. If the baseboard will go on after the wainscoting is installed, measure between the line and the floor. For now cut two or three boards to this length with a handsaw, circular saw, or mitersaw. The length of the boards may change as you move along the wall due to uneven or unlevel floors.

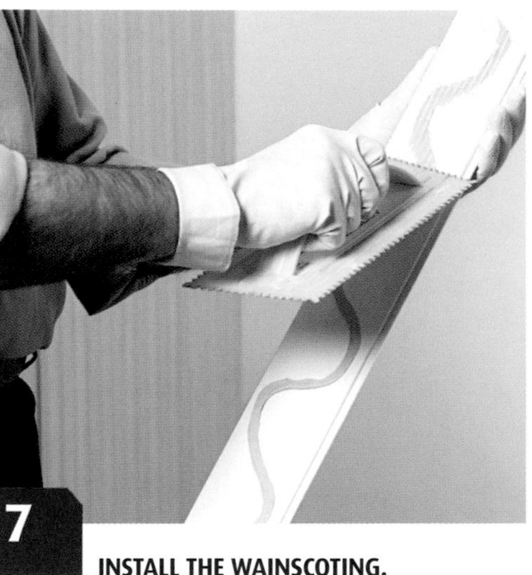

7 INSTALL THE WAINSCOTING.
Butt the grooved end of a board into a corner and nail it in place. Place the next board upside down on a drop cloth or newspapers, run a waving line of construction adhesive along the back, and spread the adhesive with a notched trowel. Apply adhesive to several boards before proceeding to the next step. Spread glue as you slip the boards into place. Slide the tongues in the grooves, leaving a 1/16-inch space between the visible edges of the boards to allow for expansion in humid weather. Align the top edges with the level line, check the edge for plumb with a level, and make necessary corrections. Press the boards with the heels of your hands to help the boards bond with the wall.

8 NAIL BOARDS OVER STUDS IN PLACE.

Once you install the boards you've cut to length, measure for the next two or three boards and cut and install them. Whenever a board is over a stud, nail it in place. If possible hide the nail in the groove along the bead or drive it through the tongue. Cut or plane as much of the last board as necessary to make it fit. Install it by slipping it down from above with its groove engaging the tongue of the previous board.

9 TAKE CARE WITH OUT-OF-PLUMB CORNERS.

If you are working toward a corner that isn't plumb, you may be able to deal with it by making small adjustments several boards away. Measure the distance between the last board and the corner at both the top and bottom of the wainscoting; divide the difference by the number of boards remaining to be installed along the wall. If it's within 1/16 inch, install the remaining beaded boards slightly out of plumb so that the last board will be flush with the adjoining wall. If the distance is more than 1/16 inch, scribe the last board to fit.

10 INSTALL THE CAP RAIL AND BASEBOARD.

Nail the cap rail in place with #6 finishing nails if they'll reach about 1/2 inch into the studs or with #8 finishing nails if they won't. Miter the rail at inside and outside corners. If the rail is especially large or complex, cope inside corners as shown for chair rails. (See "Coping a Chair Rail," page 33.) If the baseboards go on top of the beaded boards, nail them in place using #8 finishing nails in order to reach the studs. Countersink the nailheads. Fill all nail holes. If you paint the wainscoting, seal gaps with paintable caulk.

GOOD IDEA

PUSH OR PULL

It may take getting used to, but you can do a smoother job of caulking if you push the cartridge gun rather than pull it. The caulk penetrates tight corners better, and you'll make a less conspicuous bead.

Scribing to fit

If you install the first board plumb and discover the wall isn't plumb, it can create a gap. Carpenters deal with this by cutting or scribing the board to fit.

To scribe a board hold it in the corner with its edge against the problem wall. Plumb the board with a level so that it is perfectly vertical. Lay out the cut with the help of a simple compass. Set the distance between pencil and point to the width of the gap. Run the metal point along the wall and the pencil along the board to lay out the cut. (Make sure the compass setting doesn't change while you do this.) Cut along the pencil line with a saber saw.

Faux fireplace

 PROJECT DETAILS

SKILLS: Measuring, gluing, drilling, hammering

 TIME TO COMPLETE

EXPERIENCED: 2 hrs.
HANDY: 3 hrs.
NOVICE: 4 hrs.

 STUFF YOU'LL NEED

TOOLS: Stud finder, pencil, level, tape measure, liquid glue, variable-speed drill and bits, hammer, nail set, sandpaper
MATERIALS: Mantel kit and mantel cap, construction adhesive, drywall screws, molly bolt anchors, 2-inch finishing nails, wood putty, paint or stain

 DESIGNER TIP

DECORATING A FIREPLACE
If you have a fireplace, it may have become a decorating dilemma—the furniture points toward it and a few knickknacks grace the mantel, but the effect is dreary. Three key elements help play up the best features of a fireplace: the mantel, the surround, and the firebox and hearth. Give prominence to and balance out a visually weighty mantel by displaying substantial items such as a large painting with shorter, hefty items such as candles or statues. Enhance the surround (see "Good Idea," *right*). Add a decorative screen to the firebox to disguise it. Or position leafy plants, candles, or architectural pieces in front of the hearth.

▲ **A fireplace has great potential as a decorative element. This faux fireplace adds the drama without the expense of installing the real thing.**

Real fireplaces that produce heat are, of course, functional. But a fireplace outfitted with a mantel also serves as a key decorative element—often the focal point—in a room. Even if your home doesn't accommodate a functional fireplace, consider installing a mantel kit on an open wall. You may choose to line the space beneath the mantel where the fireplace typically goes with tile, as shown *above*. Paired with the right decorative objects, a mantel creates the appearance of a fireplace so warm and welcoming everyone will want to gather around it.

When installing a mantel remember that it should be mounted into the wall studs. Although the mantel may be sturdy enough to hold decorative objects, do not place more than 25 pounds of weight on it at any time. If you choose to install an actual fireplace insert or stove beneath the mantel, be certain to check local fire codes and instructions from the manufacturer before installation.

 GOOD IDEA

ENHANCE A SURROUND
Tiling is a popular technique for enhancing a fireplace surround and hearth. For a large area select basic field tiles and accent with specialty tiles. If you want a vintage style, look for architectural features such as columns or even an old mantel that can be mounted to or in place of the existing surround.

1 **MARK POSITION OF FIRST LEG.**
Use a stud finder to mark studs. Then mark where you want the first leg of the mantel to go. Try to position the legs over studs. Check for plumb and draw a line on the wall where the outside of the first leg will be positioned.

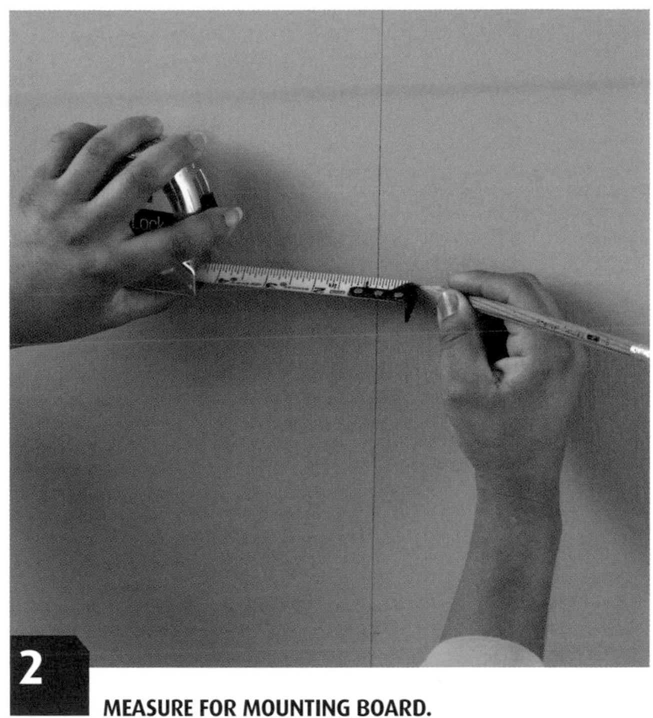

2 **MEASURE FOR MOUNTING BOARD.**
Measure in ¾ inch from the outside of the first leg. This marks the position for the mounting board. Check for plumb using a level and draw a line marking placement of the mounting board. Determine the position of the other leg and repeat steps 1 and 2 for the other leg.

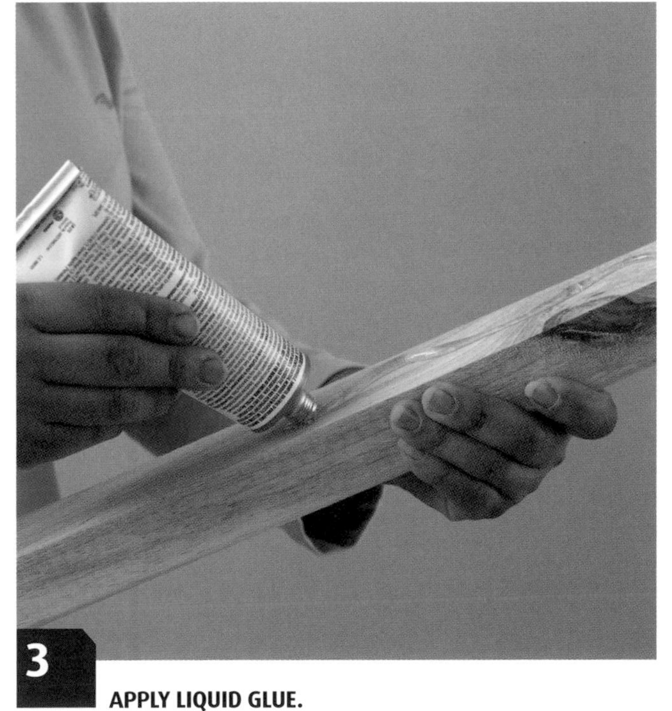

3 **APPLY LIQUID GLUE.**
To secure the mounting boards, apply liquid glue to the back of the board. Follow manufacturer's instructions. Attach the board to the wall where you marked.

4 **SECURE MOUNTING BOARD.**
Drive screws through the mounting board and into studs for the most secure attachment. If the mounting boards are not positioned over studs, use molly bolt anchors to secure them to the wall. Repeat steps 3 and 4 for the other mounting board.

5

ATTACH FIREPLACE LEG.

Position the first leg over the mounting board. Drill pilot holes through the leg and into the mounting board. If desired use construction adhesive to hold the leg in place.

6

COUNTERSINK NAILS.

Drive a finishing nail through each pilot hole and into the mounting board. To keep from marring the surface of the leg with the hammer, use a nail set to countersink the nails. Repeat steps five and six for the other leg.

7

ATTACH SKIRT.

The skirt will rest in place on the legs. Secure it by applying a thin bead of construction adhesive to the top of each leg where the skirt will rest on it. For a stronger connection drill pilot holes through the skirt into the leg support. Drive finishing nails through the skirt into the leg support.

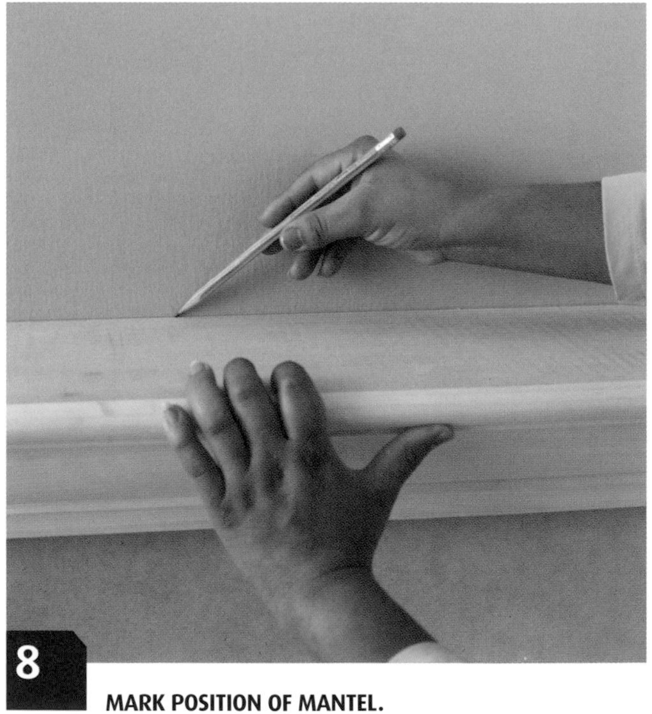

8

MARK POSITION OF MANTEL.

Rest the mantel cap on top of the skirt. Check for level. Using a pencil mark the top of the mantel cap on the wall.

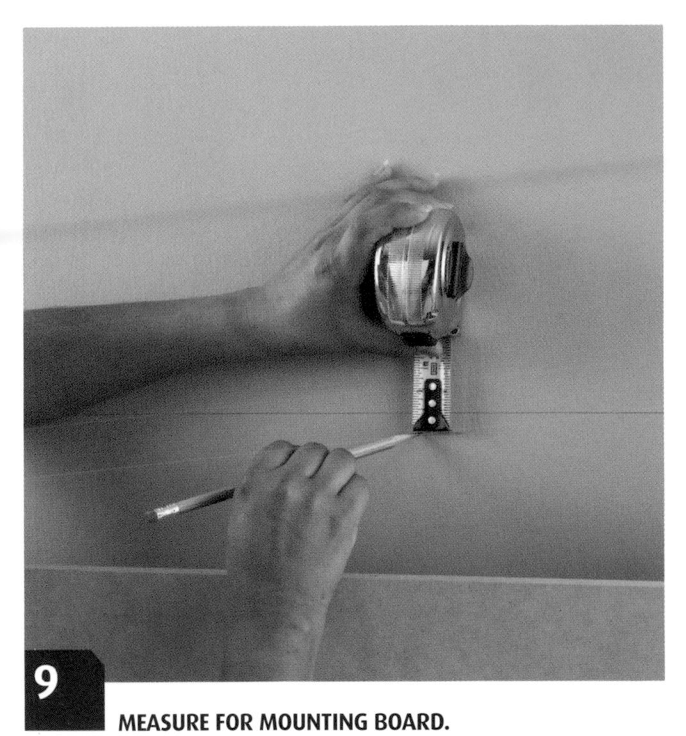

9

MEASURE FOR MOUNTING BOARD.
First measure the top board of the mantel cap to verify where to position the mounting board. From the mark you made for the top of the mantel cap, measure down 3/4 inch (or the depth of the mantel cap) and mark.

10

ATTACH MOUNTING BOARD.
Apply a thin bead of construction adhesive to the back of the mantel cap mounting board. Position the mounting board on the wall and check for level. Drive screws through the mounting board and into the wall. Be sure to drive at least three screws into studs.

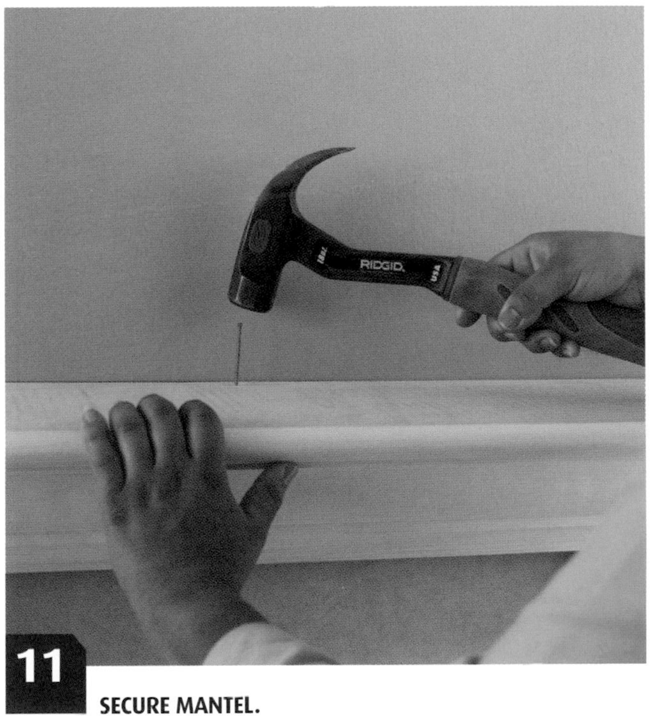

11

SECURE MANTEL.
Rest the mantel cap on the mounting board. Drill pilot holes through the mantel cap and into the mounting board. Drive finishing nails into the pilot holes, through the cap, and into the board. Use a nail set to countersink the nails.

12

FILL NAIL HOLES.
Attach the decorative caps to the bottom of each leg using finishing nails. Fill nail holes with putty and sand for a smooth finish. Apply paint or stain as desired and allow to dry. If desired apply a decorative technique—such as the tiles on this finished project—to the firebox area.

Columns

 PROJECT DETAILS

SKILLS: Marking, measuring, cutting, mounting

 TIME TO COMPLETE

EXPERIENCED: 6 hrs.
HANDY: 8 hrs.
NOVICE: 10 hrs.

 STUFF YOU'LL NEED

TOOLS: Plumb bob, pencil, tape measure, saw (hacksaw, crosscut, or saber saw), sawhorses, pry bar, wood shims, caulk gun
MATERIALS: Column, masking tape, construction adhesive, mounting brackets, screws, latex filler, paintable caulk

▲ **Columns provide dimension and focus to an otherwise large and empty space. They work well to emphasize ceiling height while linking two open portions of a room.**

Columns are a central element in classical architecture. Over the centuries they have contributed structurally and aesthetically to building composition. Although the use of classical columns for structural purposes is less common today, using them to decoratively define room spaces is popular.

Use columns to define an entryway or to divide a large room into two or more distinct spaces without imposing a wall. A pair of columns can frame a prominent window or wall unit, while a single column can enliven a nondescript corner. Half columns applied to the wall can define space without intruding into the room.

Columns are available in many styles, sizes, and materials: round, tapered, square, fluted; full columns and half columns; wood, metal, polyurethane. Columns are made up of three parts: the base, the shaft, and the capital.

In general the column shaft is cut to fit between the floor and ceiling, and it is secured with angled screws or metal brackets as well as construction adhesive. Some manufacturers assemble the base and capital in separate halves around the column after it is in place. Others are solid pieces that slide over the shaft before it is positioned and are secured to the floor and ceiling after the shaft is in place.

1 MARK THE COLUMN LOCATION ON THE CEILING AND ON THE TOP OF THE HALF-WALL.

Mark the center point of the column on the top surface of the half-wall. Use a plumb bob to transfer the center mark to the ceiling. Using the centers as starting points, lay out the shape of the column base and cap on the half-wall and ceiling to make sure they fall where you want them.

2 MEASURE THE OVERALL HEIGHT.

Measure the distance between the marks on the half-wall and ceiling to determine the overall height of the column. Transfer the measurement onto the column. Take into account the base cap, which may or may not extend above the top of the column. The top of the column is usually factory cut, and any excess is removed from the bottom of the column. Don't try for a perfectly tight fit—you'll never be able to stand the column and get it in place. Follow the manufacturer's instructions for how much to trim from the bottom to get the column into place. After it's upright shim it from the bottom. The base and cap will cover the gap.

3 CUT THE COLUMN.

A hacksaw is used to cut a polyurethane column. A standard cross-cut saw works well for a wood column. You also could use a saber saw to cut through either material and to save time. Protect the column from scratches by wrapping masking tape around the base where you will cut. Support the column on sawhorses and prevent it from rolling by slipping a thin wood shim under each side on each sawhorse.

Floor to ceiling

The column in this project is installed between a half-wall and the ceiling. The procedure is the same for installing a column from the floor to ceiling.

4 **POSITION BASE AND CAP MOLDINGS ON THE COLUMN.** The column base shown slides on before the column is stood up; it then slides into position when the column is upright. Make sure the flat part faces the floor. The neck molding was preinstalled at the factory on this column, although some neck molding is installed at this stage, and the column cap is positioned on top of the column.

5 **STAND THE COLUMN.** In this installation the column slides onto the top of the half-wall conveniently. Whenever possible stand the column in an adjacent area that has plenty of headroom. Standing the column next to the knee wall, for example, gives the installer room to work without scraping the ceiling. If you can't do this, position the base of the column near the base layout marks and stand it up. If you have to scrape the ceiling a bit to get the column fully upright, make sure it's within the area that will be covered by the column cap. A length of string tied around opposite corners of the column base prevents it from sliding down the column. Notice the slight gap at the ceiling.

6 **SHIM THE BASE OF THE COLUMN TO RAISE IT TIGHT TO THE CEILING.** Nudge the column into position on the layout marks; you may want to temporarily slide the column base down to make sure it's in the right place. Apply a bead of construction adhesive (check manufacturer's instructions for the correct type) into the gap around the top of the column. Slip a pry bar under the bottom of the column to raise it up against the ceiling, then slide wood shims under the column to hold it tight to the ceiling. Use three or four shims evenly spaced around the column. Straight columns can be checked for plumb; tapered columns require that you rely on initial layout marks.

7 **ATTACH MOUNTING BRACKETS TO COLUMN.** Follow the manufacturer's instructions for securing the column—L-brackets are a common approach. Screw the L-brackets to the column and the half-wall base (or floor). Use angle brackets at the top of the column only if you can connect to a ceiling joist. The adhesive on the top of the column and column cap should be sufficient.

8 **ATTACH THE COLUMN BASE AND CAP.** Apply construction adhesive to the flat surfaces of the column base and cap, then slide them into position. Drive screws through the column base and cap to secure them in place. For the base cap you may need to drive the screws at an angle into the column itself. Fill all screw holes with a latex filler. Caulk any gaps around the base and cap moldings.

GOOD IDEA

SQUARE UP
Home centers and hardware stores sell small packages of shims. They're inexpensive and help you do an accurate job of squaring up.

COLUMN COLOR
Faux techniques, such as stippling, marbleizing, sponging, and ragging, add luster and style to columns. Coordinate color combinations already in the room or introduce an accent color.

Carpenter's secret

To mark a straight line around a circular column, make two marks on opposite sides of the column to indicate the length. Connect the marks with a piece of wide masking tape—the wider the better—wrapped around the column. Or wrap a strip of poster board around the column and position an edge along the cut by measuring down from the straight factory edge. Trace along the edge to mark a line all around the column.

Headboard

 PROJECT DETAILS

SKILLS: Drilling, nailing, cutting, finishing, attaching

 TIME TO COMPLETE

EXPERIENCED: 4 hrs.
HANDY: 6 hrs.
NOVICE: 8 hrs.

 STUFF YOU'LL NEED

TOOLS: Tape measure, pencil, saber saw, drill, 1-inch drill bit, hammer, tablesaw, 2-inch high-quality synthetic-bristle paintbrush, tack cloth, stud finder, fine-grit sandpaper
MATERIALS: Two 1×2×72-inch premium white pine boards, four 1×3×72-inch premium white pine boards, wood glue, small box of 1¼-inch wire brads, five 1×48-inch wood dowels, 4×8-foot panel of ¼-inch maple veneer plywood cut into 11 strips each 3×60 inches, water-base satin polycrylic, two seamless eye #1 hangers

▲ **A basket weave headboard adds a finished look to a bedroom. The headboard should be firmly affixed to the wall.**

Nothing adds style to your bedroom quite like a headboard. Embellish a plain headboard using fabric, paint, or wood. Or start from scratch and build your own budget-wise version. A fireplace surround makes a dramatic headboard when mounted to the wall. Or consider affixing metal to medium-density fiberboard for a contemporary backdrop. This queen-size headboard features a pleasing basket weave pattern thanks to plywood strips that are woven in alternating rows. Regardless of the style of your headboard, if it's attached to the wall be sure to affix it to the wall studs for adequate support.

1

DRILL HOLES FOR THE FRAME.

Cut the 1×2-inch and the 1×3-inch boards to a length of $61\frac{1}{2}$ inches. Mark two of the 1×3s at $\frac{3}{4}$ inch in from the edge of the board and $2\frac{3}{4}$ inches, $16\frac{3}{4}$ inches, $30\frac{3}{4}$ inches, $44\frac{3}{4}$ inches, and $58\frac{3}{4}$ inches in from the end of the board. Drill 1-inch holes through the boards at each of these marks.

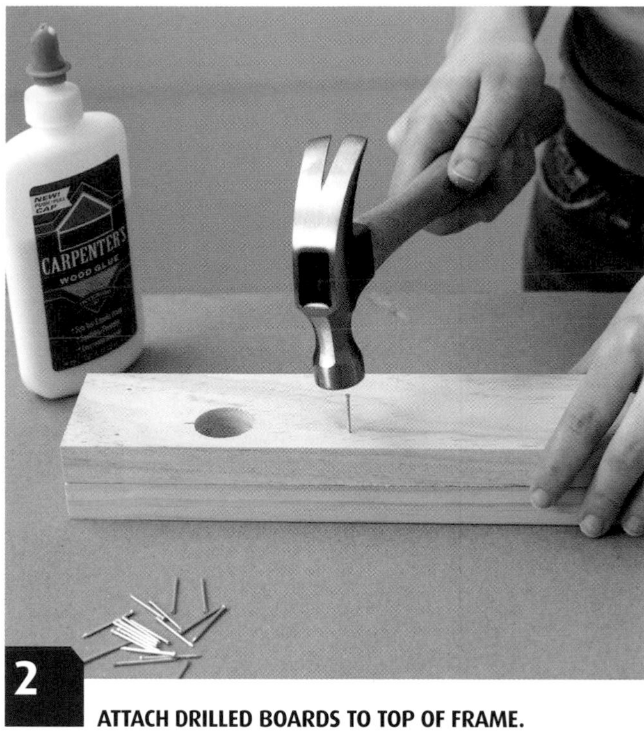

2

ATTACH DRILLED BOARDS TO TOP OF FRAME.

Glue and nail each drilled board to a 1×3-inch board that doesn't have any holes drilled in it to construct the top of the headboard frame.

3

FASTEN EDGING ON SIDE OF FRAME.

Glue and nail a 1×2-inch board to the edge side nearest the holes of the attached 1×3s to finish the top of the headboard frame. Repeat steps 2 and 3 to construct the bottom of the headboard frame.

4

RESIZE DOWELS.

Cut the five dowels to $34\frac{5}{8}$ inches. These dowels will fit between the top and bottom of the headboard and provide the framework for weaving the wooden slats.

Headboard *(continued)*

5 CUT SLATS TO LENGTH.

Cut 11 slats measuring 3×60 inches from the plywood. You will weave these slats between the five dowels.

6 APPLY FINISH TO WOOD PIECES.

You will now have what essentially looks like two 2×4-inch boards with five holes drilled in each. Sand these, the dowels, and the 11 slats. Wipe with tack cloth and finish with three coats of satin polycrylic paint. Sand lightly between coats. Allow to dry.

7 ATTACH THE DOWELS.

When all pieces are thoroughly dry, hand-fit the dowels in each of the holes in both boards. Glue the dowels in the holes of one of the rails. Fit the other end of the dowels with glue in the second rail. Lay the frame flat and square. Allow it to dry for several hours.

TOOL SAVVY

WORK SAFELY

Don't wear rings, other jewelry, watches, or loose clothing when operating a tablesaw. Wear safety glasses and hearing protection. A piece that gets caught between the rip fence and blade will kick back with force. Never stand directly behind the blade.

GOOD IDEA

TESTING STAIN

Apply stain to the slats and frame before the sealer for a different look. Stain can look a lot different on your headboard than it does in the sample brochure. Test it first on a scrap slat. A clean cotton T-shirt is a good applicator. Dip the shirt in the stain, wipe it on, and then wipe away the excess with a clean part of the shirt. When you apply stain always apply it with the grain for best results.

8 **WEAVE THE SLATS.**
Weave the plywood strips through the dowels. Alternate rows to create a pleasing basketweave pattern.

9 **FASTEN HANGERS.**
Attach hangers to the back of the headboard. Make sure to secure the wallmount portion of the hanger to studs for adequate support.

DESIGNER TIP

HEADBOARD STYLE
Design a headboard that suits the style of your bedroom. Possibilities for creative headboards are almost endless. Cover a foam board with fabric that coordinates with bedding. Center a fireplace mantel behind the bed (see page 70 for how to install one). Secure shutters or a picket fence to the wall for a fresh country look. Go for a more contemporary design with metal tread plates mounted to fiberboard. Browse the aisles of The Home Depot for more inspiration.

Medallion frame

 PROJECT DETAILS

SKILLS: Painting

 TIME TO COMPLETE

EXPERIENCED: 1 hr.
HANDY: 2 hrs.
NOVICE: 3 hrs.

 STUFF YOU'LL NEED

TOOLS: Drop cloth or newspapers, scrap wood, goggles, face mask, paint can opener, artist's paintbrush, caulk gun, hammer
MATERIALS: 20-inch (or desired size) decorative ceiling medallion, 1-inch painter's tape, white spray primer, taupe satin spray paint, semigloss white paint, disposable plate, polyurethane adhesive, 8-inch round mirror, nail with head

DESIGNER TIP

COLOR SELECTION
For a subtle effect such as this frame, use a tone-on-tone color palette. For a more dramatic effect, select a palette featuring complementary colors. See pages 10–13 for more information about using the color wheel and basic color combinations.

▲ **A ceiling medallion makes an elegant frame for a simple mirror.**

Traditionally ceiling medallions, used in conjunction with a chandelier on the ceiling of formal spaces such as the dining room, add architectural interest. With the variety of ceiling medallion styles available—from incredibly ornate to plain and simple—these decorative details are used in more places than just the ceiling. For instance a ceiling medallion makes a great frame for a mirror or may serve as a focal point above a mantel. Today's lightweight polyurethane medallions are easier to install than the original plaster-cast ones, which means the medallions can be used in places that aren't as sturdy as the ceiling. Often white ceiling medallions are left plain to match a room's trimwork. Decorative painting techniques, however, may be used before installation to make a medallion coordinate with a light fixture or match the style of the room where it is installed.

1 APPLY PRIMER TO CEILING MEDALLION. In a well-ventilated work area, cover the work surface with a drop cloth, brown paper, or newspapers. Place scrap wood pieces under the center of the medallion to raise it from the table. Secure tape around the edge of the medallion opening to keep it free from paint. Put on a safety painting mask and goggles. Spray one light coat of primer to cover the surface of the ceiling medallion. Allow to dry.

2 SPRAY BASE COAT. After the primer is dry, put on a safety painting mask and goggles. Spray paint the medallion with a light coat of taupe paint. Allow the paint to dry and then apply a light second coat of taupe spray paint. Allow to dry.

3 PREP BRUSH FOR PAINTING. After pouring a small amount of white paint on a disposable plate, dip a small paintbrush in paint. Remove the excess paint from the brush by wiping back and forth on the plate.

4 HIGHLIGHT THE RAISED AREAS. On the raised decorative portions of the medallion, brush light strokes in one direction and then the other in an X movement. Remove the tape from the center of the medallion. Allow the paint to dry.

5 APPLY ADHESIVE TO THE MEDALLION. Puncture the end of the adhesive according to the manufacturer's instructions. Place tube in the caulk gun. Press a ring of adhesive onto the center rim of the medallion.

6 PRESS MIRROR INTO PLACE. Center the mirror over the medallion and carefully press it into place. Let the adhesive dry according to manufacturer's instructions. To hang the mirror tap a nail into the wall and position the center of the medallion on the nail.

Etched mirror

PROJECT DETAILS

SKILLS: Cutting, painting

TIME TO COMPLETE

EXPERIENCED: 1 hr.
HANDY: 2 hrs.
NOVICE: 3 hrs.

STUFF YOU'LL NEED

TOOLS: Computer and printer, scissors, pencil, crafts knife, rubber gloves, foam brush, small bucket, sponge, safety glasses
MATERIALS: 18×22-inch wall mirror, computer printout of bold letters, clear tape, contact paper, etching cream for mirrors, water

▲ A simple word etched on this mirror contributes to the soothing style of this bathroom.

Etching has been used for centuries as a decorative addition to glass and mirrors. Today's methods for glass etching are much easier and safer than techniques used in the past. In fact, despite its striking appearance, only one main ingredient is used for this process—etching cream.

First you'll want to select the word, shape, or pattern you want to etch. If you are etching a word, choose the size and font for the lettering—make certain it's a bold typeface so it shows up well—and make a computer printout. The same idea applies for any shape you wish to etch: Make a printout of the object at the desired size. When etching a mirror you'll probably want to etch only words or shapes around the edges of the mirror so it can still be used. When using the etching technique on objects such as vases, however, you may wish to etch more of the object for a frosted-glass effect.

GOOD IDEA

PROTECT THE BACKING

If the mirror has a separate backing, caulk the seam with clear silicone to prevent the etching cream and water from seeping in the seam. If the mirror is without a backing piece, rinse it under a faucet instead of wiping away the etching cream with a sponge.

TOOL SAVVY

BRUSH IT ON

For a freehand etched design, use a small paintbrush to make strokes with etching cream.

1 CUT OUT THE LETTERS.

To make a computer-generated pattern, decide the size and font of the lettering. Type and print out the desired word on white paper. Cut apart the letters, leaving narrow borders at the sides of the letters.

2 COLOR THE BACK OF EACH LETTER.

Tape the letters together, keeping the spacing equal and the bottoms of the letters aligned. Color over the back of each letter with a pencil.

Etched mirror *(continued)*

3 PRESS CONTACT PAPER TO THE MIRROR.
Cut a piece of contact paper to cover the mirror. Peel off the paper backing and press the contact paper to the mirror, smoothing out the wrinkles as you place the paper.

4 TRACE AROUND EACH LETTER.
Position the taped-together printout on the contact paper where the etched word is desired. Trace around each letter with a pencil to transfer the design. Remove the paper pattern.

5 CUT OUT THE LETTERS.
Use a sharp, fine-tapered crafts knife to carefully cut away the insides of the letters. Be careful not to cut into the background.

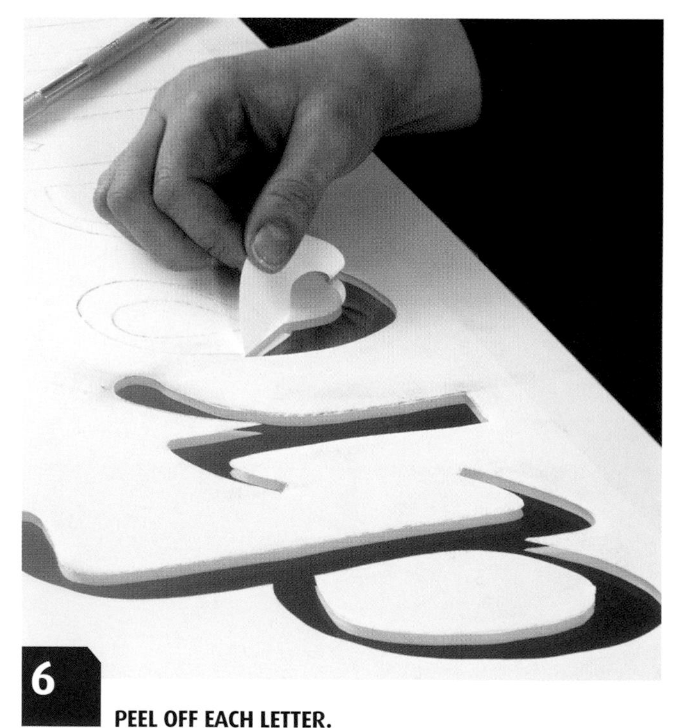

6 PEEL OFF EACH LETTER.
After cutting around the edges, carefully remove each letter. Make sure the cut edges are smooth. If not use the crafts knife to carefully cut away the necessary paper.

7

APPLY ETCHING CREAM.

Put on rubber gloves. Using a small foam brush, apply etching cream to the letter openings following the manufacturer's instructions.

8

RINSE THE ETCHING CREAM.

Fill a small bucket with water. Put on rubber gloves again. Use a dampened sponge to wipe the etching cream thoroughly from the mirror. Continue rinsing the sponge in the water and wiping the mirror until no trace of etching cream is left.

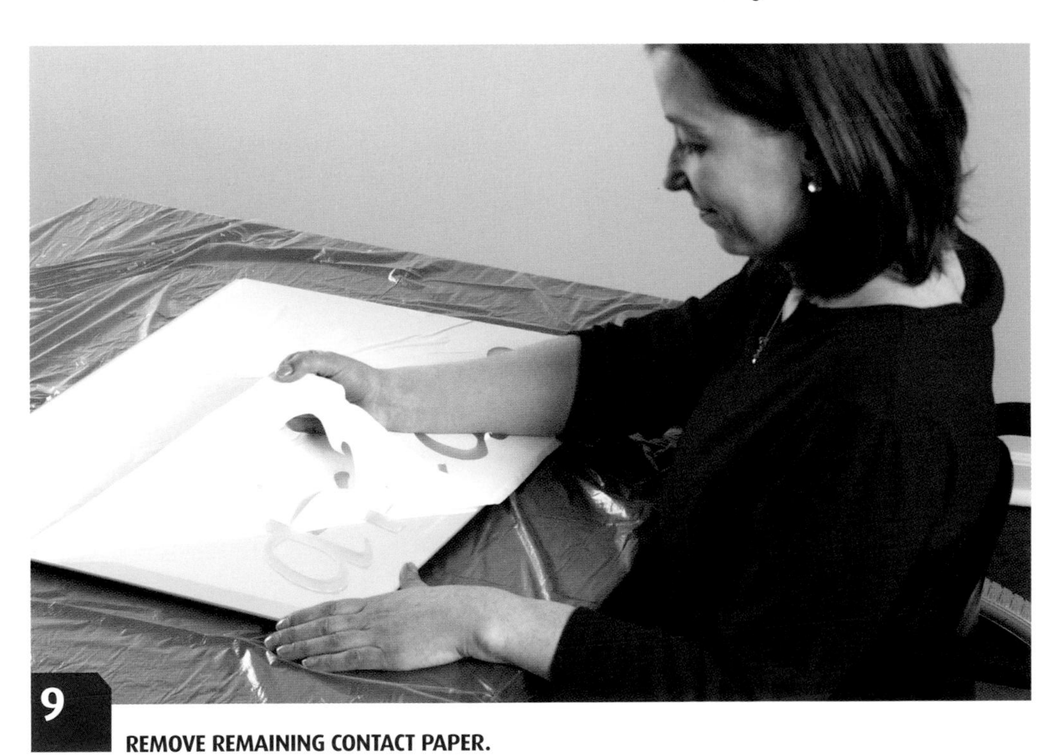

9

REMOVE REMAINING CONTACT PAPER.

Peel away the remaining contact paper. Wipe the mirror with a clean, dampened sponge.

Pictures and mirrors

PROJECT DETAILS

SKILLS: Measuring, nailing, hanging

TIME TO COMPLETE

EXPERIENCED: 1 hr.
HANDY: 2 hrs.
NOVICE: 3 hrs.

STUFF YOU'LL NEED

TOOLS: Pencil, scissors, stud finder, tape measure, drill, hammer
MATERIALS: Paper, masking tape, screw eyes, picture wire, picture hangers with nails

▲ **Test possible arrangements directly on the wall. Cut out pieces of paper the size and shape of each picture to tape to the wall. Rearrange the pieces until you find a pleasing grouping.**

Hanging art is an art. First you have the challenge of placing objects on a wall in a pleasing way. It's similar to arranging furniture. Even hanging a single picture on a bare wall can be difficult. Experiment by taping up pieces of paper cut to the sizes of your pictures. Arrange them in rows, in a circle, or randomly until you find a pleasing combination. Generally larger and darker pictures look better placed toward the bottom of a grouping. By breaking up pictures that feature particular colors, the eye is encouraged to travel around an arrangement.

Make sure your precious objects are installed securely. Use proper hanging hardware to attach them to the wall.

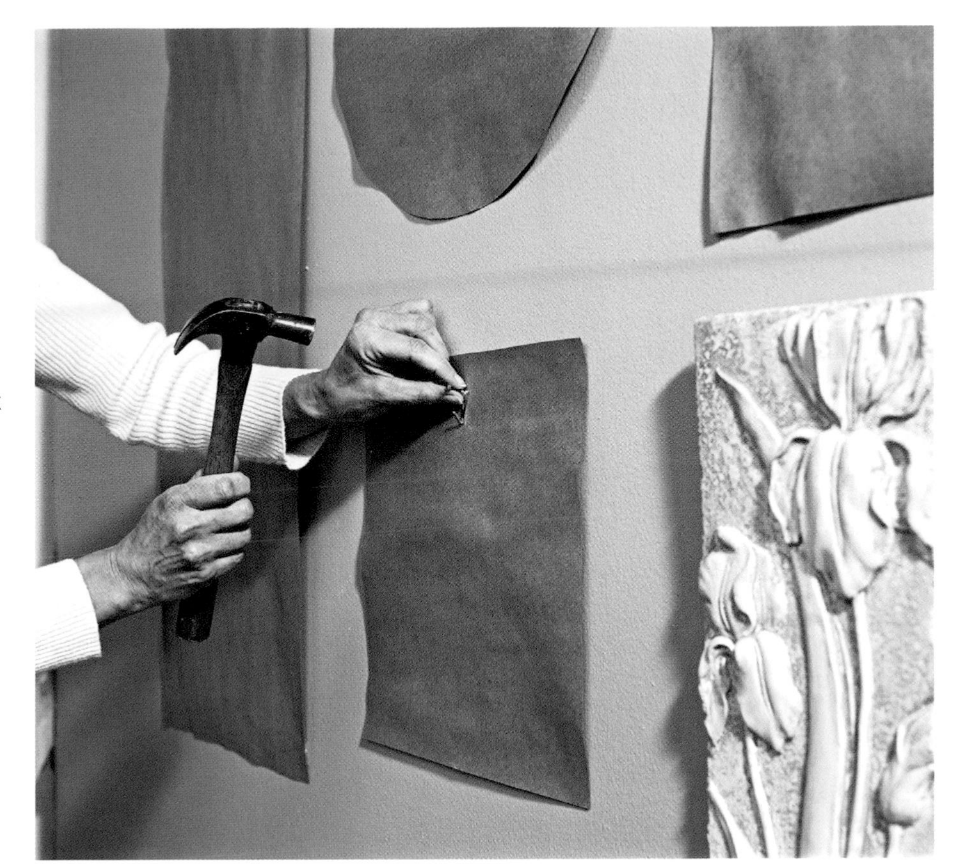

1 GROUP THE PICTURES ON THE WALL.

GROUP THE PICTURES ON THE WALL. Juggling pictures to get the right one in the right place can be difficult; instead work with pieces of paper. Trace the outline of each frame on paper that contrasts with the wall. Cut out the shapes, place masking tape loops on the backs, and experiment with grouping the pictures. For the security of anchoring heavy works and mirrors into wall studs, locate the studs with a stud finder. To support especially large objects, drive hangers into adjacent studs.

2 INSTALL EYES AND PICTURE WIRE.

Screw eyes and braided wire are sold in a range of sizes to handle framed objects of different weights. To position the eyes measure the height of the frame and mark pilot holes one-third of the way down the frame. Drill a hole slightly smaller than the diameter of the threaded portion of the eye. Drill carefully to avoid boring through the frame. Twist in the eyes by hand. To determine the length of wire to cut for a picture, measure the picture width and add 50 percent. This allows enough wire to wrap each end around a screw eye and then around itself, while preventing the frame from dropping below the hanger.

3 USE DOUBLE WIRE FOR HEAVY PICTURES.

To securely hang heavy pictures where there is no access to a stud, run two wires between the screw eyes and support each with a hanger. Space the two hangers at least half the picture's width apart.

4 NAIL A HANGER TO THE WALL.

To determine the exact position for the hanger, poke a pencil point through the paper cutout at the spot where the picture wire will be when fully stretched by the picture weight. When you find the best location for the picture, tap a nail through the hole just enough to mark the wall.

Select a picture hanger that's the right size; the weight a hanger can handle is marked on the package. To help prevent plaster from chipping, apply a small cross of tape to the wall at the point where you are driving the nail and nail the hanger to the wall through the tape.

▲ **Open staircases (*above* and *left*) are showcases for paintings, photos, and drawings. Scale is an important consideration. Note how the size of the dancer provides an anchor for the two smaller works on each side.**

GOOD IDEA

PLAN FIRST
To see how a picture grouping will look on the wall, first lay it out on the floor. You'll get a bird's-eye view and will find it easier and quicker to move objects around as you work out a preliminary arrangement.

DESIGNER TIP

THINK EYE LEVEL
Paintings and art should be hung at or close to eye level. Hang art lower in dining rooms or areas primarily used for seating; hang art higher in more general-use areas such as hallways.

DESIGNER TIP

IT'S ALL ABOUT YOU
When you decorate a room, the most important person to please is you. You live with the art and design. The decorator, designer, or even your best friend doesn't.

Arranging artwork

Collecting art and objects you love to live with requires great care. Artfully arranging them requires the same attention. Work at the display until you get patterns and groupings exactly how you want them.

A simple method of displaying family pictures and similar works of art is to align the top edges. For a variety of shapes, sizes, and subjects, hang art with the center point a specific distance from the floor. Basing arrangements on the centers of pictures breaks the monotony of perfectly aligned top edges and puts the focus of the art on possibly the most important aspect—the center of the picture. Museums typically hang art 60 to 64 inches from the floor.

For a lively grouping arrange the pictures within a circle or oval, aligning edges of some frames to give order to the arrangement.

When in doubt break the pattern. Asymmetrical groupings are informal and work well for pictures of children or folk art. Even here, however, align the edges of some frames for a continual reference point.

▲ This collection of objects and art is asymmetry in action. No two items are the same size or shape. The comfortable, inviting arrangement, which allows the eye to move randomly among the objects, is a popular country look.

▲ Images and objects in a traditional living room reinforce one another. The collection of figures calls attention to the paintings above it, while the arrangement of shorter figures flows to the tallest center figure, echoing the arc of paintings and creating a line for the eye to follow. The result is a formal look with a touch of whimsy.

▲ The antique wooden bracket in this Southwestern setting connects the two rooms to the paintings on both sides.

Hanging hardware

You'll find a variety of picture hangers in the hardware department. The common hangers shown below work in almost every situation.

Traditional hangers (A) have a nail that runs through the top of a hook that acts as a hanger. They work in drywall and plaster but tend to chip plaster.

Hangers sold as professional picture hangers (B) also work in plaster and drywall. They have a thin, sharp, hardened nail that is less likely to chip plaster. The nail is removable and reusable.

Wallboard anchors (C) are large nylon screws that house metal screws. Drive the pointed end into the drywall with a hammer, and screw the anchor into the wall with a standard screwdriver. Drive in the metal screw and hang the picture.

Anchors are available with hooks (D) to hang pictures and with special hooks to hang mirrors.

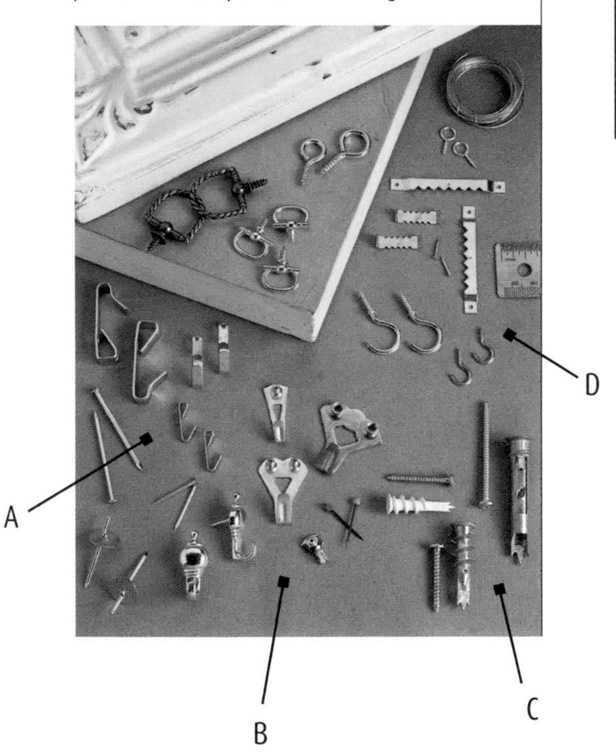

Folding screen

PROJECT DETAILS

SKILLS: Sanding, painting, drilling, hammering

TIME TO COMPLETE

EXPERIENCED: 4 hrs.
HANDY: 6 hrs.
NOVICE: 8 hrs.

STUFF YOU'LL NEED

TOOLS: Sander, sandpaper, tack cloth, 2-inch high-quality synthetic-bristle paintbrushes, gloves, pencil, utility knife, blue painter's tape, drill, hinge centering bit
MATERIALS: Six 1×8×72-inch maple veneer boards, oil-base wood finish, poster board or other heavy paper to make template, gold metallic paint, water-base satin polycrylic, twelve $^{5}/_{8}$-inch nail-on glides, ten $^{3}/_{4}$-inch brushed brass hinges

Freestanding folding screens provide privacy and distinguish living areas from one another. They're particularly useful in small spaces because the panels are hinged together for easy movement and storage. Oriental folding screen styles are common, but many of today's versions have a more modern twist. For a striking natural appearance, apply a dark wood finish to maple veneer boards. Plan out a design for the folding screen—this version features gold rectangles—and create templates to position as guides for taping off the area to be painted. After applying multiple coats of paint and removing the painter's tape, seal the boards. Once you attach the hinges to the boards, your freestanding folding screen is ready for use.

▲ Hinges blend in when painted the same gold tone as the rectangles on this easy-to-construct folding screen.

Folding screen *(continued)*

GOOD IDEA

TEST THE STAIN
It's common practice to bring home paint color samples before applying paint. It also makes sense to spend time choosing the right stain for a significant design project. When this dark-stained screen is positioned in an icy-blue room with other dark wood accents, the effect is dramatic. Look at stain sample boards and choose a stain that will coordinate with other woodtones in the room you are decorating. If you aren't sure about your selection, purchase the smallest size and try it on a scrap piece of the same wood you're going to use for the screen.

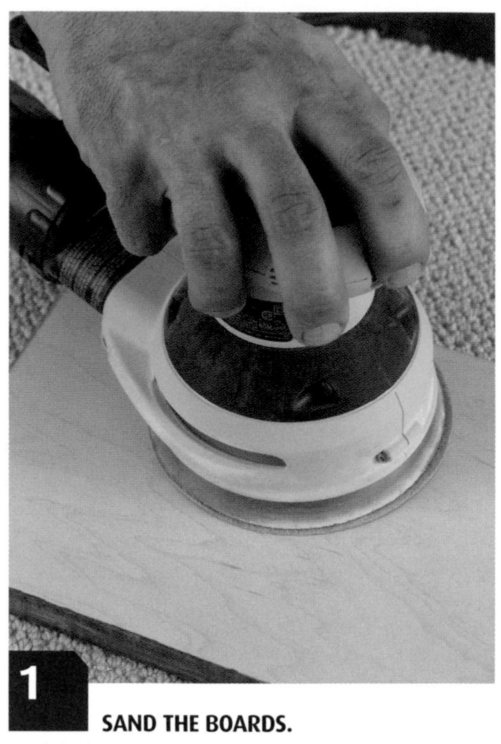

1 SAND THE BOARDS.
Sand the boards on all sides as needed. Wipe with tack cloth to remove dust before applying stain.

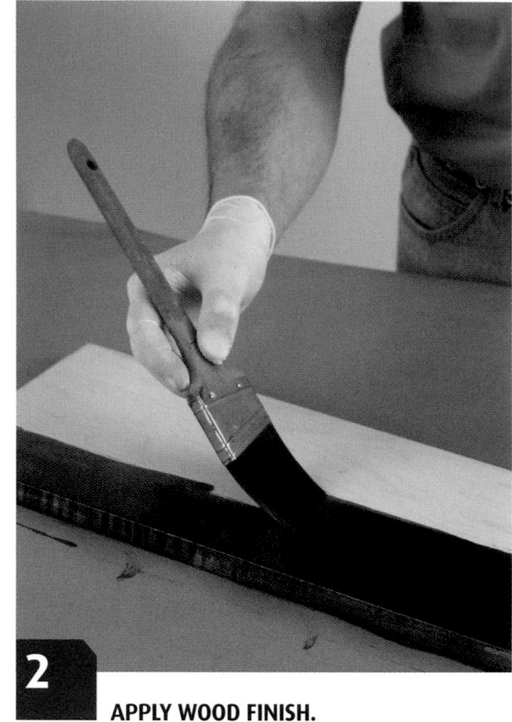

2 APPLY WOOD FINISH.
Apply stain with the grain of the wood. Allow to dry per stain manufacturer's instructions.

TOOL SAVVY

EASY CENTERING
When attaching the hinges to the screen, make centering holes easier by using a hinge centering bit with your drill. The inexpensive bit fits most standard drills.

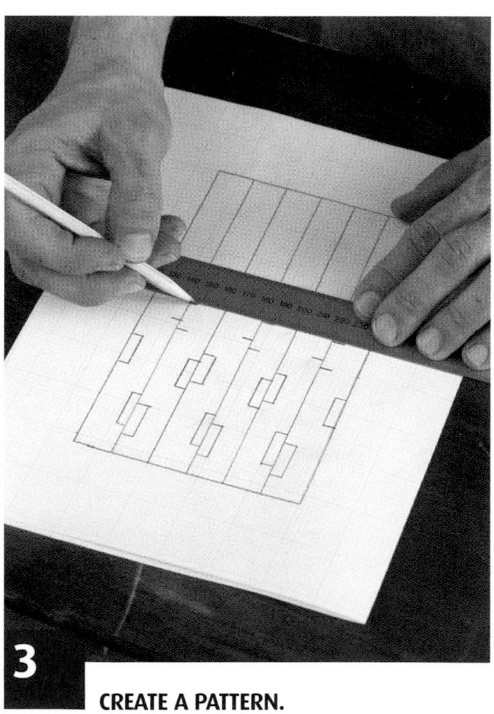

3 CREATE A PATTERN.
Using graph paper plan the design for your folding screen. Mark where hinges will be positioned and mark areas for applying paint over the stain.

4 CUT OUT THE TEMPLATES.
According to your plan draw templates for the painted areas. Cut templates for the painted pattern from the poster board.

5 **PLACE TEMPLATES FOR TAPING.**
Position templates on the boards to use as guides for taping off the area to be painted. After applying the tape remove the poster board template.

6 **APPLY PAINT.**
Paint taped areas with two to three coats of gold paint. Apply paint in one direction for the most even coverage and best final appearance. Allow to dry.

GOOD IDEA

ASSEMBLY LINE
You'll be able to work more efficiently if you tape off the design on all the boards before you start painting. That way you won't have to wrap your brush when you're finished with one board while you tape off the next. Move directly from one board to the next.

3 WALLS, CEILINGS, AND FLOORS

7 **FINISH BOARDS WITH SATIN WATER-BASE SEALER.** When paint is dry apply three coats of polycrylic to each board. Allow sealer to dry between coats according to manufacturer's instructions. Apply stain with the grain for best finished appearance.

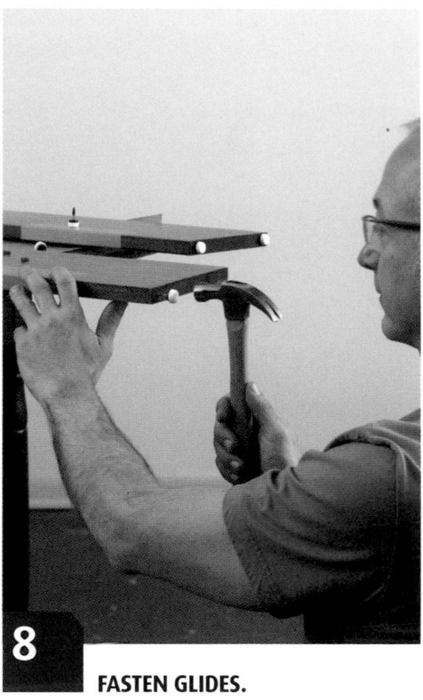

8 **FASTEN GLIDES.**
Attach nail-on glides to protect flooring surfaces and to make it easier to reposition the screen.

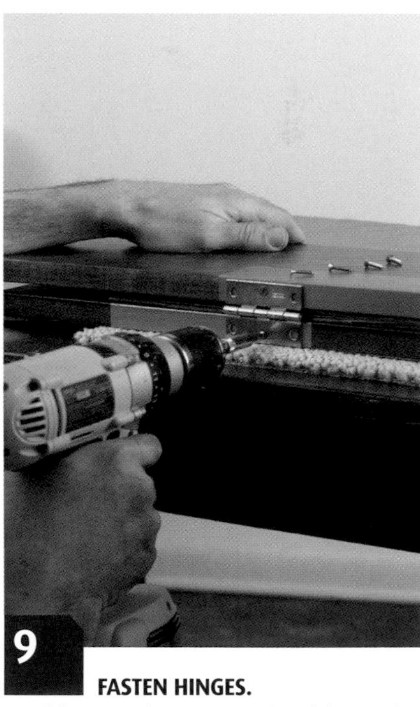

9 **FASTEN HINGES.**
Attach hinges with screws on sides of the panels. Position the hinges in areas that have been painted gold so they blend in.

Ceiling fans

Selecting Fan Blade Size

Determine the size of your room to ensure selection of the proper fan.

Room Size (square feet)	Fan Blade Diameter (inches)
100	36
144	42
225	48
400	52

SMART & SAFE

FAN-RATED BOXES
Ceiling fans should be properly anchored to an electric ceiling box designed to hold a heavy fixture. Purchase a fan-rated box when you purchase a new fan.

▲ **The traditional style and dark blades of this ceiling fan create a standout addition to a bedroom.**

Ceiling fans are designed to cool the air—and with so many styles available, they're also pleasing to the eye. Think of a fan as another component in your decorating scheme rather than a utilitarian afterthought. Once you have a basic design plan for the room, look for a fan that complements and enhances the decor. Styles vary in the shape and size of blades, materials and finishes for the blades and fan body, overall profile, and features such as lights. Hanging a ceiling fan is not mechanically difficult and most fans come with good installation instructions, so you'll be enjoying cool breezes in no time.

Selecting a ceiling fan

For the best cooling effects, first select a fan for function, then consider style. Several basic choices impact the function of a ceiling fan: downrod versus ceiling hugger design, the size of the blades, blade angle, and light fixture options. High-quality fans should remain balanced and in good working condition and have motors that will operate quietly for years. Inexpensive fans—though they may look good when new—likely will wobble and wear out after a short time. Consider these items when selecting a fan:

Fan position. If you have ceiling high enough to accommodate it, purchase a fan with a downrod to position the fan blades at least 10 inches from the ceiling. Ceiling hugger fans position blades too close to the ceiling to circulate air effectively. Make sure that height clearance to the blades is no less than 7 feet from the floor.

Blade size. Select fan blade size according to the size of the room (see "Selecting Fan Blade Size," *above left*). No matter the size of the fan and room, position the fan so the blades swing no closer than 18 inches to the nearest wall.

Blade angle. The greater the angle of the blade, the more air it will circulate through the room. See "Cost-Effective Comfort" on page 98 for more information about the latest in blade technology.

Light fixtures. Many ceiling fans have an integrated light fixture that provides ambient light for the room and enhances the look of the ceiling fan. Some fans are designed with the option of installing the light fixture or installing a cap at the base of the fan body instead of the light. Make a lighting plan for the room before finalizing your choice of a ceiling fan. See page 136 for more information about lighting plans.

▲ **Many ceiling fans are rated for outdoor use, making them ideal for cooling a covered porch or patio. This nautical-style fan features sailcloth canvas blades.**

▲ **The contemporary design of this white ceiling fan with metal-finish blades adds a bright, streamlined touch to a bedroom filled with dark furnishings.**

WORK SMARTER

ASK FOR HELP

Ceiling fans are heavy and awkward to handle, so have a helper watch the ladder and lend a hand.

▲ An interesting new design makes this ceiling fan an almost sculptural contribution to the room. Two pairs of blades are attached at two levels on the fan housing.

Cost-effective comfort

New Aero Breeze Blade Technology has been developed for Hampton Bay fans available exclusively at The Home Depot. These fans feature aerodynamically optimized fan blades that move up to 40 percent more air than standard blades. You'll save energy with these environmentally friendly fans by operating the fans on lower levels while still maintaining the comfort level associated with higher speeds on fans with standard blades. The Aero Breeze series of fans is available in a variety of styles.

▲ Fan pulls can be a subtle decorative element in their own right. Purchase a separate decorative pull that coordinates with the room decor.

Custom design your fan

Mix and match components to custom design the fan of your choice. Choose components from the Hampton Bay custom program at The Home Depot. Start with a fan housing unit in rustic, *shown below*, or white finish. Then choose from one of three light kits—lantern, onion, or acorn—each available in a rustic or white finish. The rustic onion light kit is shown here. Finally select from two blade styles—leaf and bamboo. The leaf blade style is available in maple (shown on fan), washed black, honey, ivory, and white (not shown). The bamboo blade is available in mahogany, tan, olive, and white (not shown).

RUSTIC STYLE

LEAF BLADE

BAMBOO BLADE

Turn it on

Gone are the days when you had to stretch for a pull chain to adjust the speed of a ceiling fan. Look for a fan that comes equipped with a remote control receiver that can be operated from anywhere in the room. The remote allows you to turn the fan on and off, adjust the speed, and control the light fixture. If the fan of your choice doesn't come with a remote, you can purchase a separate add-on kit for a universal fan remote. Or install a fan wall switch with separate controls for the fan light fixture—many come with a dimmer function—and the fan speed.

REMOTE CONTROL

WALL CONTROL

Faux-plaster rosette

PROJECT DETAILS

SKILLS: Marking and drilling

TIME TO COMPLETE

EXPERIENCED: ½ hr.
HANDY: 1 hr.
NOVICE: 2 hrs.

STUFF YOU'LL NEED

TOOLS: Pencil, electronic stud finder, drill and driver, caulk gun, cloth, paintbrush
MATERIALS: Polyurethane rosette, latex adhesive caulk, 2½-inch trim-head screws, water, latex paint

Older stately homes were given lavish molding details to enhance their appearance. Rosettes—round decorative plaques traditionally molded of plaster—were mounted in the center of ceilings to surround light fixtures. Popular again, ceiling rosettes accent almost any room decor, making an ordinary light fixture exceptional or an elegant chandelier grand.

Ceiling rosettes are available in traditional plaster, but they are heavy and difficult to mount—especially to drywall ceilings. Lightweight rosettes made from gypsum or polyurethane are comparatively easy to install. Sizes range from 9 inches to 36 inches in diameter.

▲ **This rosette and the molding look like plaster, but modern materials let you install these items with a minimum of tools for maximum effect.**

1

TRACE ROSETTE ON CEILING AND LOCATE THE JOISTS.
With the fixture out of the way, center the rosette over the ceiling box. Lightly trace a pencil line on the ceiling around the perimeter of the rosette. Remove the rosette and use an electronic stud finder to locate the ceiling joists that pass above the rosette. Mark joist locations along the perimeter line of the rosette. Reposition the rosette and mark screw hole locations on the rosette where they will meet the joists. Select areas of the rosette where a transition between details will conceal the screw holes. Predrill holes through the rosette for the screws.

Prep work

Before you install a rosette, turn off the power to the light fixture, disconnect the wiring, and remove the old fixture. Depending on the thickness of the fixture and the type of electrical box in the ceiling, you may have to use longer screws or a longer threaded tube to accommodate the ceiling rosette. After the rosette is in place, reinstall the fixture and turn on the power.

2

APPLY ADHESIVE TO THE CEILING.
Apply a bead of construction adhesive or latex adhesive caulk to the area within the rosette outline. Keep the adhesive an inch or so away from the edge of the outline to minimize squeeze-out.

3

ATTACH THE ROSETTE TO THE CEILING.
Position the rosette to align the screw holes with the joist marks and press the rosette into the adhesive. Drive screws into the joists and tighten gently to avoid crushing the rosette. Wipe off excess adhesive immediately. Remove the pencil marks at the joists with warm water and a cloth. Patch the screw holes with latex caulk or putty; paint the installed rosette.

Lighted crown molding

PROJECT DETAILS

SKILLS: Marking, cutting, drilling, painting

TIME TO COMPLETE

EXPERIENCED: 8 hrs.
HANDY: 10 hrs.
NOVICE: 12 hrs.

STUFF YOU'LL NEED

TOOLS: Stud finder, pencil, tape measure, circular saw, square, drill, screwdriver, fish tape, hammer, nail set, saber saw, trim brush
MATERIALS: 1×6 or wider backerboard, receptacle and cover, 2×4 for nailer block, clamp, bench, crown molding, cable lights, finishing nails or screws, wood putty, mounting clips, paint or varnish

FINISHING TOUCH
The bottom edge of the backerboard is flat, square, and dull. Dress it up with a piece of molding. Check sample boards at The Home Depot and pick one that you think will work well. It need not be specifically designed to work with crown molding. Try base cap molding designed to go on a baseboard. Other possibilities include chair rail, door trim, or window trim. Cut and install the molding, coping the inside corners as explained on page 32.

▲ Lighting in crown molding creates a subtle sense of warmth and accents the perimeter trim.

Installing lights in crown molding combines a classic decorative element with a modern, functional purpose. Although most lighting is focused downward, lights such as some sconces and torches are designed to reflect light off the ceiling and wall surfaces. Uplights in crown molding add warm, subtle, indirect light in a room and augment other primary lighting sources.

Cable lights provide the simplest approach to installing lights in crown molding. They are made up of tiny long-life bulbs strung together and encased in clear, flexible PVC tubing. Individual cable lengths join together at the ends with screw-together fittings and can be strung as long as 150 feet. They also can be cut every 18 inches along any cable to fit a given space.

Part of the job of adding lighting to crown molding is to install a new outlet near the ceiling to provide power to the lights.

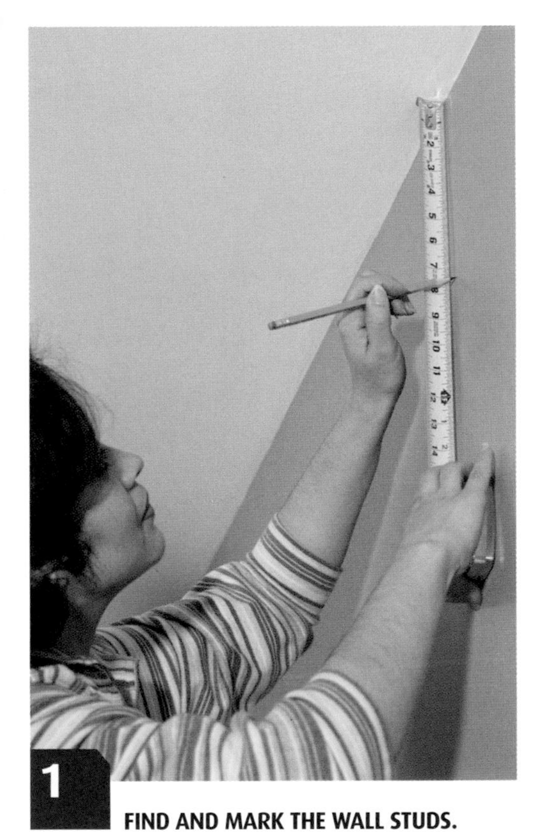

1 FIND AND MARK THE WALL STUDS. The backerboard, which supports the crown molding, needs to be attached to the wall studs for support. Use a stud finder or tap on the wall with a hammer to find the studs—the sound pitch will go up and become less hollow at the studs. Wall studs are typically spaced 16 inches on center, so once you have found one, you'll know approximately where to look for the others. Mark the locations on the wall just below where the bottom edge of the backerboard will be.

2 CUT THE BACKERBOARDS TO LENGTH. If you don't have access to a radial-arm saw or a sliding mitersaw, make the cuts with a circular saw guided by a square, like the one shown. Lay out the cut, position the saw, and put the square against the saw before making the cut.

GOOD IDEA

PREFINISH MOLDING

Prefinish the molding components as far as practical before installing. This means priming molding that will be painted and applying all but the final coat on stained and clear-coated molding.

Choosing crown molding

The larger the molding, the wider the swath of light projected against the ceiling. A small crown molding does not allow much light to project from behind the molding. A 4½-inch-wide crown is the smallest to consider. The one used in this installation is almost 5 inches wide across its face. For proper lighting leave at least 2½ inches of space above the top edge of the crown molding.

Lighted crown molding *(continued)*

3 NAIL OR SCREW THE BACKERBOARDS TO THE WALL.
If you install a new outlet for the wall, cut an opening for it as explained in "Wiring Crown Moldings Lights," page 105. After you cut the opening, install the backerboard by driving drywall screws along the bottom half of the board and into the studs. The crown moldings, when they are attached, conceal the screws. Drive finishing nails or finishing screws into the upper half of the backerboard, which will be visible. Inside corners can be butted one piece to the other. Ideally outside corners should be mitered. Set nails and drive screws that will be visible so they're below the surface of the wood. Fill the holes with wood putty.

4 CUT A CONTINUOUS NAILER BLOCK.
A nailer block, shown here clamped between the molding and the backerboard, gives the molding the support necessary because the molding is not nailed along the top edge. The block needs to be cut at an angle that matches the angle of the molding. Determine this angle by making a full-scale drawing of the molding and backerboard. Rip the nailer blocking from straight pieces of 2×4 material or have it cut at The Home Depot. Decide on the location of the molding and strike a line to show where the nailer block will go. Test the fit of the nailer block by clamping the backerboard, nailer block, and crown molding together on a bench.

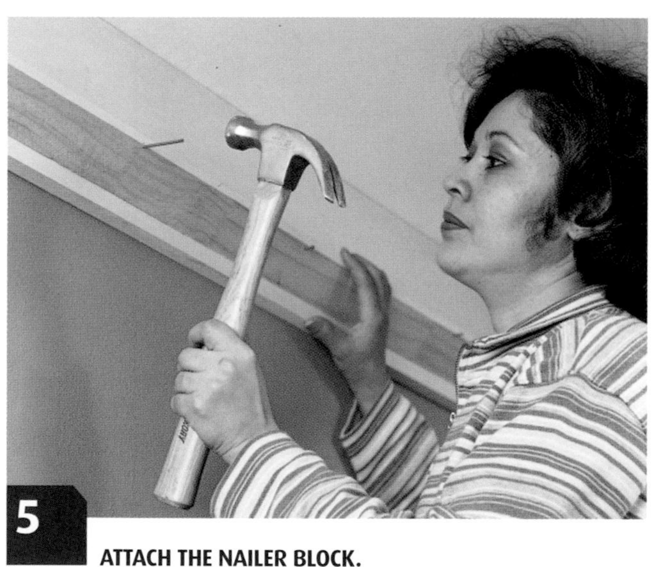

5 ATTACH THE NAILER BLOCK.
Before you nail the nailer block, determine the location of the light cable. The light cable can be attached to the backerboard or to the top of the nailer block, whichever is easier. You may want to temporarily nail up a short piece of the crown molding and hold the light cable in place with the power on to determine the best light position. Small adjustments in position change the amount of light that is cast against the ceiling. In general the light cable should be an inch or so below the top level of the installed crown molding.

6 ATTACH MOUNTING CLIPS FOR CABLE.
Attach the cable mounting clips to the backerboard or nailer block. Some nail in place; others are screwed on. Check manufacturer instructions for proper installation method. Locate the clips every 18 to 24 inches. Before completely installing the lights check that all the lights work.

7

ATTACH THE LIGHT CABLE.
Press the light cable into the mounting clips. Bend the cable gently around corners. Connect additional lengths of cable as needed. If you haven't already, connect the power and check that all lights work.

8

CUT AND FIT THE CROWN MOLDING.
Now you're ready for a typical crown molding installation. Cope the inside corners and miter the outside corners. If the molding will be painted, attach it to the backerboard and nailer block by driving finishing head screws along the bottom edge of the molding. If the molding is stained and varnished, attach it with finishing nails, which leave smaller holes. (See "Crown Molding," page 39, for a full treatment of crown molding installation.)

9

SET NAILS, FILL, AND PAINT THE MOLDING.
Sink all the nailheads below the surface of the wood with a nail set. Fill all the nail or screw holes with a latex filler that matches the finish. Paint the molding.

Wiring crown molding lights

Running wires from floor to ceiling usually involves cutting holes in the wall. Fortunately this job requires almost no wall repair. Check The Home Depot's *Wiring 1-2-3* for specific instructions for running wires. Here are the basics: Cut the hole for the new outlet box above the nailer block and directly above an outlet along the floor. Fit the outlet box in the opening. Connect new cable to the outlet and fish the wire up the wall to the new outlet. Run more cable from the outlet to the switch. If you remove the baseboard and cut out part of the wall behind it, you can run the wire and then replace the baseboard to cover the work.

Sisal area rug

PROJECT DETAILS

SKILLS: Drawing, painting

TIME TO COMPLETE

EXPERIENCED: 2 hrs.
HANDY: 3 hrs.
NOVICE: 4 hrs.

STUFF YOU'LL NEED

TOOLS: Marker, crafts knife, foam board, 2-inch fine-tip brush, small artist's brush
MATERIALS: Brown crafts paper, stencil sheet, 5×7-foot sisal rug, interior flat enamel paint in cream and leaf green

GOOD IDEA

PERSONALIZED PATTERN
You can make just about any simple shape into a stencil. Look to the room you are decorating for inspiration. The pattern in window treatments, upholstery, or an art piece might provide ideas. If possible trace a simple shape onto a stencil sheet. Or for very basic shapes, draw the design freehand. Minimize complex cutouts and fine lines for best results, especially on a rough surface such as sisal.

Painting a sisal rug is a low-commitment, relatively inexpensive way to add a decorative element to your floor. Rather than undertaking the daunting task of hunting for a rug with the perfect colors and pattern to match your decor, painting a plain rug is an easy way to get the exact look you want.

You can paint almost any simple design on a sisal rug—just remember that sisal really absorbs paint, so you'll need quite a bit of paint to achieve good coverage. If you purchase a sisal rug without a border, you may wish to paint a border on the rug as well. Just remember that, unlike an unfinished edge, a finished edge such as the one featured here won't fray.

▲ Applying paint to a sisal area rug allows the covering to be customized to fit the color and style of the room.

1 **DRAW STENCIL.** Make a trial copy of the design first. Determine whether it's too large or too small for the finished look you want. Trace or freehand draw the outline for the stencil on a stencil sheet.

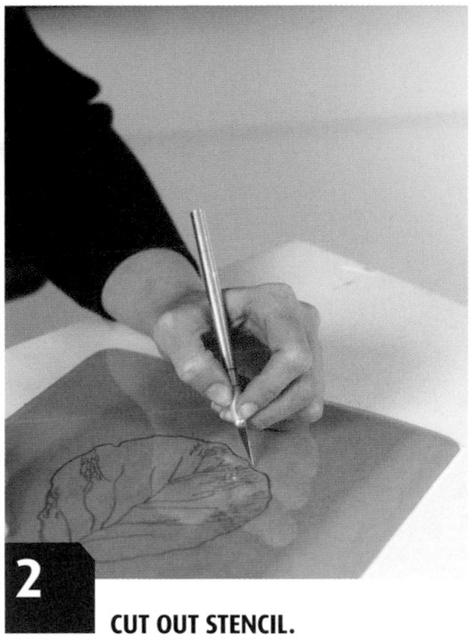

2 **CUT OUT STENCIL.** Cut out the stencil with a fine-tapered crafts knife that has a new, sharp blade. Practice on a scrap piece first. To protect the cutting surface, place the work over a piece of foam board as you cut.

3 **POSITION THE STENCIL AND APPLY PAINT.** For a random pattern position the stencil on the surface. Press the stencil to the rug. Apply the paint with a dabbing motion until the cutout is all painted. Repeat until you achieve a pleasing pattern.

4 **FILL IN FINE LINES.** Because sisal absorbs paint, fine lines may not show up after the pattern is removed. Fill in any fine lines using a small artist's brush.

5 **PAINT ADDITIONAL COLORS AND DETAILS.** Fill in details by hand on a simple design for a more natural look. Wait until the base color is dry. Then using a fine artist's brush, apply a second color to each leaf in the design of veins.

TOOL SAVVY

CLEAN CUTS

Hold the crafts knife like a pencil and always draw it toward you. Either turn the transparent sheet as you work or move yourself around the worktable. Make two distinct cuts in corners—cutting into them, not out of them. Use a continuous motion without lifting the blade to make curved cuts. Use a straightedge to guide straight line cuts.

Decorative wood floor inlay

PROJECT DETAILS

SKILLS: Nailing, routing, gluing

TIME TO COMPLETE

EXPERIENCED: 2 hrs.
HANDY: 3 hrs.
NOVICE: 5 hrs.

STUFF YOU'LL NEED

TOOLS: Pencil, hammer, router, flush-trim bit, nail set, corner chisel, caulk gun, notched trowel, mallet, wood block
MATERIALS: Medallion, template, #4 finishing nails, construction adhesive, drywall screws, glue

Prep work

Some installers put tar paper over the subfloor. It's optional but helps to deaden the sound made by walking over the floor.

Dos and don'ts

DO double-check to make sure the medallion and the floor are the same thickness. Sanding down one or the other more than a little is virtually impossible without damaging both.

DON'T get stuck. Use construction adhesive to hold down the medallion and use glue to put the covers over the screws. Whatever you use is bound to squeeze out—and glue is easier to clean up than adhesive.

▲ **Inlaid borders are made by installing contrasting floorboards. This medallion is purchased preassembled; templates and router bits come with it to simplify installation.**

Make a beautiful floor spectacular by using decorative inlays. Decorative inlays were once the domain of highly skilled flooring installers. Now preassembled inlays are available through many flooring products manufacturers. An inlay becomes the focal point in an entryway, at the base of a stairway, or in front of a fireplace.

Inlays are available in several thicknesses, as well as finished or unfinished, to match existing flooring materials. Inlays match most off-the-shelf flooring from home centers, though they may have to be special ordered. The installation procedure for an inlay depends on the manufacturer. Some provide a template with each inlay; it requires a router to cut the recess into the surrounding floor. The special router bit is included in the installation kit. This approach, *opposite*, is nearly foolproof. It's also ideal if you want to install an inlay in an existing floor. The inlay will have to match the thickness of the existing floor. To measure remove a threshold or baseboard to expose an edge of the floor.

1 LOCATE INLAY ON THE FLOOR.
Take time to position the inlay on the floor with straight edges parallel to floor strips to prevent awkward seams. When you have it where you want it, use a pencil to trace around the perimeter of the inlay onto the floor.

2 NAIL THE TEMPLATE TO THE FLOOR.
Lay the template on the floor so the inside edges line up with the pencil lines traced from the inlay. Nail each corner of the template to the floor with #4 finishing nails.

3 **ROUT AGAINST THE TEMPLATE EDGE.**
Lock the router bit in a router and adjust the router to make a 1/8-inch-deep cut into the excess flooring. (The first cut should be deep enough to skim across the top of the tongues on the boards.) Start the bit into the flooring about an inch away from the template to avoid damaging the template. Guide the router clockwise around the template. Blow out the dust and examine the cut; look for exposed nail holes where the cut passes over a tongue edge and set any exposed nails all the way down through the boards. Lower the bit 1/8 inch and repeat the process until you have cut all the way through the floor strips—three passes is recommended in 3/8-inch-thick flooring. Remove the floor strips within the inlay area. Use the chisel that came with the kit to knock out the corners and check the fit of the inlay.

4 **APPLY ADHESIVE TO THE FLOOR.** Use high-quality construction adhesive available in caulk tube form. Evenly spread the adhesive with a small notched trowel (the kind sold for applying base cove molding adhesive) around the entire surface of the inlay area.

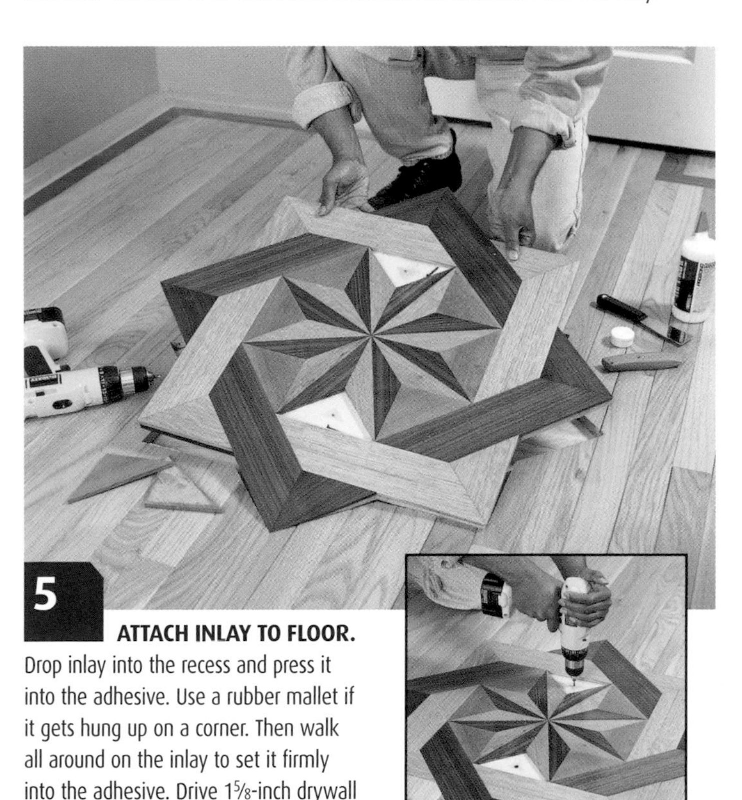

5 **ATTACH INLAY TO FLOOR.**
Drop inlay into the recess and press it into the adhesive. Use a rubber mallet if it gets hung up on a corner. Then walk all around on the inlay to set it firmly into the adhesive. Drive 1 5/8-inch drywall screws into the predrilled holes to secure the inlay to the subfloor.

6 **GLUE IN SCREW COVERS.**
Apply yellow or white glue to the back of the loose pieces of the inlay that cover the screws. Set the pieces into the recesses and tap them down with a block of wood and hammer. Let the glue set for at least an hour before sanding the inlay.

Floor stenciling

PROJECT DETAILS

SKILLS: Sanding, measuring, marking, painting

TIME TO COMPLETE

EXPERIENCED: 6 hrs.
HANDY: 8 hrs.
NOVICE: 12 hrs.

STUFF YOU'LL NEED

TOOLS: Stencils, stencil brush, sander or rubber sanding block, 180-grit sandpaper, tape measure or ruler, pencil, masking tape, paper plate palette, single-edge razor blade, lamb's-wool varnish applicator for floors
MATERIALS: Flooring, plywood or cardboard for practice, stencil paint, painter's tape, clear polyurethane, tack cloth

Stencils offer a foolproof method for applying uniform decorative patterns. Spice up a floor with decorative border stencils to define space and highlight architectural features, such as doorways, a fireplace, or built-in furniture. The traditional way to achieve this effect is with costly inlaid borders, which is impractical for an installed floor. Painted border stencils work on any wood floor, from classic oak with a natural or stained finish to yellow painted pine floor. Combining stenciling with faux-finishing techniques simulates wood inlays, adding another level of decorative accent.

▲ **Add color to your floor with stencils. This Southwestern pattern, originally designed for walls, proves that imagination and inspiration are what decorating is all about.**

Same technique, different surface

Although wall stenciling is a common decorative application, stenciling a pattern on the floor is also a classic decorating technique. In many ways it's also easier to do. You won't be running up and down a ladder or working above your head, the paint won't run down the wall, and laying out the design is less difficult. Floor stencils work well with almost any decorating style, but the technique really shines as part of a Southwestern, colonial, country, or Victorian scheme. Choose a kit especially made for a floor or use a wall border version. And, of course, you can make your own.

Painter's secret

When you reach a corner that ends with less than a full stencil pattern, use an even increment within the pattern. (This stencil has three repeats of the pattern.) When that doesn't work fudge the spacing a little.

1 MAKE A SAMPLE STENCIL.
Make a sample stencil to get a preview of the pattern and the colors. If you have an extra piece of matching flooring, use that. Otherwise use a piece of plywood or cardboard. Tape the stencil to the sample material and paint the sequence of colors.

2 SAND THE FLOOR.
Slightly abrade the surface with 180-grit sandpaper so the stencil paints adhere. Make a quick pass with either an electric orbital sander (*above*) or with a paper-wrapped sanding block. Vacuum the dust or wipe with a tack cloth.

Make your own stencils

Wall stencils work equally well for floors. Make your own stencils at a copy center. Find a pattern you like—a leaf, a wallpaper detail, or a pattern from a book. Photocopy it onto transparency film—the sheets of clear plastic sold at office supply stores for overhead projectors. Take home the photocopy and cut out the pattern with a mat knife to make the stencil. Tape the stencil in place and begin. Most photocopiers enlarge or shrink images, allowing infinite control over the size of your pattern.

3 MEASURE AND MARK LAYOUT LINE.
While you can lay a stencil against the wall or baseboard, a border looks better away from the wall. Measure and mark several spots along the wall, then connect the marks with a band of painter's tape for a stencil guide. The tape is easier to remove than a pencil line.

4 PLAN THE STENCIL LAYOUT.
The hardest part of stenciling is making the pattern turn corners cleanly. It's easy with some patterns but difficult with others. Start at the most visible corner of the room and work out. Inevitably one or more of the corners will end up with an incomplete pattern, but they'll be less conspicuous than a main focal point. Map out how the pattern will fall in the corners by making several photocopies of the stencil, cutting them out, and laying them along the wall.

Floor stenciling *(continued)*

DESIGNER TIP

WHOLE-FLOOR STENCILING
Pick an easy pattern that requires only one color. Randomly stencil the entire floor, providing accents by changing the color from time to time. When the floor is dry, sponge paint the space between the stencils. For a different effect color-wash the floor first and then stencil over it.

5 POSITION THE STENCIL ON THE FLOOR IN THE FIRST POSITION. When you decide on the best starting point, position the stencil on the layout line and tape it to the floor. Use masking tape or painter's tape to cover the parts of the stencil that don't receive the first color.

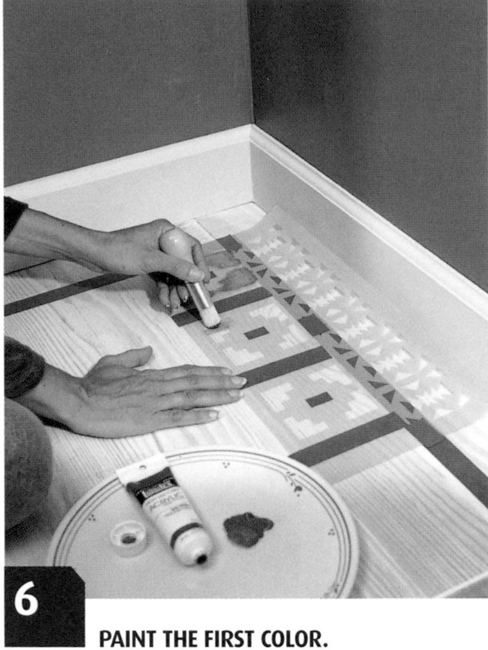

6 PAINT THE FIRST COLOR. Pour paint onto a paper plate. Lightly dip the stenciling brush into the paint and apply it to the floor. Use either stippling or swirling to apply stencil paint. Stippling maintains the stencil outline more crisply, and swirling looks more fluid and may allow some paint to bleed under the edges of the stencil. Experiment with the paint and the brush to decide which looks best; maintain that approach throughout your project.

7 PAINT ADDITIONAL COLORS. Remove the tape covering the stencil parts that receive the second color and tape over the portion that received the first color. Use brown painter's masking tape for this step. It covers a wide area, comes in many widths, has adhesive along only one edge, and is easy to remove.

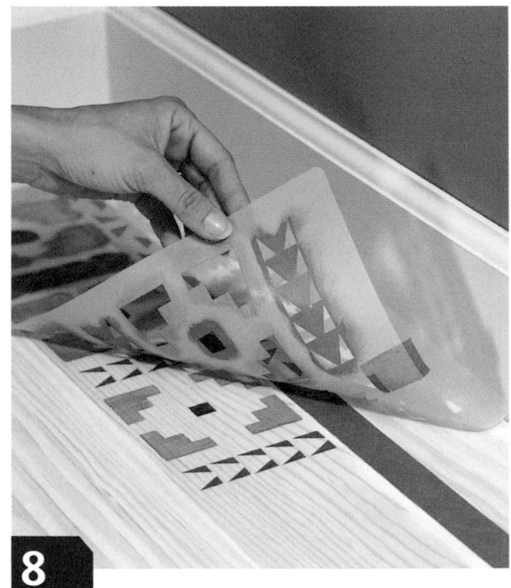

8 REMOVE THE STENCIL. After all the stencil colors have been applied, remove the tape and carefully lift the stencil from the floor. If some paint has bled under the stencil, allow the paint to dry thoroughly and scrape off the excess paint with a single-edge razor blade. Do not blot the paint while it is still damp.

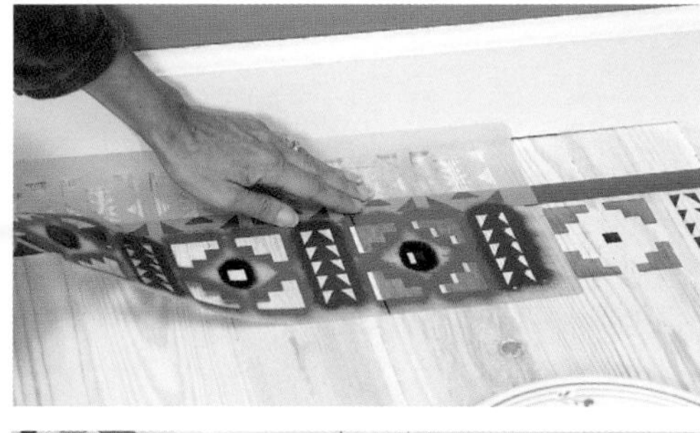

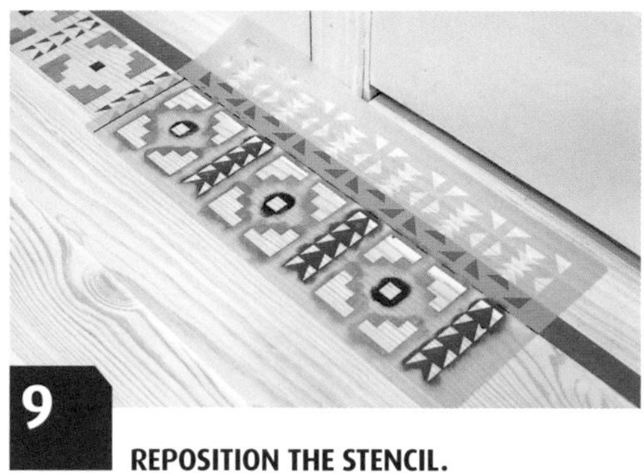

9 **REPOSITION THE STENCIL.**
Move the stencil to the next position. Align the registration marks that ensure regular spacing of the pattern (the solid line on the left side of the stencil), as well as the marks that align with the layout line (the broken line running lengthwise through the stencil).

10 **CONTINUE THE PATTERN AROUND CORNERS.**
Restart the stencil pattern when turning corners. Depending on the pattern, you may have to turn the stencil facedown to match the pattern. If so, be sure to clean the painted side completely.

11 **SAND LIGHTLY.**
Let the paint dry thoroughly for a day or two; sand it lightly. If you want to impart a slightly aged look to the stenciling, sand a little heavier in some areas to simulate wear.

12 **APPLY A CLEAR FINISH COAT.**
To lock in the crisp colors in the stencil and to prevent the paint from wearing off, apply a coat of clear polyurethane. If you apply the polyurethane to only the stenciled area rather than the entire floor, match the sheen that's on the rest of the floor.

Vinyl floor tiles

 PROJECT DETAILS

SKILLS: Measuring, snapping grid lines, cutting

 TIME TO COMPLETE

EXPERIENCED: 2 hrs.
HANDY: 3 hrs.
NOVICE: 4 hrs.

 STUFF YOU'LL NEED

TOOLS: Pencil, tape measure, chalkline, marker, straightedge, wire-cutting scissors
MATERIALS: Vinyl floor tiles

▲ **A simple checkerboard pattern of muted stone-look vinyl tiles completes this easy fresh country look.**

Vinyl flooring tiles are ideal for creating visual variety—and installation is as easy as creating a grid pattern, peeling off the adhesive backing, and affixing each tile to the floor. Vinyl is conducive to creating interesting flooring patterns—you can cut tiles to form fancy mosaic designs and borders or keep it simple with the checkerboard design shown here. Although it isn't as inviting for sprawling on the floor as some other materials, vinyl is easy to clean, which makes it a great choice for high-traffic areas such as the kitchen, mudroom, or entryway. And should floor damage occur, it's easy to pull up and replace only the damaged tiles instead of installing an entire floor. Be sure to plan your design in advance because you may have to mark and cut some tiles to fit along the edges of the room where full tiles won't fit.

1 SNAP GRID LINES.
Measure out from both ends of the longest wall to the center of the room and mark. Snap a chalkline between the points. Continue measuring and snapping lines to create a grid.

2 REMOVE BACKING.
Starting in the center of the room, peel the backing off a tile and lay the tile in place.

3 POSITION THE TILE.
Once the backing is removed, position each new tile using the grid lines as a guide. Alternate the color of tile in each row to form a checkered pattern.

4 MARK FOR PARTIAL TILE.
Most layouts require some tiles to be cut. Place the tile to be cut on the last one secured to the floor. Mark the tile to be cut where it meets the last full tile.

5 MARK THE CUTLINE.
Use a straightedge and marker to join the marks on the back of the tile to be cut.

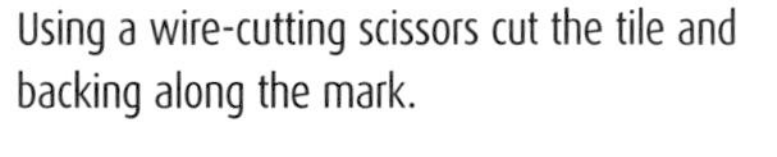

6 CUT THE TILE.
Using a wire-cutting scissors cut the tile and backing along the mark.

7 POSITION PARTIAL TILE.
Remove the backing from the partial tile and secure the tile in place on the floor. If necessary install baseboard molding to complete the floor.

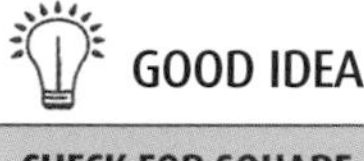

GOOD IDEA

CHECK FOR SQUARE
Many rooms are out of square. Rather than relying on adjoining walls to be at right angles, you can test for square. Measure out from both ends of the longest wall and snap a chalkline. The do the same for the next longest adjoining wall. From the intersection of chalklines, measure and mark three feet on one line and four feet on the other. If your grid is square, the diagonal between the points will be five feet. If not adjust the shorter line and snap in a new color until the diagonal measures five feet.

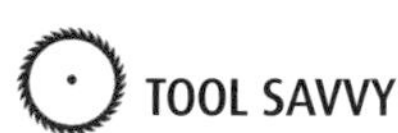

TOOL SAVVY

CLEAN LINES
Before you snap the line on the floor, shake off some of the chalk. Too much chalk will make a muddy line that can be hard to read, especially if you're checking for square.

Carpet floor tiles

 PROJECT DETAILS

SKILLS: Measuring, snapping grid lines, cutting

 TIME TO COMPLETE

EXPERIENCED: 2 hrs.
HANDY: 3 hrs.
NOVICE: 4 hrs.

 STUFF YOU'LL NEED

TOOLS: Pencil, marker, tape measure, chalkline, heavy scissors or wire cutter, straightedge
MATERIALS: Carpet floor tiles

▲ **Carpet tiles are an easy flooring idea and solution for a homework space.**

Just as the vinyl floor tiles shown on page 114 add visual variety to areas like kitchens and entryways, carpet floor tiles are an interesting variation on standard carpeting for living areas. Although carpet tiles offer fewer design possibilities than vinyl tiles because they lock into place and feature a wavy edge that must be matched up exactly, they are available in a variety of colors, patterns, and textures that look particularly appealing when laid in a stripe pattern. Carpet floor tiles are a boon for areas frequented by children, because spills and other damage easily are remedied by pulling up and replacing single tiles rather than an entire room of carpet.

 DESIGNER TIP

BASIC DESIGN
These carpet tiles are designed for easy installation. You won't even have to peel off the backing. Two ends of the tiles are curved to help "lock" them together. As a result these are best suited for simple designs—stripes as shown, or a solid. If you want a more complex floor design, check out vinyl or ceramic tiles.

 GOOD IDEA

KID-FRIENDLY FLOORS
Carpet tiles are probably one of the more child-friendly flooring surfaces. They provide a softer surface for floor games than any other material. Each tile is also simple to swap out if spills mess up one area of flooring.

1 SNAP GRID LINES.
Measure out from both ends of the longest wall to the center of the room and mark. Snap a chalk line between the points. Use the width of a tile for your measurements. Continue measuring and snapping lines to create a grid.

2 POSITION THE CARPET TILE.
Starting in the center of the room, lay the carpet tile in place. Use the grid lines as a guide to position the tiles. To form a stripe pattern, alternate the color of each row.

3 MARK FOR PARTIAL TILE.
Most layouts require some carpet tiles to be cut. Place the tile to be cut on the last full one in place on the floor. Mark the tile to be cut where it meets the last full tile.

4 MARK THE CUTLINE.
Use a straightedge and marker to join the marks on the back of the carpet tile to be cut.

5 CUT CARPET TILE.
Use a wire cutter or other heavy scissors to cut the tile along the mark.

6 POSITION PARTIAL TILE.
Position the partial carpet tile in place. Vacuum the floor after all carpet tiles are in place to help disguise the seams where the pieces are adjoined.

Chapter 4 highlights

Windows and doors

Windows and doors are intricate pieces of work—although windows, with their movable frames, complex joinery, and the physics of letting in light while keeping out the heat, cold, and bugs, often seem much more so.

Windows also present technical and design challenges because they are tricky to paint and require tough choices in regard to color, form, and the elements that embellish them. Thoughtful use of roller shades, horizontal blinds, valances, and interior shutters is the key to keeping the design of your window treatments consistent with other design features in your room.

Doors are important too, particularly because they are the first and last part of a room you see. Like the first and last lines of a well-executed speech, a door should make a good impression. One easy way to do that is to include door trim that coordinates with the molding in the room. Doors that fit the style of your home help unify your decor while creating pleasing transitions from room to room.

Roll-down shades

PROJECT DETAILS

SKILLS: Measuring, painting, mounting hardware

TIME TO COMPLETE

EXPERIENCED: 1 hr.
HANDY: 2 hrs.
NOVICE: 3 hrs.

STUFF YOU'LL NEED

TOOLS: Tape measure, air filter, wire cutters or tin snips, 1-inch blue painter's tape, two 4-inch extra-smooth foam rollers, paper towels, two small paint trays
MATERIALS: Two roll-down vinyl shades (one for practice), two half-pints of paint in two shades, shade bracket for hanging

▲ An air filter grid finds creative use as a stencil design on this embellished roller shade.

Add personal style to a purchased roll-down shade by embellishing it with paint. Roller shade kits are available at window-treatment specialty shops and home centers as well as by mail order. Buy an extra shade to use for practicing the proper amount of paint and pressure before you begin creating the finished product. Unroll the shade on a hard, flat surface and affix a fiber filter on the shade, using painter's tape to create stripes. Select two colors—such as the brown and blue shown here—to paint in alternating stripes on the shade. Begin rolling color from the bottom of each stripe to the top in one motion, then roll back down the full length of the stripe and repeat until the paint is smooth and even.

GOOD IDEA

BLOCK THE LIGHT
An inside-mount shade like the one in this project may admit more light around the perimeter than you want. Inside-mount shades give a cleaner look than outside mounts and show off trimwork. If light control is important to you, however, use an outside mount.

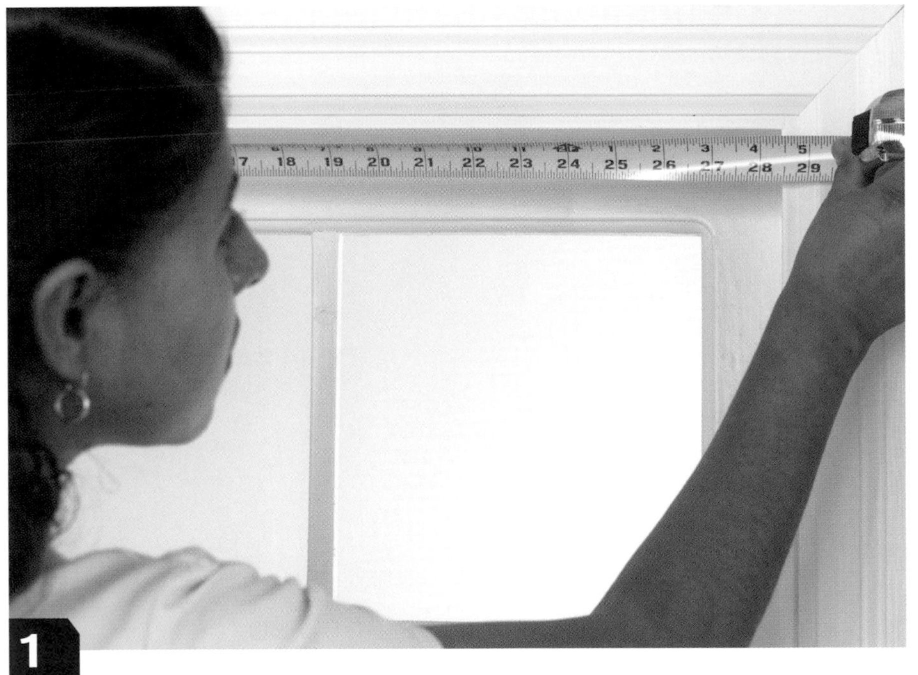

1

MEASURE FOR SHADE.
Measure the inside window opening to determine the correct size roller shade to purchase.

DESIGNER TIP

ADD A PULL
Attach a simple ornamental pull to the bottom center of the roller shade for an additional decorative touch. Choose a pull that complements the design of the shade and the room decor.

2

CREATE THE GRID.
Peel back the cardboard frame from the air filter. Separate the metal grid from the fiber filter. Lay the first metal grid on top of the shade with a solid edge of the grid positioned toward the bottom of the shade. Center the grid from right to left.

Roll-down shades *(continued)*

3

SECURE GRIDS WITH TAPE.
Trim the top edge of the grid with a tin snips or wire cutters. Apply tape around the edge of the grid, securing it to the shade. The tape should bisect a line of circles on each side of the grid. Add extra widths of tape to the outside edges of the sides and bottom to help prevent any overrolling. Any paint that finds its way outside the lines dries quickly and is very difficult to remove. Tape around the sides of individual stripes to make a symmetrical pattern. This works best if the stripes are the width of or more narrow than the roller being used. Lay the second grid above the first and tape in place the same way. Add extra widths of tape above the second grid to prevent overrolling.

4

PREPARE THE ROLLER FOR PAINTING.
Wet the foam roller with water and squeeze it dry with a paper towel so it is just moist. Use a stick to drizzle blue paint in the top flat part of the small paint tray. (Imagine that you are drizzling icing on a Danish.) Roll the roller back and forth to distribute the paint evenly on the roller. The roller should be almost "dry" to prevent paint from bleeding under the grid.

5

TEST THE ROLLER.

Roll the roller on the practice piece of vinyl to ensure it rolls evenly and the paint is not too heavy.

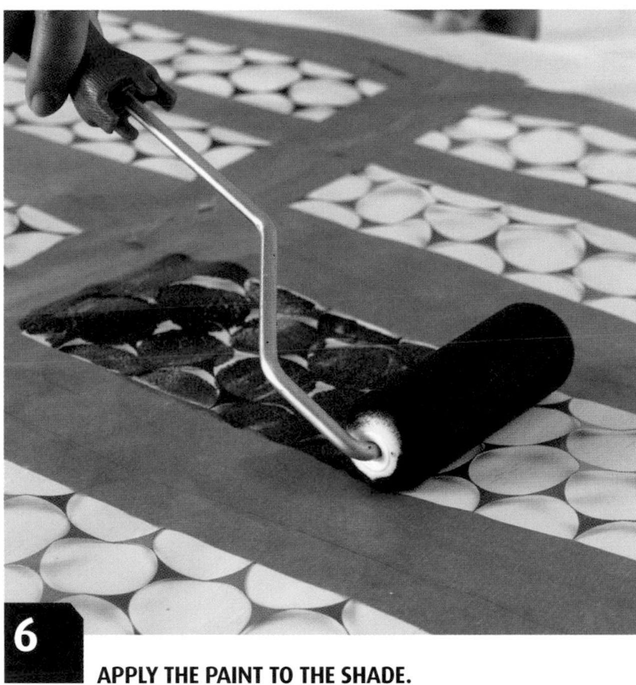

6

APPLY THE PAINT TO THE SHADE.

Begin rolling color from the bottom of a stripe and roll to the top of the stripe in one motion. Roll back down the full length of the stripe. Roll back and forth until the paint is smooth and even. You shouldn't need to add paint to the roller during this process. You should be able to paint the three bottom blue stripes without adding paint. Repeat the process and paint the top three blue stripes. Cover the paint trays and rollers with plastic wrap when not in use to prevent them from drying out.

7

TEST AND APPLY SECOND PAINT.

Repeat the process for the brown stripes. Be sure to practice with the brown paint because although it is the same brand of paint, it may handle differently. Carefully peel the tape and remove the grids. Allow the paint to dry.

8

ATTACH MOUNTING HARDWARE.

Following manufacturer's instructions secure mounting hardware for the roller shade to the interior of the window frame. Insert the rod in the bottom of the shade. Hang the shade.

Horizontal blinds

PROJECT DETAILS

SKILLS: Measuring, leveling, drilling

TIME TO COMPLETE

EXPERIENCED: ½ hr.
HANDY: 1 hr.
NOVICE: 2 hrs.

STUFF YOU'LL NEED

TOOLS: Tape measure, level, drill and bits, screwdriver
MATERIALS: Blinds, screws, anchors if necessary, brackets

SMART & SAFE

CHILD-SAFE WINDOWS
To prevent young children from becoming entangled in control cords, install cleats to keep the cords out of reach. Or shorten the cords by sliding up the knob, retying the knot that secures the knob, and cutting off the excess. Choose blinds that use wands instead of rope to open and close.

▲ **Adjust the horizontal movable slats to control light levels and to filter and direct the light.**

BUYER'S GUIDE

PREVENT BLOWING BLINDS
Some manufacturers offer hold-down brackets to keep lowered blinds from swaying. A pin in each bracket fits into a hole in the bottom rail. Request this feature when ordering.

Horizontal blinds with variable-pitch slats regulate light levels, ranging from gentle filtering to near darkness. Slats are made of aluminum, vinyl, PVC, or wood and come in many widths. Micro blinds average just ½ inch, minis about 1 inch, and standard-width slats 2 inches. Some blinds fold into compact stacking height—just 3 inches or so for a 6-foot blind. Wood blinds have a handsome, substantial look and provide a warm glow as outdoor light passes through them. But 6-foot wood blinds may have a stacking height of 8 inches or more. The longer the blinds are, the heavier they get and the more difficult to raise and lower. Consider installing several narrower blinds rather than one large one.

Blinds are installed two basic ways: mounted inside or outside the window opening. An outside mount makes the window look large because the stack goes above the window. A valance mounted on the wall can conceal the raised slats. Inside-mount blinds look trim. Because they don't overlap the window opening, they admit more light around the edges. Careful measurement is important to ensure that they'll fit the space.

WORK SMARTER

MOUNTING STYLE
Choosing between an inside and outside mount is usually a matter of depth and style. But if your windows are out of square, your best bet is an outside mount. To check for square, measure the window diagonally—top left to lower right of the opening, and from the top right to lower left. If measurements differ by more than ½ inch, go with an outside mount.

1 MEASURE WINDOWS FOR THE BLINDS.

Decide whether to mount inside or outside the opening.

A. For an inside mount, measure the width at the top, middle, and bottom. Use the smallest figure. Unless specified by the manufacturer, do not measure for clearance. That will be accounted for when the blinds are cut to size. Measure the height at the left and right sides and center. Use the largest figure.

B. For an outside mount, measure the overall width and add at least 8 inches to allow a generous overlap on each side to block light. Measure the height, adding at the top to account for the mounting brackets and enough at the bottom for a satisfactory overlap.

2 INSTALL THE BRACKETS.

Note that on some units, the same brackets are used for inside and outside mounting. Hold the end brackets (and central bracket if included) in place and mark for pilot screw holes. Use a level to make sure each set of holes is even with the others. Drill the holes for the screws and install the brackets. In wood or wood framing, drill the hole slightly smaller than the screw you'll use. If you aren't going into wood trim or wood framing, use wall anchors, toggle bolts, or other hardware and follow the directions supplied.

3 INSTALL THE HEAD RAIL.

Place the head rail into the brackets and lock it in place. If blinds hang long check the directions for removing some of the slats from the bottom.

4 ATTACH THE VALANCE.

If the blinds have a decorative valance, attach it as instructed. Also attach the wand for adjusting the vanes.

Valances

 PROJECT DETAILS

SKILLS: Measuring, drilling

 TIME TO COMPLETE

EXPERIENCED: ½ hr.
HANDY: 1 hr.
NOVICE: 2 hrs.

 STUFF YOU'LL NEED

TOOLS: Stepladder, tape measure, pencil, drill, screwdriver
MATERIALS: Valance, pole or rod with mounting brackets, mounting hardware, finials

4

WINDOWS AND DOORS

BUYER'S GUIDE

TAKE HOME SWATCHES
If you are slightly unsure about which fabric to use for a window treatment, take home swatches of your favorites. Look at them next to upholstered furniture and paint samples in the room you're decorating, ideally under both daytime and nighttime lighting conditions.

▲ **This richly patterned valance adds texture to the room, especially when paired with a bamboo shade. The colors in the valance pick up tones from the wall, furnishings, and artwork.**

Valances are typically used to disguise the mounting hardware and ends of blinds, roller shades, and traversing drapes. The additional fabric from the valance can also add a more formal, traditional touch to a room than a blind or shade alone. Choose a fabric for your valance that coordinates with and enhances the other treatments on the same window, as well as upholstered furnishings and paint in the room. Select from an astounding array of decorative finials for wooden rods and metal poles. Styles are made to complement the decor or to add a bit of whimsy.

1 **MEASURE THE WIDTH.** Measure between the outer edges of the window molding or extend this distance beyond the molding to make a narrow window look wider. Though a valance doesn't require a careful measure of the height of the window, measure for the desired height of the valance. Extend the distance above the window to make a short window look taller. Position the valance just above the window molding if little clearance exists between it and the ceiling.

2 **MEASURE FOR THE BRACKETS.** Measure the width of the mounting bracket and the location of the hardware that attaches to the wall. Transfer this measurement to the desired location on the wall. Mark with a pencil.

3 **INSTALL THE MOUNTING HARDWARE.** Attach the brackets that support the pole or rod, driving screws, toggle bolts, plastic anchors, or specialty mounting systems into wall studs or the window molding. The keyhole-shape holes in the back of the bracket for this valance slip over the heads of screws anchored in the wall.

4 **THREAD THE VALANCE.** Slide the pole through the opening at the top of the valance, leaving room at each end to attach the decorative finials.

5 **ATTACH FINIALS.** Screw a decorative finial to each end of the rod or pole.

6 **INSTALL THE ROD OR POLE.** Rest the pole or rod on its brackets.

Interior shutters

PROJECT DETAILS

SKILLS: Measuring, cutting, mounting hardware, chiseling

TIME TO COMPLETE

EXPERIENCED: 1 hr.
HANDY: 2 hrs.
NOVICE: 3 hrs.

STUFF YOU'LL NEED

TOOLS: Tape measure, plane or saw (if necessary), pencil, drill, screwdriver, utility knife (if hinges are mortised), wood chisel (if hinges are mortised), hammer (if hinges are mortised), cardboard or cedar shims, straightedge, drill
MATERIALS: Shutters with installation hardware, paint or stain (optional)

▲ **Mulitpurpose louvered shutters control the level of light, provide ventilation, and offer privacy in a room.**

In an era before screens and blinds, interior shutters graced many homes. A practical window treatment, they conserve heat in the winter and allow ventilation and privacy in summer. Shutters provide architectural elegance and a sense of structure different from the flounce and flow of draperies, curtains, and other fabric treatments.

Shutters can be installed in several configurations: full height, double hung (*left*), as separate shutters for the bottom and top halves of the window, and cafe-style with shutters at the bottom half of the window.

Typically interior shutters have operable louvers connected with a tilt bar to moderate light, but they also are available with fixed louvers. A version that's suited for country, traditional, and Victorian styles is the solid frame-and-panel style.

MEASURE FIRST
Before you order shutters measure all the windows in the room. It's tough news to learn that some of your made-to-order shutters don't quite fit.

1 MEASURE THE WINDOW OPENING.
If the installation will be outside the opening, measure so that the shutters will slightly overlap the jamb. If the shutters are to be placed inside the window opening, measure the width and height of this space at several places; use the narrowest measurement for the width and the smallest measurement for the height. Measure for inside-mount shutters to the nearest ⅛ inch.

2 TRIM THE SHUTTERS IF NECESSARY.
If a shutter is too large, plane or saw equal amounts from the outside edges of both stiles (the vertical frame members) or both rails (the horizontal members) as needed. Do not remove so much stock as to compromise the appearance or the strength of the shutters. Test the fit by wedging the shutters in the opening, considering whether you will recess the hinges in mortises. Plane or cut again if necessary. If the shutters aren't already finished, paint or stain before installation.

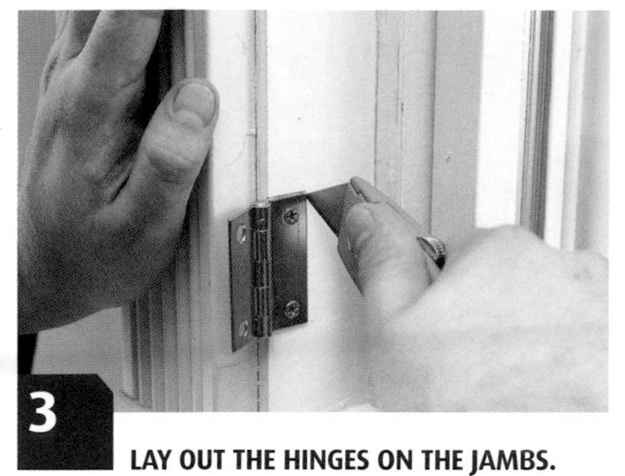

3 **LAY OUT THE HINGES ON THE JAMBS.** Hinges are usually placed 1½ inches from the top and bottom of the shutter; if the shutter is over 3 feet tall or especially heavy, add a third hinge midway. Note that shutters fit more closely to the sides of the window opening when the hinges are set into mortises, both on wood window trim and on the shutters. Before cutting the hinge mortises, mount the hinges temporarily on the jambs, then use a utility knife to outline them. Drill pilot holes for the screws if necessary.

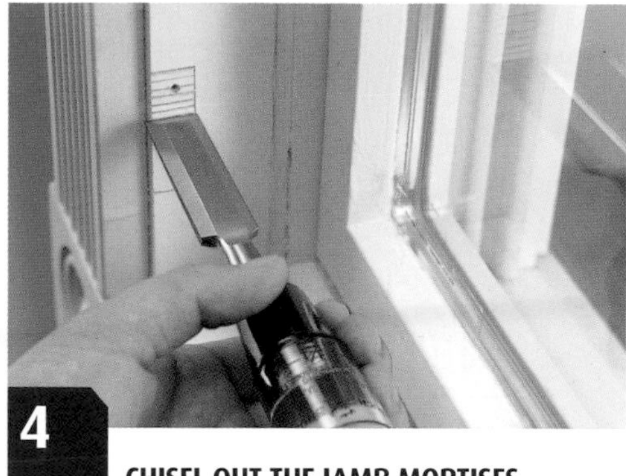

4 **CHISEL OUT THE JAMB MORTISES.** If the instructions for the shutters direct you to mortise the jambs for the hinges, use a chisel and hammer to remove the wood, working to a depth that makes the leaves of the hinges flush with the surface. Place each hinge in its mortise, mark for pilot holes, drill, and temporarily install with just one screw for each hinge.

5 **LAY OUT AND CHISEL THE MORTISES.** Temporarily wedge the shutters in place with cardboard or tapered cedar shims and check for proper clearance all around. Make sure they open the right way and operate freely, then trace the hinge outlines on the shutter stiles. So that the hinge mortises will have crisp, true edges, go over the pencil lines with a utility knife held against a straightedge.

6 **FINISH INSTALLING THE SHUTTERS.** Remove the shutters and mortise them for the hinges if directed to do so. Drill pilot holes and install the shutters. Adjust the jamb hinges if necessary, then drive the remaining screws.

Refinisher's secret

Why are interior shutters so often stained? It could be just for the dark, handsome look, but convenience also may have something to do with it. Painting louvered shutters with a brush is tricky, but stain can be wiped on quickly using a rag.

GOOD IDEA

PROTECT WOOD SHUTTERS
If wood shutters will be used in a high-humidity area—over the kitchen sink or in the bathroom, for instance—prime and paint every surface, or condition, stain, and finish with a coat of polyurethane.

Mounting interior shutters

Interior shutters are installed either outside or inside the window jamb. Decide which method suits your needs before measuring and ordering them.

Outside mount is the most common mounting method. If the window has no trim, attach the hang strip to the wall and hang the shutter from it. If the window has trim, mount the hang strip to it.

Inside mounts are tricky because mismeasured shutters or an out-of-square window opening may leave light gaps around the perimeter. Also you need two or more inches of jamb depth for the shutters to operate without interfering with the operation of the window.

The two types of inside-mount shutters are as follows:

- **Direct Mount:** If the window opening is surrounded by a wood jamb, use a direct mount, with one-half of the hinge attached to the jamb and the other to the shutter.
- **Indirect Mount:** If the window jamb is drywall, use an indirect mount, with one-half of the hinge attached to a hang strip and the other to the shutter. This installation method is also used to deal with an opening that is out of square because the strip position can be adapted to allow the shutter to operate properly.

Gallery of window treatments

After the rest of the room is in shape, it's time to dress the windows. Choosing the right treatments is a challenging design decision. You may want to seek advice from a design professional at The Home Depot. Designers and window treatment specialists will share basic knowledge of styles, materials and fabrics, hanging methods, and accessories to help you select a version that best suits your room.

Choose from three options for purchase: custom, semicustom, and off-the-shelf. For unusual or complex treatments, talk to a design staff member about manufacturing treatments to your specifications. Design centers also carry a wide assortment of semicustom draperies, which include basic designs in several different materials, lengths, and widths ranging from simple to elaborate. You can also find basic options on the shelves at The Home Depot, often with a range of standard lengths and widths. In addition look for rods and poles, finials, and hangers suited to the treatment you select and that will match almost any decor.

Layering for Effect

Most successful window treatments are a combination of several elements rather than a single blind or roller shade. The base layer of a window dressing is typically a blind or shade. These offer light control and, depending on the material, additional protection from UV rays. Fabric panels typically are added at the sides of the base layer or may be wide enough to close over a sheer base fabric. A valance, swag, or cornice tops the window.

When draperies are used to frame a window rather than to close it off, interior shutters are a good partner. Whether the shutters are full height or halfway, they can be closed to provide privacy and to dim the room. Use shutters with these window treatments:

- **Swags** sweep dramatically from the top of the window and aren't operable. Couple a swag with a side jabot, joining the two with a rosette. Make sure that the shutters clear the swags or shutter only the bottom half of the windows.
- **Valances** balance the tops of windows covered with cafe shutters on the lower half.
- **Curtains** duplicate the area covered by shutters. They allow flexibility in moderating light, privacy, and the appearance of the room.

For a cohesive look plan for the window dressing before shopping and then select all the elements to work together. Start with the blind or shade. They are crisply attractive in their simplicity and efficiency. Even if blinds alone don't seem to suit a plush, traditional living room, when you add a swag, valance, or traversing draperies, you'll soften the look.

FOR MORE THAN WINDOWS
Use tall shutters as freestanding room dividers and smaller shutters as cabinet doors.

▲ **Natural-stain wooden blinds partner with a soft denim valance for a comfortable look appropriate for fresh country style.**

▲ **A delicate floral-pattern valance in a classic black-and-white color scheme contributes formality when partnered with a soft, light-diffusing pleated shade.**

Selecting blinds and shades

Shopping for blinds and shades requires time and research. The Home Depot carries huge displays showcasing hundreds of colors and styles. Improvements in operating mechanisms make blinds and shades easy to install. Innovations in design and materials offer choices for privacy and light diffusion. Perforations in plastic and metal blinds allow more light without sacrificing privacy. Cellular shades and honeycomb shades, which have horizontal tubes of fabric that are barely visible when raised, are soft variations of blinds. When lowered they provide soft, diffused light with little insulation. Double- and triple-cell shades increase resistance to heat flow—the R-value. Shades operate in several ways—from the top down, bottom up, or both. And the top can be sheer, while the bottom is opaque. Wallpaper and fabric inserts change the personality of vertical vanes, which is handy if you redecorate or repaint the room.

▲ **White on white is a natural window dressing for a cheerful kitchen. The lacy border on the valance softens the sharp horizontal lines of the shade.**

Door trim and molding

 PROJECT DETAILS

SKILLS: Measuring, nailing, mitering

 TIME TO COMPLETE

EXPERIENCED: 2 hrs.
HANDY: 3 hrs.
NOVICE: 4 hrs.

 STUFF YOU'LL NEED

TOOLS: Combination square, pencil, miter box and backsaw, hammer, clamps, drill, nail set
MATERIALS: Molding, #6 and #8 finishing nails, glazing putty or wax stick for filling nail holes

Carpenter's secret

Hide nails by driving them into one of the grooves in the molding. After you set the nail, fill the hole with glazing putty if you paint. If you stain, stain and varnish before putting up the molding, as shown in this project. After the trim is up, fill the nail holes with colored wax sticks sold in paint departments. Pick a stick that matches the stain and rub it across the nail hole until it is filled.

▲ **Door trim makes a statement about your decorating scheme. Plain moldings are contemporary; corner blocks are Victorian. It's all in the details.**

Door trim, door molding, and door casing refer to the same material—the wood that goes around a door. There are several styles of door trim and a couple of techniques for installing it. The most common method, shown here, is also the oldest. The trim pieces are mitered where they meet. A more decorative approach is to install blocks at the base and at the top of the door trim with a straight stretch of molding running between. This was a Victorian solution that, although simple to install, used more wood. As the cost of wood went up, miters again became fashionable. You can still get Victorian-style trim; see how it's installed in "No Miter/No Cope Baseboard," page 44.

Obtaining a good substitute for old-fashioned molding may be easier than you think. The wood-molding industry long ago standardized molding profiles. You should be able to match a standard molding in your home with one in the lumberyard, even if the molding is decades old. Be prepared for slight variations—the profile actually changes as the cutters wear down. If you have difficulty finding what you want, contact architectural millwork houses that make moldings and other trims. They can reproduce molding or create a custom profile for you.

Carpenter's secret

When installing door trim some carpenters begin with the vertical pieces (called legs); others prefer to hang the top trim first. Installing the top first has the advantage of offering precise control over the most finicky part of the installation—the miters. Once the top trim is up, install the legs one at a time, positioning each so that the miter is perfect. If you do the legs first, you'll have to fit the top trim on both miters simultaneously. Unless both miters are perfect and the legs perfectly parallel, you're bound to get gaps you can't close.

1 LAY OUT THE REVEAL.

The door trim is never flush with the edge of the jamb; typically it sits back from the edge by about ⅛ inch. The space, or reveal, leaves enough room for the hinge barrel and provides a margin of error if the jamb dips. The frame on a prehung door is likely to have a layout line on it that marks the edge of the reveal. If you work on a door frame that isn't already marked, set a combination square to ⅛ inch and guide it and a pencil along the frame. Mark the reveal on both sides and above the door.

2 MEASURE AND MITER THE TOP TRIM.

First cut a 45-degree miter on one end of the top trim piece; hold it in place to mark the inside point of the second miter cut. Lay out the cut with a combination square and cut it with a miter box and backsaw.

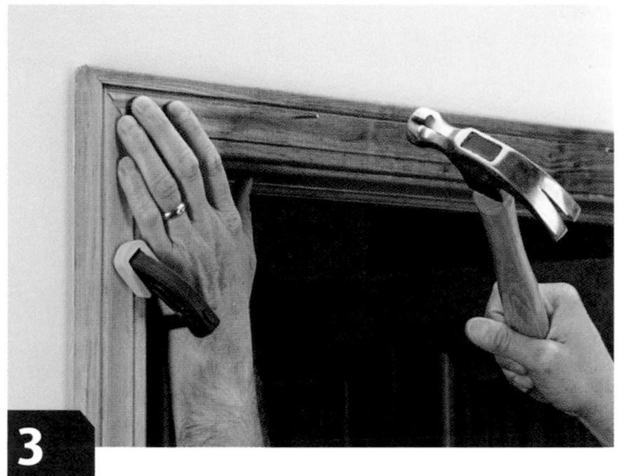

3 NAIL THE TOP TRIM IN PLACE.

To help position the trim, miter two short pieces of molding, and clamp them in place along the sides of the door frame. Put the top trim in place and adjust as necessary to get a tight miter. When you're satisfied with the fit, nail the trim into the jamb with #6 finishing nails; drive #8 finishing nails through the trim and into the studs. Drive the nails only partway, leaving at least ⅛ inch exposed in case you need to remove them.

4 MITER THE LEGS.

Mitering a piece to fit can be tricky. Make it easy on yourself by mitering the legs before you square them off. Then place the legs against the frame so they're upside down. This leaves the miter on the floor and the full length of the trim extending toward the ceiling. Mark where the top trim touches the leg, and cut the leg square at the mark.

5 NAIL THE LEGS TO THE DOOR FRAME.

Start at the top, holding the leg so the miter closes tightly, and drive a #6 finishing nail through it and into the jamb. Work down the leg, flexing it if necessary so that it aligns with the line that marks the reveal. When you're satisfied drive #8 finishing nails into the framing behind the wall. Repeat on the opposite leg and set all the nails.

To keep the corners tight, predrill and drive a #6 finishing nail at an angle up through the edge of the leg, through the miter, and into the header molding.

The Victorian approach

Victorian molding took a more decorative—and simpler to install—approach toward doors. Plinth blocks were installed at the bottom trim and rosette blocks at the top corners. Molding was then cut to fit between the blocks.

An advantage of this approach is that there are no miter joints to cut; another is that it adds style.

Plinth blocks, rosettes, and reversible pilaster trim are available in packaged kits. Install the blocks first with construction adhesive, then crosscut lengths of trim to fit between them.

TOOL SAVVY

MEASURE WITH LIPSTICK

Lipstick makes quick work of measuring. On a door trim rub lipstick against the point of the miter. When you put the leg against the miter, it makes a bright mark where you need to make the cut.

Use the same technique to install drywall. To lay out the hole for a switch or outlet, rub lipstick on the junction box. Put the drywall in place and push gently in the general area of the box. You'll get a bright mark on the back of the drywall showing the location of the box.

爱
Love
财
Wealth
喜
Happiness
THE
SECRET
WOMAN
Victoria
Holt
THE
Troubled

Chapter 5 highlights

Lighting

Lighting is first about function—good lighting quality is essential for how you utilize a room. After function comes form. Light fixtures do as much to define the style and look of a room as other elements in the space.

You'll find many options for light fixtures—home centers and lighting specialists bring a high level of sophistication to the process of matching lights to a particular room. As you shop for light fixtures, be aware of the size, style, and wattage that will best fit your room.

Also consider how various types of lighting reflect and impact the style of the room. Recessed lights disappear discreetly into the ceiling, while surface-mounted track lighting protrudes into the room. Pendants, table and floor lamps, chandeliers, and wall sconces are as integral to the style of the room as are the furnishings and accessories. Once you've selected the right fixtures, each may be fitted with a variety of bulbs to achieve the quality of light best suited to the way you use the room and to the specific purpose of the fixture.

Lighting plans

The right lighting can make any room in your home more attractive. Rather than installing a single lighting component, think in terms of the total effect of the room. Layering several types of lights makes a room more comforting and inviting. One goal is flexibility, so you can set a variety of moods by brightening or dimming the entire room or part of the room.

Try to include each of these types of lighting:

Ambient lighting produces a daylight effect. Flush ceiling fixtures or track lights spread light more evenly than recessed can lights or pendants. Windows and skylights are great sources of light during daylight, but they need help in the evening and in gloomy weather. Dimmer switches for ambient light fixtures make it easier to achieve the lighting effect you desire. **Task lights** provide illumination for common work such as reading. **Accent lights** highlight architectural and decorative features. Accent lighting, the most decorative of the three main types of lighting, has many forms.

Recessed can lights are a good solution for improving the lighting in almost any room. These lights vary in intensity and angle. The higher your ceiling the more floor space a light will illuminate. In general recessed cans should be six feet from each other. Of course most rooms are not sized to accommodate this spacing so adjust your plans according to the size of your room. Recessed canister lights enhance your decorating strategy with three techniques:

Wall washing. To light up a large wall area, install cans with wall-wash trims that are 24 to 30 inches apart and the same distance from the wall.

General accent lighting. Spotlight a painting, fireplace mantel, or other feature with a can that has an eyeball trim. Place it 18 to 24 inches from the wall, centered on the object.

Grazing. To dramatize an unusual vertical surface, such as a fireplace or a textured wall, place cans six to 12 inches apart.

▲ **Before recessed lights and an art light were installed, this living room seemed dark and shadowy, particularly in the corners. The textures and subtle color variations of the stone fireplace wall were not highlighted effectively.**

▲ The lighting plan for this living room includes a grid of recessed canister lights for general lighting and a ceiling fixture, not shown, in the center of the room. An art light highlights the painting next to the fireplace. A recessed light with fish-eye trim also would work to spotlight the wallhung painting. The table lamp and floor lamp provide task lighting for reading.

Chandelier replacement

PROJECT DETAILS

SKILLS: Connecting wiring

TIME TO COMPLETE

EXPERIENCED: 1 hr.
HANDY: 2 hrs.
NOVICE: 3 hrs.

STUFF YOU'LL NEED

TOOLS: Ladder and support platform, screwdriver, wire strippers, electrical tape
MATERIALS: Chandelier, appropriate ceiling electrical box, wire nuts

SMART & SAFE

USE WIRE TAPE
Once you've connected the wires with wire caps, wrap electrical tape around the wire and the cap. It's not always necessary, but it will help keep the wire from popping free and charging the metal parts of the chandelier with electricity.

▲ A chandelier usually is used to illuminate dining tables. Plan the placement of one as carefully as you would plan a good meal. To give off a pleasing light, a chandelier should be centered over the table and about 30 inches above it. For a chandelier with one socket, use a single 100-watt bulb. For two sockets use two 60-watt bulbs. For three or more sockets, use 40-watt bulbs.

Lighting fixtures impact the ambience of a room. Besides the quality of light they produce, consider the appearance of the fixtures, especially because they are prominent room features.

Although "chandelier" may bring to mind ornate lights with sparkling crystals, for practical purposes it refers to any ceiling-mounted fixture that hangs from a chain or wire. This includes an incredibly wide range of fixtures that complement any style of decor, from Early American candle types to stained-glass Arts and Crafts designs.

Despite the variety, installation of ceiling-mounted fixtures is similar, regardless of the style. The biggest issue is determining whether the electric box that houses the wiring connections in the ceiling is adequate to support the weight of the chandelier. If you replace a hanging fixture with a fixture about the same weight, the existing box is probably fine. If the new fixture is heavier, you may need to replace the box with one rated to hold a heavy fixture.

See The Home Depot's *Wiring 1-2-3* for detailed information about wiring and lighting fixture installation.

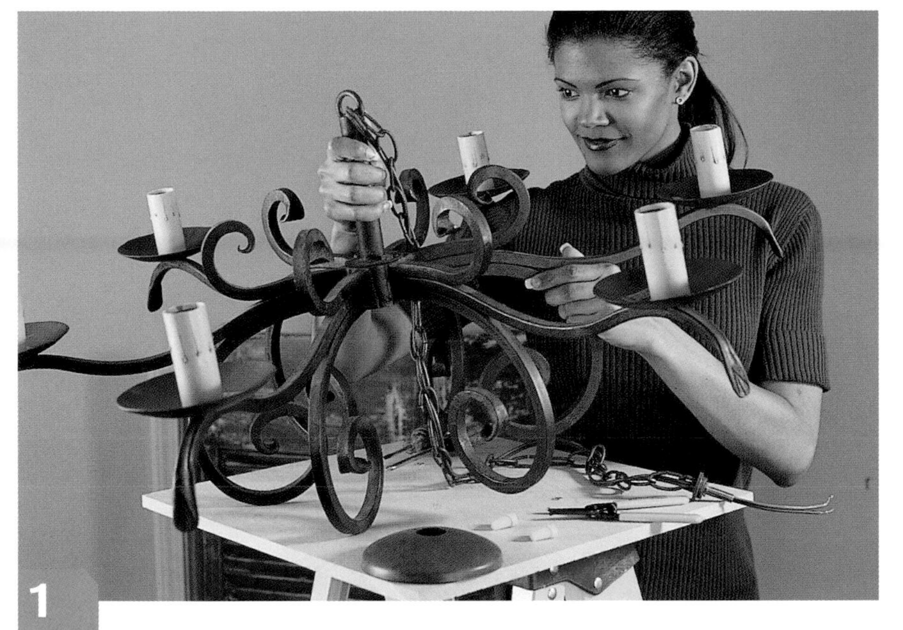

1

ASSEMBLE THE CANOPY AND HANGING HARDWARE.
Remove any components that can be installed after the fixture is hanging (globes, glass panels, lightbulbs, etc.). Follow the specific instructions provided with the fixture. Remember to slide any necessary parts over the wiring and hanging chain.

Support the fixture close to the ceiling by screwing a platform to the top of a stepladder with a few drywall screws. This provides a good work surface and should put the chandelier close enough to the ceiling to allow you to do the wiring without having to hold it in midair. Having a second person on a second ladder also may work but can be difficult with a heavy fixture.

Fixtures usually come with a new mounting strap—a strip of metal that screws into the junction box in the ceiling. You often can use the existing strap, but if not, unscrew the old strap and screw the new one in place.

Electrician's secret

Break something while you were working on the chandelier? Many—but not all—parts of a chandelier or lamp are interchangeable. Take the broken part to an electrical department or a lighting store. Brass globes, threaded fittings, and brass stems almost always can be replaced.

2

CONNECT THE WIRING.
Shut off power. Then check the supply wires for fraying or damage. If necessary cut the wires and strip off about $^3/_4$ inch of insulation. On older fixtures, like this one, the wires aren't color coded. Newer fixtures have a black and a white wire. Connect the black fixture wire to the black supply wire and the white fixture wire to the white supply wire. Twist the bare end of the black supply wire with the bare end of the black fixture wire and twist on a wire nut. Repeat with the white wires. Carefully tuck the wires into the junction box. Put a bulb in the fixture to check that connections work before finishing.

3

HANG THE FIXTURE.
Thread the fixture's mounting stem into the mounting strap on the ceiling box. The fixture is now securely hanging from the ceiling, but the box and mounting hardware are still visible. Slide the canopy up against the ceiling to cover the mounting hardware and tighten the locknut against the canopy.

Chandelier embellishment

 PROJECT DETAILS

SKILLS: Drilling, painting

 TIME TO COMPLETE

EXPERIENCED: 1 hr.
HANDY: 2 hrs.
NOVICE: 3 hrs.

 STUFF YOU'LL NEED

TOOLS: Gloves, drill, mask
MATERIALS: Chandelier, cotton balls, hammered-silver spray enamel, antique-brass spray enamel, two packages of 3-inch crystal prisms, two packages of 2-inch crystal prisms, one package of 1½-inch crystal prisms, clip-on belle shades

 SMART & SAFE

THE RIGHT LIGHT
Older fixtures don't have labels stating maximum bulb wattage. Be safe: Use small low-wattage, low-heat bulbs in an older chandelier. The resulting light will be more pleasing and prevent overheating that could result from larger bulbs.

▲ **Update an old chandelier with spray paint and crystal prisms.**

An inexpensive chandelier looks stunning when it's embellished with the right combination of paint finishes and accessories to complement your decorating scheme. For instance, a light mist of silver spray paint followed by a layer of brass paint tones down an overly bright brass chandelier. Remove the chandelier from the ceiling before adding embellishments. When painting allow each coat to dry before applying another. Further additions include prisms hung in predrilled holes and clip-on belle shades. The shades come in several colors and, in addition to dressing up the chandelier, provide softer light for a dining area. After completing the embellishments see page 138 for replacing the chandelier.

ACCESSORIZE
Other accessories may be used to embellish a chandelier. Prisms are a classic choice because the facets on them will scatter and reflect light from the chandelier for a glittering effect. Pearlized beads, glass beads, and fabric are other options. Choose lightweight objects that coordinate with the look of the room.

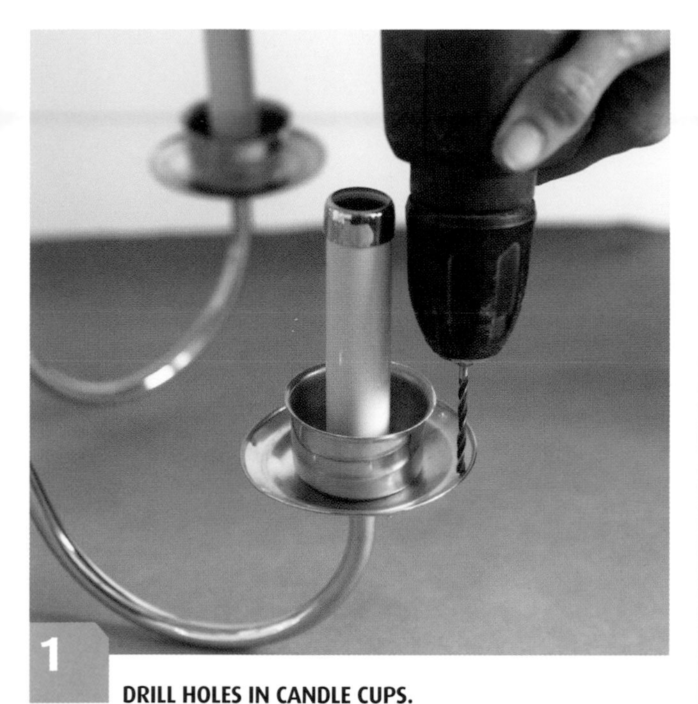

1

DRILL HOLES IN CANDLE CUPS.
Remove bulbs from the chandelier as well as any other parts that can be installed after the fixture is hanging, such as globes or glass panels. Place the chandelier on a sturdy worktable. Using a drill evenly space six holes around each candle light saucer. Position the holes close to the outside edge of the saucer. You will suspend prisms from these holes.

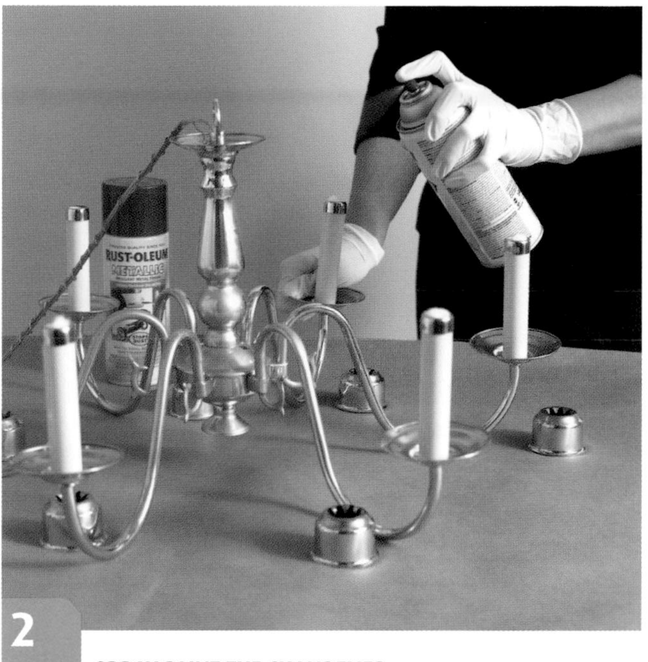

2

SPRAY PAINT THE CHANDELIER.
Place cotton balls in the space for each bulb to protect the socket from paint. Using the hammered-silver spray paint, lightly mist sporadically over the chandelier. Allow paint to dry. Using the antique brass spray paint, lightly mist sporadically over the chandelier. Allow to dry. Paint the chain and any removable parts that need to match the body of the chandelier.

3

HANG PRISMS.
After the paint is dry, attach the prisms by threading the hook on a prism through one of the holes you drilled in the light cups. Continue adding prisms until the holes are filled. Hang additional prisms from the center of the chandelier as desired.

4

ATTACH SHADES.
Remove the cotton balls from the sockets in the chandelier. Replace the bulbs. Clip on coordinating belle shades to complete the new look.

Wall sconces

PROJECT DETAILS

SKILLS: Connecting wiring

TIME TO COMPLETE

EXPERIENCED: 1 hr.
HANDY: 2 hrs.
NOVICE: 3 hrs.

STUFF YOU'LL NEED

TOOLS: Screwdriver, wire strippers or combination tool, electrician's pliers, nylon cord or coat hanger
MATERIALS: Wire nuts (if old ones need replacing)

5

LIGHTING

DESIGNER TIP

USE SCONCES
Sconces are perfect as accent lights above the mantel or beside the fireplace. They provide subtle light without taking up floor space.

▲ A wall sconce—whether it's new, a reproduction, or an antique—is a small investment that makes a big difference.

Replacing a wall sconce is one of the simpler ways to dress up a wall, whether your reasons are practical or aesthetic.

Taking out an old sconce involves removing a couple of screws and untwisting a couple of wires. Installing the replacement is just the opposite. A pointer: Connect similar-colored wires to each other and twist them together before applying the wire nut.

Be smart and safe. Before you start turn off the power at the panel, not just at the switch.

SMART & SAFE

AVOID FAULTY WIRING
Faulty wiring may send currents into the body of an electrical fixture. The grounding wire in the cable safely diverts the electricity. If the box is plastic, connect the fixture's grounding wire to the one in the cable. (Grounding wires either are uninsulated copper or have a green plastic coating.) If the box is metal, attach the grounding wires to a third wire and connect the third wire to the electrical box. Ask The Home Depot's electrical department for advice if the wiring in your home makes grounding difficult.

Electrician's secret

It may require more than two hands to hold a light fixture as you twist the wire connections on or off. If you don't have a helper, temporarily support the fixture by tying a nylon cord to the mounting strap on the electrical box. If there's no mounting strap, hang the fixture on a hook made from a hanger.

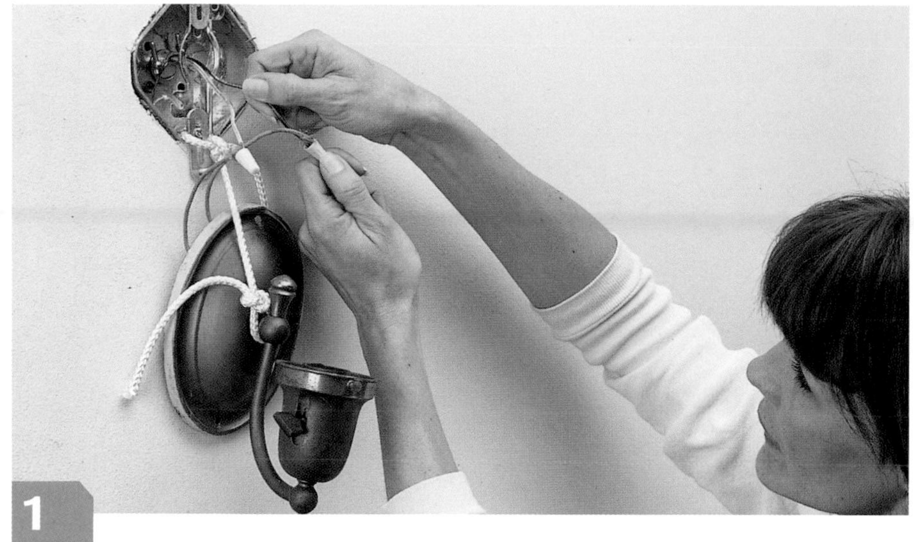

1

REMOVE THE EXISTING FIXTURE.
Turn off the power to the fixture at the fuse or circuit breaker box. Remove the glass globe or shade and bulb. Remove any nuts or screws holding the fixture in place, then carefully pull the fixture from the wall. Pull gently in case the fixture has been painted in place and to avoid yanking on the wires. After you remove the fixture, twist off the wire nuts that connect the wires.

2

INSPECT THE WIRES AND INSTALL THE MOUNTING STRAP.
Check the condition of the wires in the electrical box. If the metal is nicked, scratched, or twisted, it may break off after you install the light. Clip the wire flush with the end of its insulation, then strip off about an inch of insulation with wire strippers.

Sconces mount in a couple of different ways; check the manufacturer's directions. Most mount on a strap that is attached to the junction box in the wall. The strap usually comes with the fixture. Screw the strap to the junction box.

Once the strap is in, the lamp probably is attached with either a pair of boltlike threaded studs or with a single, hollow-threaded rod called a nipple. Twist the studs, or nipple, into the mounting strap.

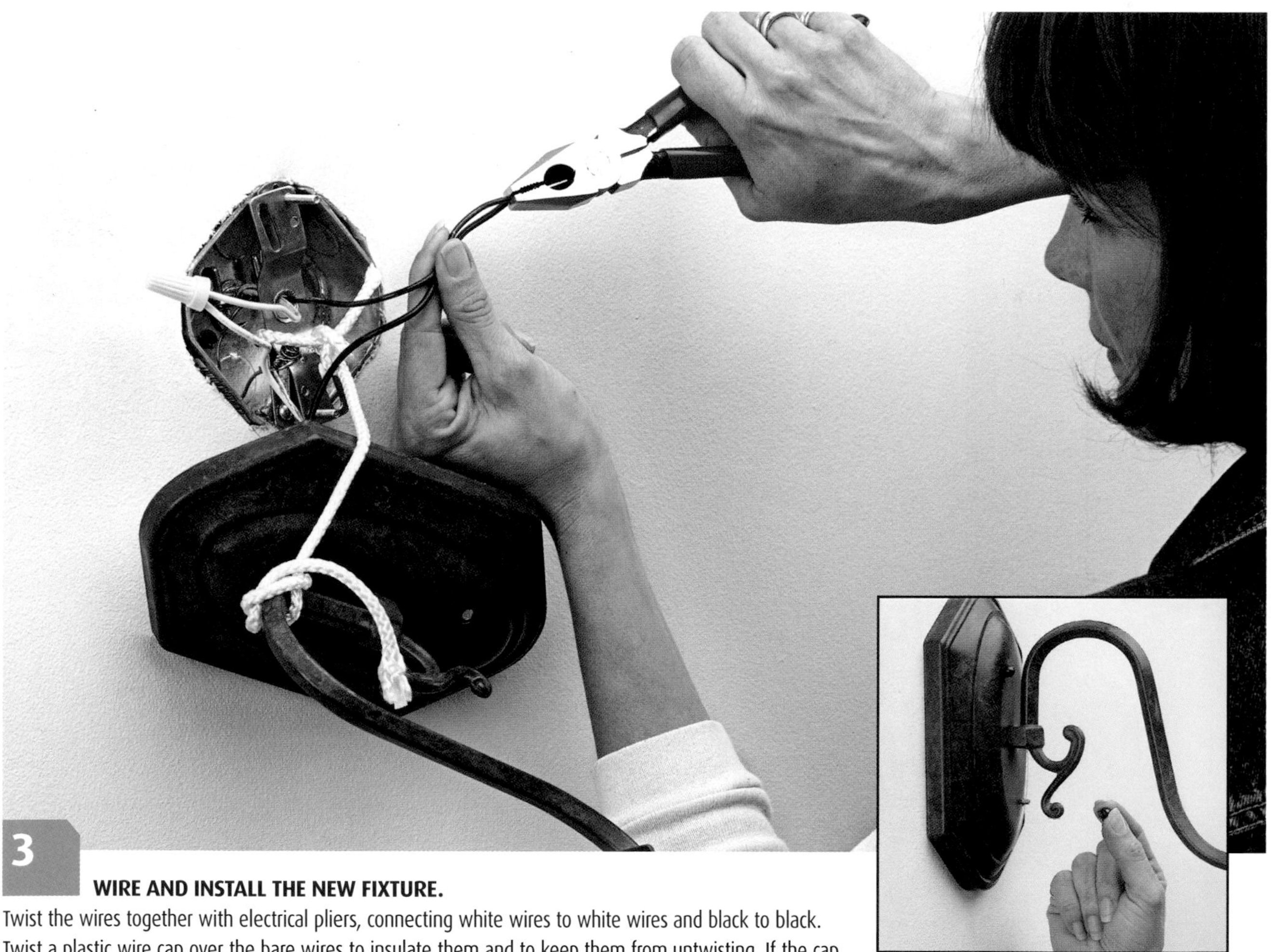

3

WIRE AND INSTALL THE NEW FIXTURE.
Twist the wires together with electrical pliers, connecting white wires to white wires and black to black. Twist a plastic wire cap over the bare wires to insulate them and to keep them from untwisting. If the cap doesn't cover the bare wire, remove the cap, trim the bare wire a bit shorter, and reattach the cap. Carefully fold the wires into the junction box, place the fixture over the studs or nipple, then attach the fixture with the ornamental nuts provided. (See inset, *right*.)

Trapeze lights

PROJECT DETAILS

SKILLS: Anchoring screw hooks, splicing wires

TIME TO COMPLETE

EXPERIENCED: 1 hr.
HANDY: 2 hrs.
NOVICE: 3 hrs.

STUFF YOU'LL NEED

TOOLS: Drill, screwdriver, longnose side-cutting pliers, wire strippers
MATERIALS: Trapeze light kit, wire nuts, cable anchors

▲ **Trapeze lights show off their hardware rather than hiding behind a canopy or globe. These fixtures may be positioned to cast light directly on a focal point area, like a shelf displaying artwork.**

These halogen fixtures are stylish, energy-efficient, and—because you easily can point them where they're needed—versatile. The exposed wires are not dangerous because they carry very low voltage. Remove an existing ceiling light and attach a canopy transformer to the ceiling box (as shown in step 2) or place a plug-in transformer into a switched receptacle.

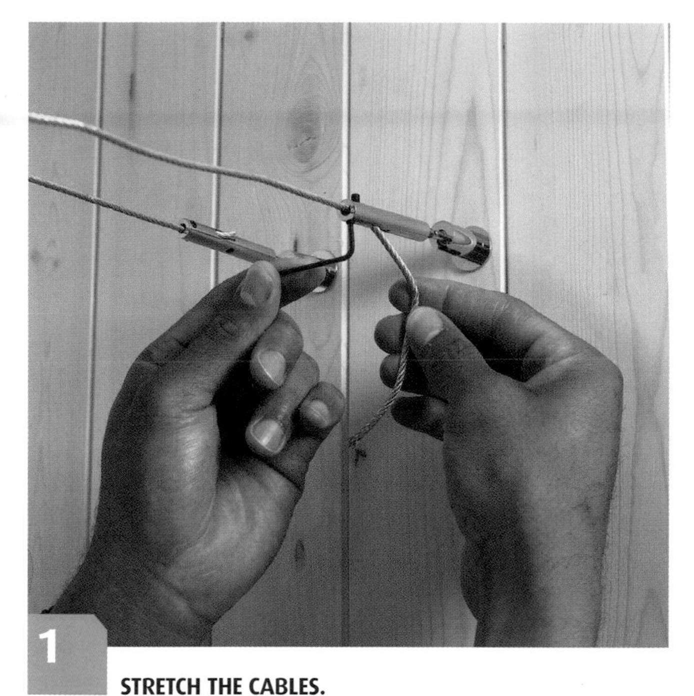

1

STRETCH THE CABLES.
Shut off power. Remove the light fixture or install and run cable to a ceiling box where you plan to install the lights. Attach two cable anchors on the walls between which the unit will hang. Cut two lengths of cable to span the length of the installation. Fasten cables to the anchors and tighten the turnbuckle until the cables are taut.

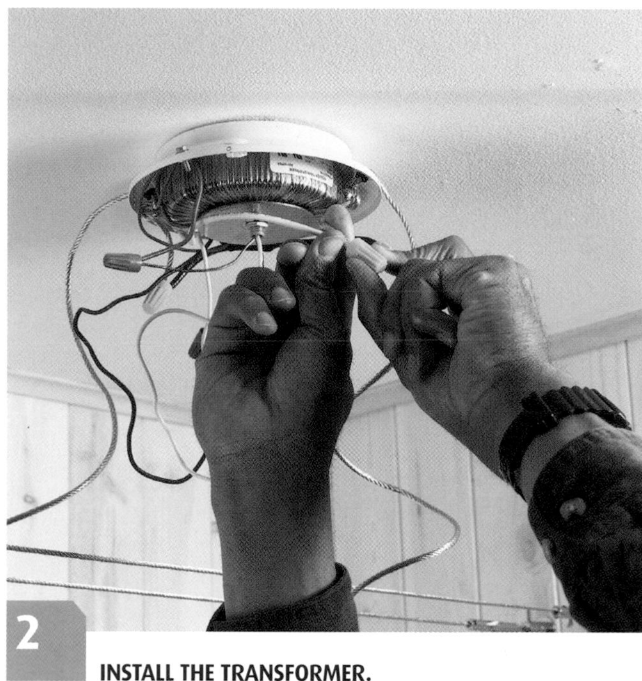

2

INSTALL THE TRANSFORMER.
Install a strap on the ceiling box. Mount the transformer on the strap. Splice the canopy transformer's red lead to the house's black wire and splice white wires to white wires. Connect the green lead to the ground wire (the thin copper one). Cap connections with wire nuts.

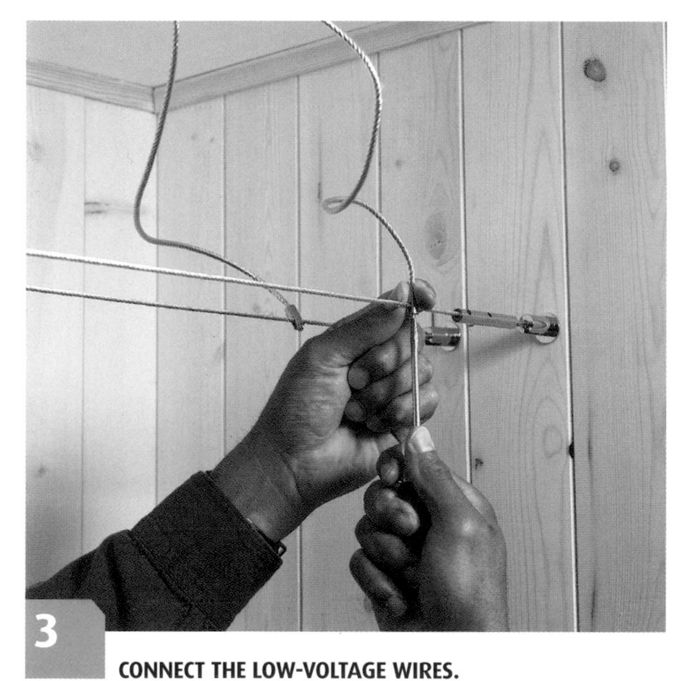

3

CONNECT THE LOW-VOLTAGE WIRES.
You may have to cut the low-voltage leads to the right length, restrip the clear insulation, and reattach the leads to the transformer. Clamp the leads onto the stretched cables using the fasteners provided with the kit. Attach the cover to the transformer.

4

HANG THE LIGHTS.
Hold a halogen bulb with a cloth (oil from your skin will damage it) and push the pins into a light arm. Slip the spring clamp over a wire, position the light arm on the cable, and clip the spring clamp onto the cable. Restore power and test. Adjust the lights while the power is on. The voltage is low enough to ensure safety.

Table lamp

PROJECT DETAILS

SKILLS: Cutting, drilling, wiring, gluing

TIME TO COMPLETE

EXPERIENCED: 2 hrs.
HANDY: 3 hrs.
NOVICE: 4 hrs.

STUFF YOU'LL NEED

TOOLS: Geometric compass, drill, saber saw, sandpaper, blue painter's tape, 5/16-inch drill bit, tape measure, scrap wood, 1/8-inch drill bit, screwdriver, hammer, hot-glue gun, utility knife

MATERIALS: 3/4-inch medium-density fiberboard (MDF), four drawer pulls, surface-mount porcelain lamp holder, lamp cord set, two 5/16×48-inch wood dowels cut to four dowels at 22 1/4 inches, 40-watt tube appliance bulb, 23-inch-wide matchstick Roman shade, two hose clamps to fit 7-inch diameter, in-line off/on switch (optional)

GOOD IDEA

CORD SWITCHES

Rather than plugging in the lamp each time you want light and unplugging it each time you want it off, equip it with a quick-install cord switch. An inexpensive rotating switch is fine for occasional use. Determine the best spot for the switch along the length of the cord. With the lamp unplugged cut a 1-inch-long slit to divide the cord where you want the switch, then snip the smooth (hot) wire. Insert the wire into the switch and screw the two halves of the switch together.

▲ **This table lamp with a bamboo shade brightens a hallway display area and contributes to the artistic arrangement.**

When it comes to lighting, a freestanding lamp is one of the more multifunctional items for your living spaces. Depending on the size of the lamp and where it's placed, it may provide ambient lighting that helps create an overall glow for the room, task lighting that illuminates a certain area for reading or other activities, or even accent lighting that highlights decorative objects such as a collection displayed on a table. Rather than purchasing a standard lamp base and shade, create your own lighting element by affixing a lampshade constructed from a matchstick Roman shade to a tall frame made from medium-density fiberboard and wooden dowels. The result is a contemporary fixture that provides subdued accent lighting in any setting.

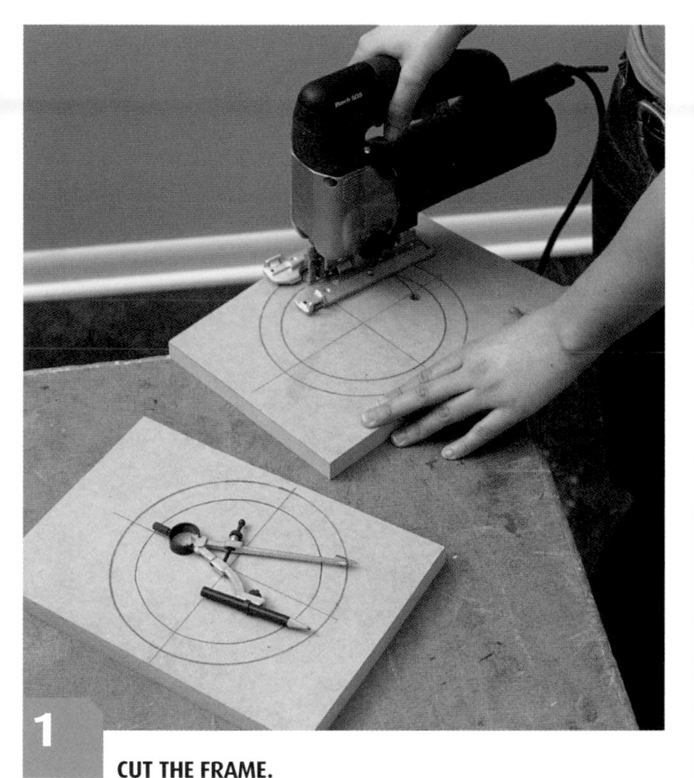

1

CUT THE FRAME.

With the compass, draw a 6 3/4-inch-diameter circle on two pieces of 3/4-inch MDF. Draw a 5 3/4-inch-diameter circle inside of the larger circle using the same midpoint. On one of the pieces of MDF, drill a hole inside the smaller circle to accommodate the saber saw blade. Insert the saw blade and cut out the smaller circle. Cut around the perimeter of the larger circle so you end up with a ring 6 3/4 inches in diameter. Cut around the perimeter of the 6 3/4-inch circle on the second piece of MDF. Sand the cut edges if needed to smooth and even them out.

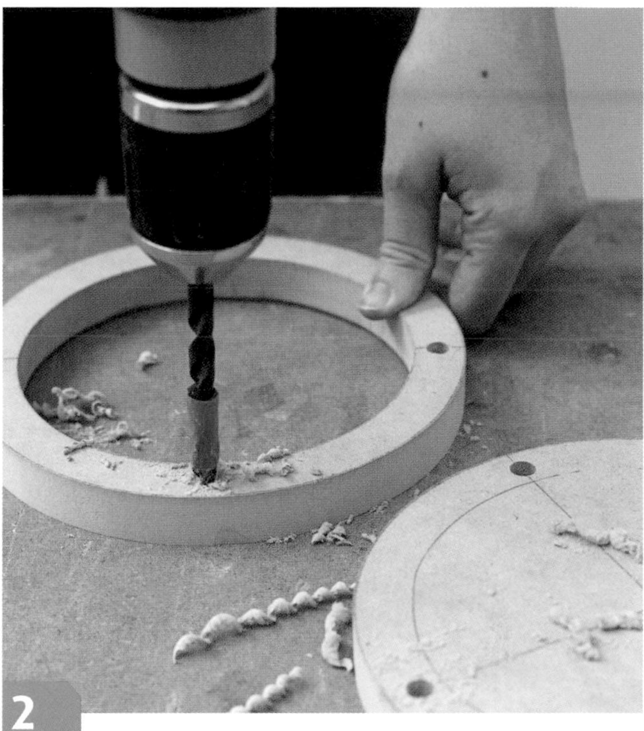

2

DRILL HOLES IN THE FIBERBOARD.

Wrap blue painter's tape around the 5/16-inch drill bit to gauge a drilled depth of 1/2 inch. Check depth by drilling into a piece of scrap wood. Drill 1/2-inch-deep holes in the MDF ring at four equidistant points. Drill corresponding 1/2-inch-deep holes in the solid MDF circle.

Wiring a lamp is an easy project. If you want to rewire a lamp, purchase a lamp rewire kit for the specific type of lamp. To make your own table lamp, purchase an individual surface-mount lamp holder and lamp cord set.

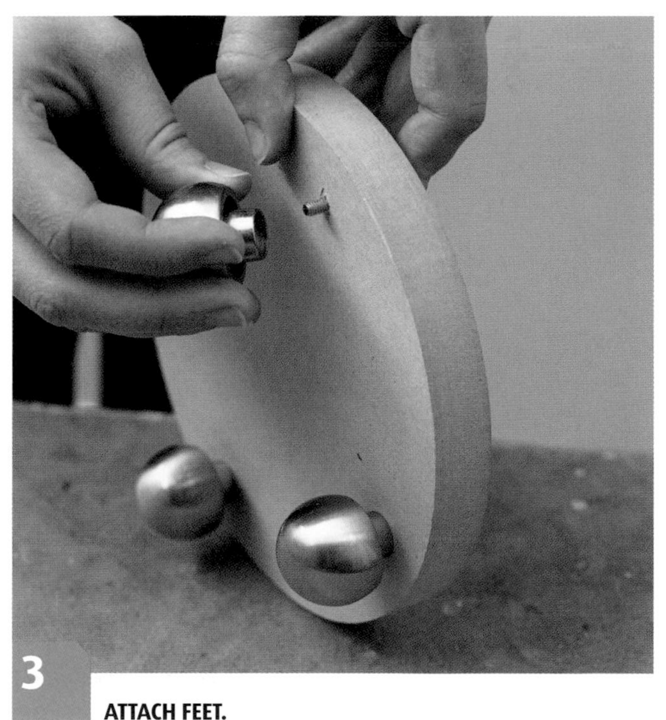

3

ATTACH FEET.

With the 1/8-inch bit drill four holes equally spaced 1 inch in from the edge of the circle and attach drawer pulls as feet.

Table lamp *(continued)*

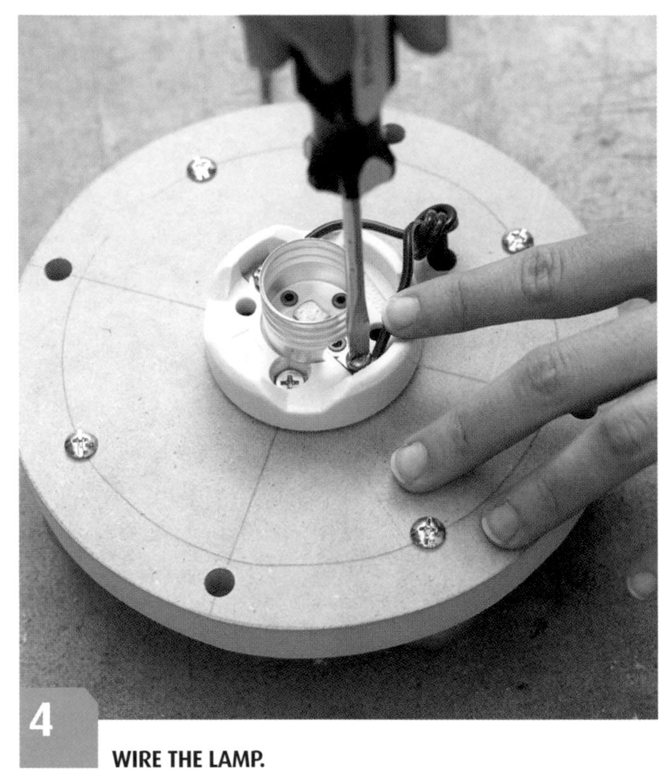

4 **WIRE THE LAMP.**
Mount the porcelain lamp holder in the center of the solid circle. Drill a 5/16-inch hole just to the outside of the lamp holder to feed the lamp wire through. Knot the lamp wire to prevent it from being pulled back through the hole. Attach the wire ends to the lamp holder contact screws.

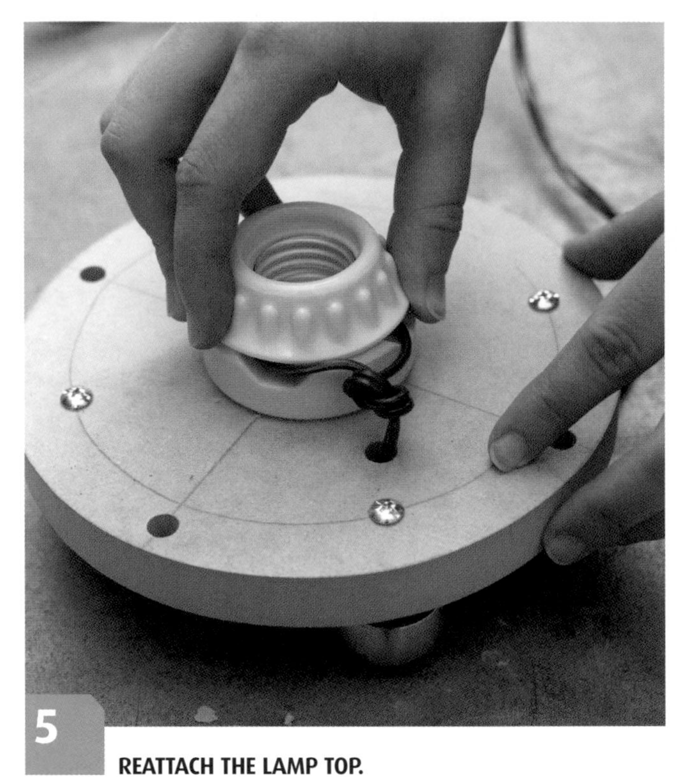

5 **REATTACH THE LAMP TOP.**
Reattach the porcelain top to the base.

6 **RESIZE THE WOOD DOWELS.**
Cut the two 5/16×48-inch wood dowels to four dowels at 22 1/4 inches each.

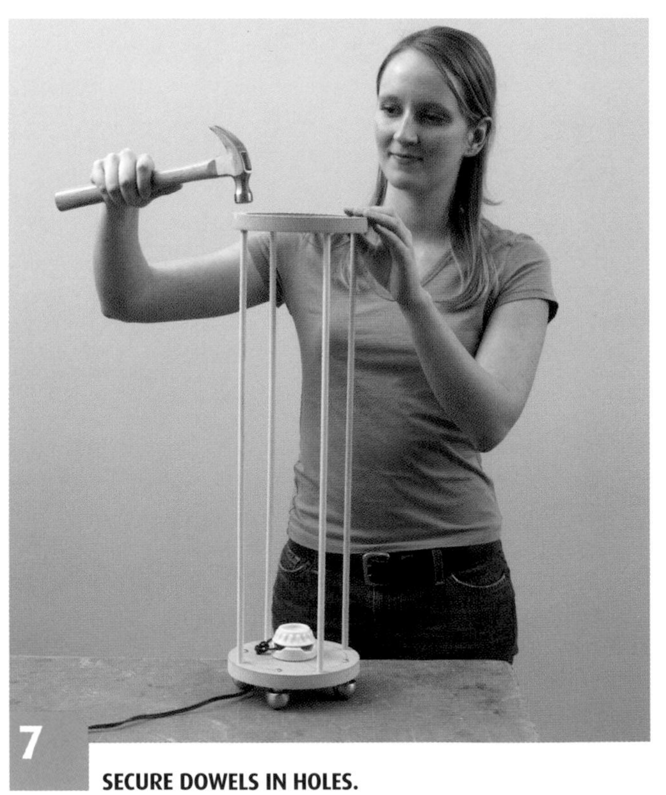

7 **SECURE DOWELS IN HOLES.**
Insert a wood dowel into each of the four 1/2-inch-deep holes. Set the ring on top of the dowels and match them to the holes in it. Tap with a hammer to fit evenly. Screw in a lightbulb.

8

GLUE LAMPSHADE.
Unroll the shade and remove the drawstring and any hardware that will be in the way. Hold the shade up and stretch it around the lamp frame to determine where to cut (there shouldn't be any overlap). Dab hot glue on the binding strings on matchsticks on each side of where you plan to cut. Flip the shade over and do the same on the back.

9

CUT THE SHADE TO LENGTH.
Cut the string with a utility knife. Make sure you have glued along the edge where you are cutting so that the shade will not unravel.

10

GLUE SHADE TO FRAME.
Fit the shade around the lamp frame and use spots of hot glue to hold it in place.

11

SECURE THE SHADE.
Attach a hose clamp at the bottom edge and tighten with a screwdriver. Next attach the second hose clamp at the top of the lamp.

GOOD IDEA

DRESS IT UP
You easily can embellish an old lamp that's in working condition. If you like the base but the shade is looking worn, simply purchase a new shade. Select one with a size proportional to the base. Or decorate the existing base and shade. Paint is always a simple enhancement. Use a paint stamp to add color to the shade. If you like an industrial look, apply grommets or other light hardware to the shade in a random fashion. If the base needs a new look, paint pens enable you to draw freehand designs and are suitable for use on glass, metal, ceramics, and other surfaces.

Chapter 6 highlights

Furnishings

Furnishings are a key element in interior design. You probably select furnishings before you choose paint colors and flooring. The types of furnishings you like probably also influence elements in the room like the trimwork and doors. How you arrange the furnishings should have an impact on lighting design.

Furnishings are very much about style but should also be about comfort. Upholstered goods should create a welcoming environment and should offer comfortable seating. Likewise, furnishings need to be about more than function. Case goods not only provide storage but they also are an important element for adding character to any room. Constructing custom furnishings such as a display shelf, ottoman, or side table affords you the pride of having built it yourself and allows you to design a piece that fits your needs and your style.

Beloved but old furniture gains new life when refinished, updated, or painted. Paint treatments, inset panels, and veneer finishes are options for revitalizing a tired piece.

Custom bookcase

PROJECT DETAILS

SKILLS: Measuring, cutting, mitering, basic carpentry

TIME TO COMPLETE

EXPERIENCED: 4 hrs.
HANDY: 5 hrs.
NOVICE: 6 hrs.

STUFF YOU'LL NEED

TOOLS: Clamps, drill, countersink or combination bit, screwdriver bit, hammer, nail set, pry bar, miter box and backsaw, stud finder, pencil, level, utility knife, hot-glue gun, caulk gun, sandpaper, paintbrushes
MATERIALS: Two basic pine bookcases (no face frame or trim, with a recessed toe-kick 2 to 3 inches high) approximately 24 or 30 inches wide by 72 or 84 inches high, tapered wood shims, 1¼-inch drywall screws, 1×3- or 1×4-inch wood for plinth base (depending on height of base molding and height of bottom shelf), #6 finishing nails, one piece of 1×6×8-inch wood for bottom fascia (rip to width if necessary), one piece of 3¼×8-inch wood for crown molding, approximately 7 feet of base molding (to match existing baseboard), 2- and 2½-inch drywall screws, four pieces of 1×3×8-inch wood for face frame, 1×2-inch support blocks, approximately 42 feet of ¼×¾-inch triple-bead screen molding (plus additional screen molding for shelf edges), #4 finishing nails

▲ **Once-standard freestanding bookcases take on a traditional, custom look with molding and paint.**

You'll probably find two extremes when shopping for bookcases—beautifully finished expensive units and unfinished, bare-bones versions that cost less and don't look as good. Even the best bookcases tend to have an institutional look—cases lined up against a wall, one next to the other. Functional, yes; attractive, not necessarily.

With basic carpentry skills, however, you can turn inexpensive, basic bookcases into an attractive integrated unit. The key is to use stock moldings to blend the separate cases into well-composed pieces of furniture.

The project shown connects two bookcases side by side, raising them slightly on a base (or plinth) and adding a face frame, base molding, columnlike trim called pilasters, and crown molding. The moldings are off-the-shelf profiles, commonly available at The Home Depot.

Because inexpensive bookcases often are made of several species of wood, getting a smooth, consistent stain is difficult. Finish the bookcase with paint; you'll save money because painting allows you to use less expensive paint-grade moldings.

1

SCREW TWO (OR MORE) BOOKCASES TOGETHER.
Nestle the bookcases side by side and hold them together with clamps. Make sure the front and top edges align. It may help to slide shims under the cabinets if the floor is uneven. Predrill holes for screws through the side of one case and partway into the other; countersink the holes with a countersink bit. Space the holes evenly along the front and back of the side, drilling a hole every foot or so. Drive 1¼-inch drywall screws into the holes to hold the cabinets together.

2

BUILD A PLINTH BASE.
Most bookcases have a nondescript base—a recessed toe-kick at the front and nothing along the sides. A plinth base raises the assembled bookcases to create a base at least as high as the baseboard in the room. Choose 1×3-inch or 1×4-inch material, depending on the height of the baseboard. If the baseboard in the room is low (3½ inches or less), build a plinth base in any event. (The bookcase will look better sitting on it.) Nail the plinth base together with #6 finishing nails.

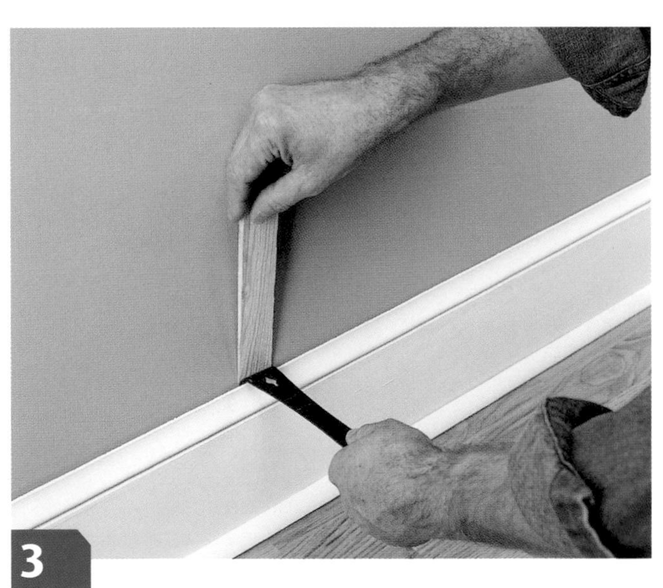

3

REMOVE THE EXISTING BASEBOARD.
Bookcases should be attached to the wall to prevent them from tipping over. To attach the bookcase remove the baseboard. Hold a wood shim between a pry bar and the wall to avoid damaging the wall and push the pry bar down behind the baseboard. Pry the baseboard away from the wall. The baseboard may be built from several pieces of molding. Cut off a few inches from each, take them to The Home Depot, and buy molding to match—get enough to go around the bottom of the bookcases.

TOOL SAVVY

USE A COMBINATION BIT
A countersink is a cone-shape hole in a work surface that houses the head of a screw. You can drill the hole with a countersink bit although it's faster and easier to use a combination bit that simultaneously drills the countersink and a hole for the screw.

Cabinetmaker's secret

When two boards—such as the face frames of the bookcases—meet, it's rarely a perfect match. One might be too thick, too thin, or out of square enough to cause a gap. Cabinetmakers camouflage the gaps by sanding a small bevel on the front edges of all vertical pieces and on the visible face at the end of each horizontal. (On this project sand a bevel no more than 1/16 inch wide.) This creates a shallow V-groove wherever two pieces meet. It looks like a decorative detail, but in fact it's a cabinetmaker's secret.

Custom bookcase *(continued)*

4 LEVEL THE PLINTH BASE AND SCREW IT TO THE WALL.
Locate the studs in the wall with a stud finder and mark them. Use a level to extend these marks up the wall just beyond the finished height of the bookcases. Then level the plinth base, sliding tapered shims underneath it as necessary.

Screw through the back of the plinth base into the wall studs with 2½-inch drywall screws. Trim the shims with a utility knife.

5 SCREW THE BOOKCASES TO THE WALL.
Make sure the bookcases sit evenly on the plinth base. If you see a slight overhang (or gap), center the bookcase so the mismatch is equal on all sides. Attach the bookcase backs into the wall studs with 2-inch drywall screws. If gaps exist between the back edge of the bookcase and the wall, slide a shim into the gap and trim the shim. Caulk the gaps later.

6 CUT AND ATTACH FACE-FRAME PIECES.
Start with the vertical pieces. Cut them to the full height of the unit. When you install them the side verticals are even with the outside edge of the bookcase. The center vertical overhangs the walls of the individual bookcases evenly. Nail the vertical pieces in place with #6 finishing nails and countersink the nailheads. Next cut the horizontal face-frame pieces to fit between the verticals. The bottom horizontal face-frame pieces, or fascia, should be flush with the top of the bottom shelf. Nail the pieces in place.

7 CUT THE MOLDING SUPPORT BLOCKS.
Cut support blocks; these are short 1×2-inch blocks with the end cut to 50 degrees (the angle of the crown molding). Set the miter box to 50 degrees and cut enough blocks to place one roughly every foot along the bookcase.

8 **ATTACH THE CROWN AND BASE MOLDING.**

Attach the blocks you cut in step 7 with hot glue. Then cut the crown molding. Nail the crown molding to the top edge of the cabinet but not to the blocks—they're for positioning and added support. The base molding is cut and fit much like the crown molding—mitered at the corners and butted to the wall along the sides. It should match the baseboard. The profiles are standard, and The Home Depot should be able to match them.

After cutting the molding and nailing it in place, reinstall the old baseboard along the wall and fit it to the new base molding on the cabinet with a scribed joint.

9 **CUT AND NAIL ON SCREEN MOLDINGS. FINISH AS DESIRED.**

Apply two strips of beaded screen molding centered on the three vertical face frames. These pieces butt into the edge of the crown molding at the top and into the base molding at the bottom. Cut the strips to length and nail them onto the vertical face frames with #4 finishing nails. Also cut strips to fit across the front of the shelves and nail them in place.

Seal any gaps between the bookcase and wall or between any of the pieces of molding with paintable caulk. Sand, prime, and apply two top coats of paint.

Perfect fit for crown molding

Once the crown molding is cut to fit, tack it in place with hot-melt glue. Dab a small amount of hot-melt on the support blocks and then press the molding in place. Hold it for 30 seconds while the glue grabs. If it fits nail the bottom edges of the molding to the cabinet. If it needs adjustment pry off the molding, remove the dried hot-melt glue, and cut it again.

Painter's secret

For a smooth and glossy finish, fill imperfections, prime, sand, and apply two coats of finish color with a soft-bristled brush.

Cabinet door insert

PROJECT DETAILS

SKILLS: Cutting, measuring

TIME TO COMPLETE

EXPERIENCED: 1 hr.
HANDY: 2 hrs.
NOVICE: 3 hrs.

STUFF YOU'LL NEED

TOOLS: Jigsaw or circular saw, black marker, flathead screwdriver, tape measure, heavy gloves, wire cutters or tin snips, staple gun, rubber gloves
MATERIALS: Side table or nightstand, roll of poultry netting, staples, spackle

▲ **Inserting mesh in a cabinet door allows the items within to be on display.**

Adding a panel to the center cutout of a cabinet door is a great way to refresh dated cabinetry. Depending on the material, panels also allow items inside to be on display. Choose a material for the insert that works with the design of the room. You have lots of options. For this project poultry netting teamed with a color-wash paint finish gives a freestanding piece French country style. The center panel of the cabinet door was cut out before installation of the wire netting. After the poultry netting was cut to size, it was stapled and spackled in place.

DESIGNER TIP

SELECTING AN INSERT
Many new cabinets can be purchased with glass panel inserts. Manufacturers typically offer several options from clear to nearly opaque and decorative finishes such as rice paper.

WORK SMARTER

DOOR ORDERS
If you are purchasing new cabinetry and want inserts, order the doors without a center panel to avoid cutting out the center or select from panel options available from the manufacturer. They will arrive already installed.

1 CUT OUT CENTER PANEL.

Use a jigsaw or circular saw to cut the center panel from the door. Cut approximately $\frac{1}{2}$ inch inside the face frame. If the door has a groove in which the center panel rests, use a screwdriver to pry loose any pieces of the center panel that remain in the groove.

2 MEASURE AND CUT THE NETTING.

Measure the new opening and add $\frac{1}{4}$ inch to all four sides to allow material to fit into the groove. Transfer these measurements to the poultry netting. Wearing heavy gloves use wire cutters or tin snips to cut the poultry netting.

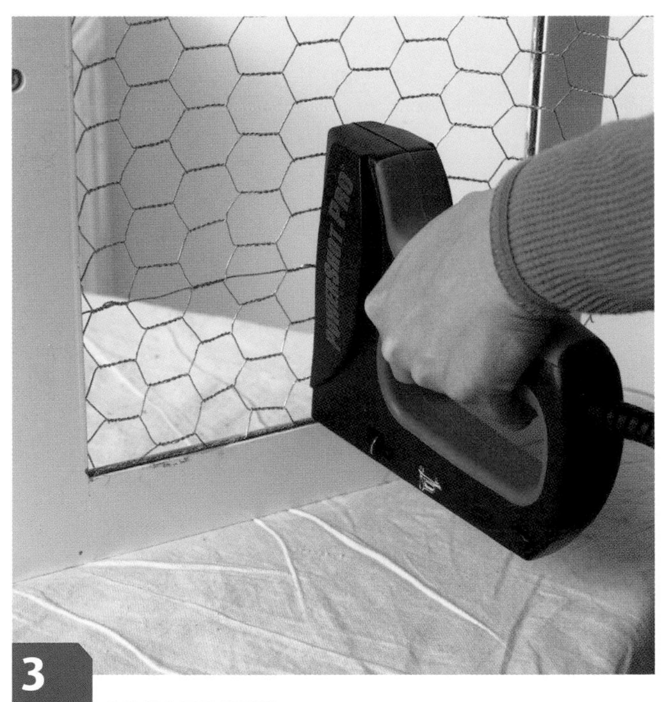

3 STAPLE THE MESH.

Position the poultry netting inside the new opening and work the ends into the groove. You may need to bend the netting slightly to slide it into the groove. Working your way around the perimeter of the opening, staple the poultry netting in place. Staple at an angle toward the back of the door.

4 APPLY SPACKLE.

After stapling the netting in place, apply spackle to the groove around the perimeter of the opening to help secure the netting. Wear rubber gloves and apply the spackle with your finger to work it into the gap. Allow the compound to dry. Reattach the door to the cabinet.

Wood veneer

PROJECT DETAILS

SKILLS: Measuring, cutting, ironing, staining

TIME TO COMPLETE

EXPERIENCED: 1 hr.
HANDY: 2 hrs.
NOVICE: 3 hrs.

STUFF YOU'LL NEED

TOOLS: Screwdriver, tape measure, pencil, scissors, iron, rubber gloves, rags
MATERIALS: Veneer in ⅞-inch red oak, veneer in 2-inch white birch, varnish in honey maple

▲ **Dress up an old cabinet with easy-to-apply veneer strips and stain.**

Old cabinets can benefit from a facelift. Although paint is a standard pick-me-up, wood veneer is a good alternative if you want to maintain a stained finish. This project features thin strips of veneer typically used to finish the thin edges of plywood. It's easier to work with than larger pieces of veneer. This type of veneer is also made to iron on, which means it is a simple technique for improving the look of the cabinet door. When two types of veneer strips are alternated—white birch and red oak for this project—it results in an interesting texture with seams that are part of the design rather than something you have to attempt to disguise.

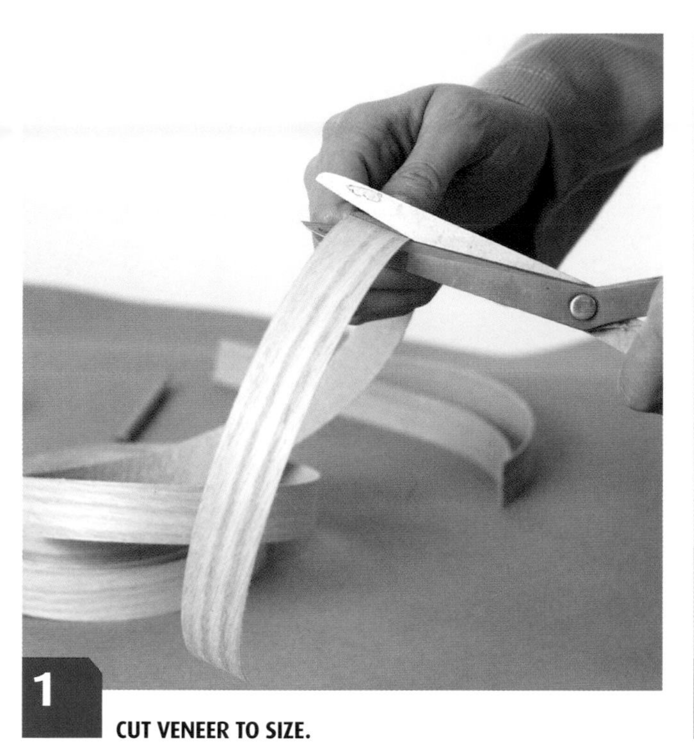

1

CUT VENEER TO SIZE.

Remove the doors from the cabinet. Remove any knobs. Clean and dry the surface. Measure the length and width of the inside door panel. Calculate how many strips will cover the panel. Transfer the measurement of the panel length to the wood veneer and mark with a pencil. Mark and cut enough strips to cover the door.

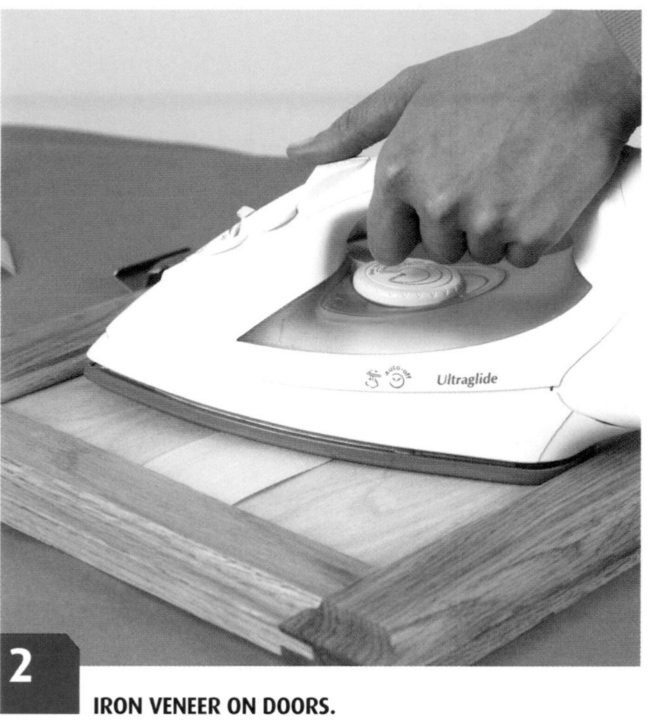

2

IRON VENEER ON DOORS.

This type of veneer strip is designed to adhere with the heat from an iron. Beginning with the center strip, position the strips on the face of the door. You may need to cut the outer strips to get a precise fit that is centered on the door. Heat an iron to a cotton setting but do NOT use water or steam with the iron. Start at the center and heat the veneer with the iron to make it adhere. Allow the strips to cool and set.

3

APPLY STAIN.

After the veneer is cool, wear gloves to apply varnish with a rag. Wipe off any excess after the varnish has absorbed into the veneer for three minutes. Check manufacturer's directions for applying various types of varnish. Allow to dry and attach the doors and knobs.

GOOD IDEA

UNEVEN EDGES

If the door panel is slightly uneven, cut each strip slightly longer than you need it. Tack down the center of the strips and then use a crafts or utility knife to trim the edges of the veneer to match the center panel. Finish securing the strips.

CLOSER LOOK

WORKING WITH VENEER

Large rolls of veneer are available if you want a seamless look for cabinets. Bigger pieces are more difficult to work with, however. Most large pieces of veneer need to be adhered with contact cement. The contact cement is brushed on the door and the back of the veneer with a paintbrush. Once the cement dries the veneer is pressed into place. It's nearly impossible to lift and reposition the veneer, so you need to align it carefully. Use a rubber roller to remove any air bubbles.

Toe-kick feet

 PROJECT DETAILS

SKILLS: Measuring, cutting

 TIME TO COMPLETE

EXPERIENCED: 2 hrs.
HANDY: 3 hrs.
NOVICE: 4 hrs.

 STUFF YOU'LL NEED

TOOLS: Tape measure, pencil, straightedge, jigsaw, sandpaper and sanding block, drill, paintbrush
MATERIALS: Base cabinet, wood feet, screws, latex paint

▲ **Adding feet help tranforms this base cabinet into a freestanding island. Toe-kick feet also can be added to standard base cabinets for an unfitted, furniture look.**

Cabinet feet are a popular feature in traditional and retro-style kitchens. When applied to base cabinets, they give standard cabinets a freestanding appearance. For this project feet were applied to a standard base cabinet finished to function as a freestanding kitchen island. An alternative to this project is to tuck similar feet into the toe-kicks of several base cabinets along the walls of the kitchen to create the look of freestanding furniture. In addition to cabinet feet, corbels, turned legs, and other decorative wood details lend character to kitchen cabinetry and can help personalize stock cabinets.

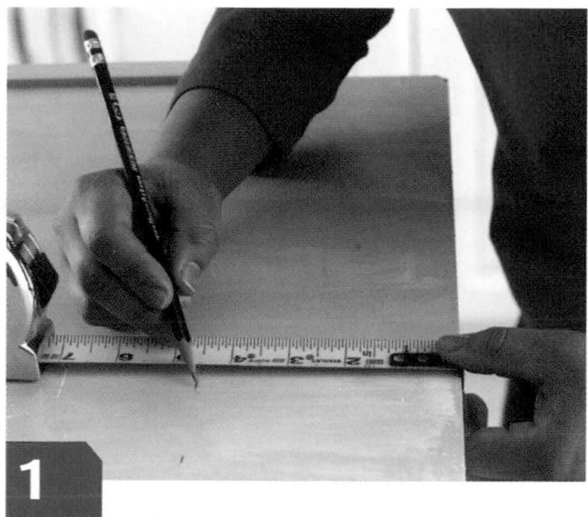

1

MEASURE THE TOE-KICK.

Using a tape measure, measure and mark the toe-kick on the front side of the cabinet. This should be the same distance as from the floor up to the bottom of the cabinet. Use a straightedge to connect the marks for a cutting line.

2

CUT OFF THE TOE-KICK.

You will be removing the toe-kick to add the feet to create a freestanding island. Set the cabinet on its side and jigsaw around the cabinet following the pencil line. You now should have a level cabinet bottom.

3

SAND LIGHTLY.

Lightly sand the rough edges smooth where you cut. Depending on the cabinet you may need to prime and paint the sides and back of the cabinet to create surfaces suitable for a freestanding island. If so allow to dry.

4

DRILL HOLES FOR FEET.

Mark the same distance from each of the four corners. Check that the feet won't protrude past the sides. Drill pilot holes into the four corners of the cabinet base.

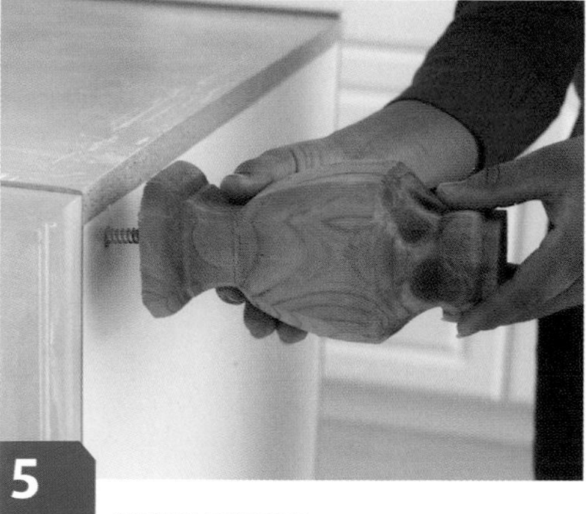

5

ATTACH THE FEET.

With the cabinet still on its side, tightly screw the feet into place. Once you have turned the cabinet upright in step 6, you may need to make slight adjustments to the height of the feet so that the cabinet is level.

6

PAINT THE FEET.

Before turning the cabinet upright, apply latex paint in the desired color and finish. Allow the paint to dry. Once the finish is dry, turn the cabinet upright.

DESIGNER TIP

GATHER IDEAS

Before selecting toe-kick feet peruse kitchen magazines and books for ideas. See which shapes and profiles look best in kitchens with decor similar to yours. Then purchase a similar style or design your own (see below).

DESIGNER TIP

MAKE YOUR OWN

You can draw a simple pattern for toe-kick feet to add to standard base cabinets. Use graph paper to plot a straightforward shape that you can transfer to blocks of wood. Measure the toe-kick space to make sure the foot will fit. Adjust the size if necessary and transfer the drawing to the wood. Use a jigsaw to cut out the pattern. Secure the feet with finishing nails or screws.

Custom molding shelf

PROJECT DETAILS

SKILLS: Measuring, cutting, mitering, gluing, nailing

TIME TO COMPLETE

EXPERIENCED: 3 hrs.
HANDY: 4 hrs.
NOVICE: 5 hrs.

STUFF YOU'LL NEED

TOOLS: Pencil, tape measure, clamps, miter box and backsaw, drill with 1⁄16-inch bit, scrap wood, vise, hammer, nail set, fine-grit sandpaper, tack cloth, staining pads
MATERIALS: 4-foot 1×6-inch pine board, 5⁄8-inch embossed molding , 3⁄4×3-inch beaded casing, wood glue, nails, wood filler, 5⁄8-inch square dowel, two keyhole shelf hangers, prestain wood conditioner, pine wood stain, clear semigloss polyurethane

▲ **Embossed molding and beaded casing provide a traditional look for this custom display shelf.**

Decorative shelves are a popular element for displaying collectibles. Although you can purchase premade shelves, you are likely to pay a hefty price and won't necessarily get a style or finish that works with your room's design. Making a shelf by combining decorative moldings allows you the creativity to design one that is best suited to your style. Select from numerous molding profiles to combine pieces to achieve the style and size you want. Finish the shelf with stain or paint. Plan the depth of the shelf to accommodate objects you plan to display. You can create a composition on a single shelf as illustrated above or group several shelves—odd numbers work best—to make them part of the overall composition.

1

CUT THE BOARD.
To make a pair of 2-foot-long shelves, cut a 4-foot board into two equal lengths using a miter box to guide cutting.

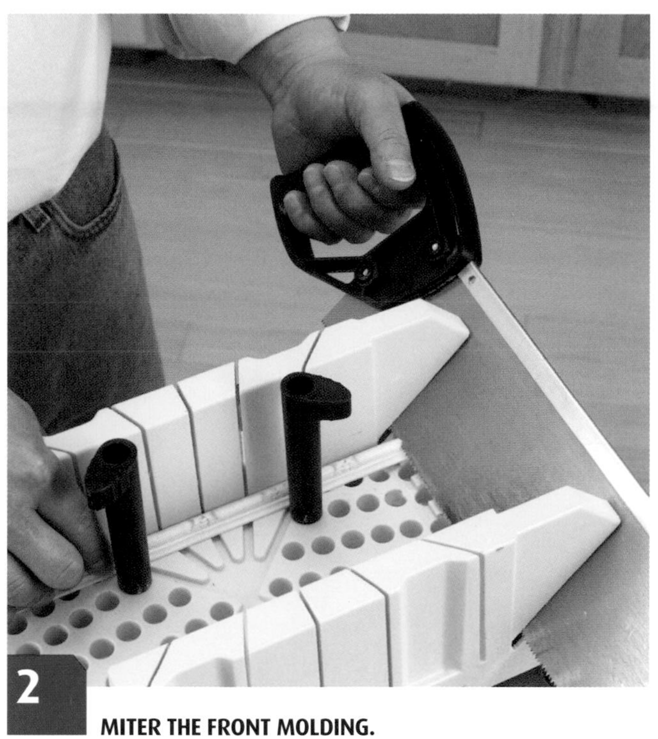

2

MITER THE FRONT MOLDING.
For each shelf, on the front embossed molding piece, measure and mark 24 inches for the inside miter, allowing at least 1 inch at each end to accommodate miters. For the side molding pieces, measure and mark 6 inches for the front corner miter, allowing 1 inch at the front for miter cut. Use a straight cut at the end that is flush with the wall. Secure the molding in the miter box and cut at a 45-degree angle where marked.

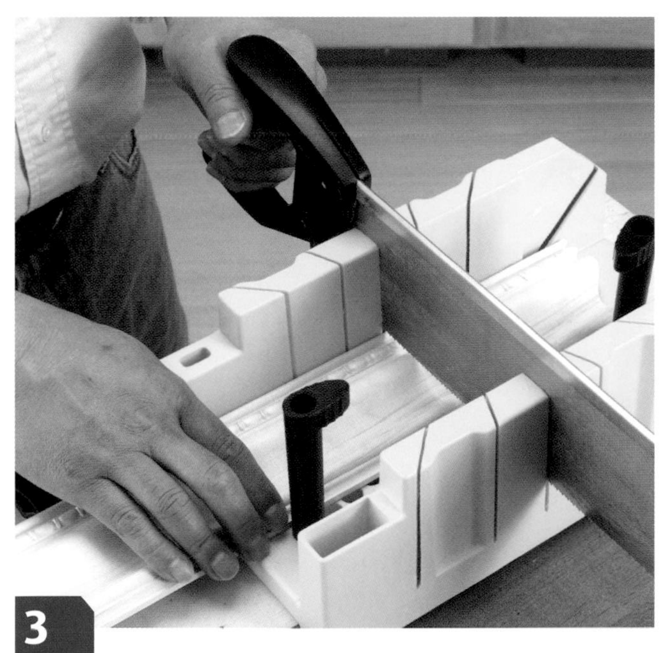

3

CUT THE BEADED CASING.
To cut the front beaded casing piece for the shelf bottom, measure and mark 21 inches for the inside miter, allowing 1 inch at each end for mitering. For the side casing pieces, measure and mark 4½ inches for the front corner miter, allowing 1 inch on front and at each end for miters (the end that is flush with the wall remains a straight cut). For each molding piece secure in miter box and cut each end at a 45-degree angle where marked. Cut only one end of each side molding piece at a 45-degree angle.

DESIGN OPTIONS
From a Mission look to contemporary, you can change the style of the shelves by using different moldings and beaded casing materials.

SANDED SMOOTH
Sand wood filler lightly when dry for a smooth surface.

Custom molding shelf *(continued)*

4 **DRILL PILOT HOLES.**
Using a 1⁄16-inch bit, drill guide holes through the side casing pieces where they meet the front casing piece, drilling in the widest part of the casing.

5 **APPLY WOOD GLUE.**
With an end up place the front casing piece between two wood scrap pieces in a vise. Apply a small amount of wood glue to the mitered edge of the short side piece of molding. Align the miter cut on the side and front pieces and press together. Wipe away any excess glue.

6 **NAIL TOGETHER.**
Gently tap nails into the pilot holes to secure the front and side beaded casing pieces together. Use a nail set to countersink the nails slightly. Repeat steps 5 and 6 for the remaining side piece.

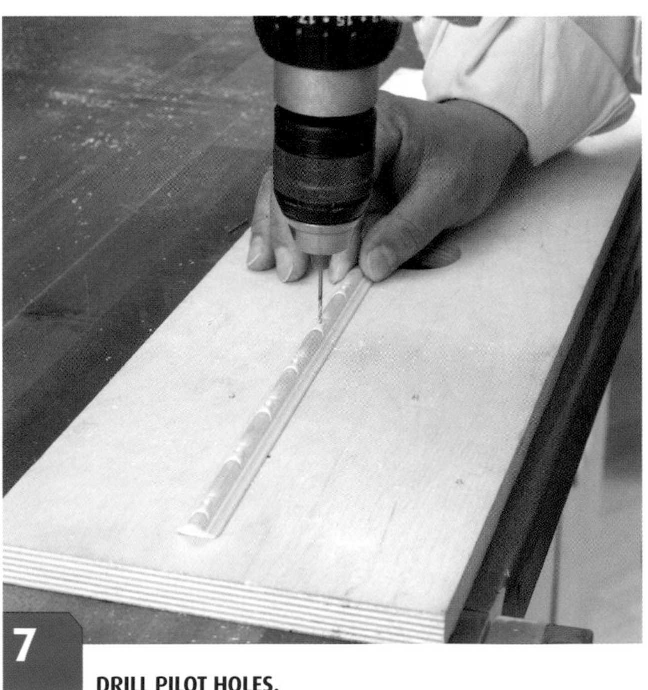

7 **DRILL PILOT HOLES.**
Using a 1⁄16-inch bit drill two or three guide holes through the narrow molding for the front and side trim.

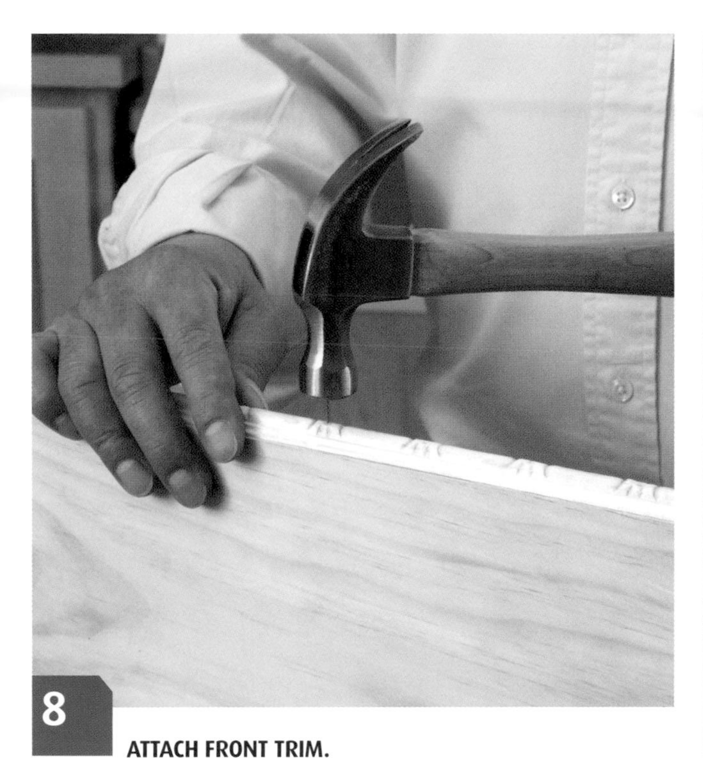

8

ATTACH FRONT TRIM.

Apply a thin bead of wood glue to the narrow molding. Gently nail the trim to the shelf edges. Use a nail set to countersink the nails slightly. Cover the nailheads with wood filler. Allow the glue and wood filler to dry.

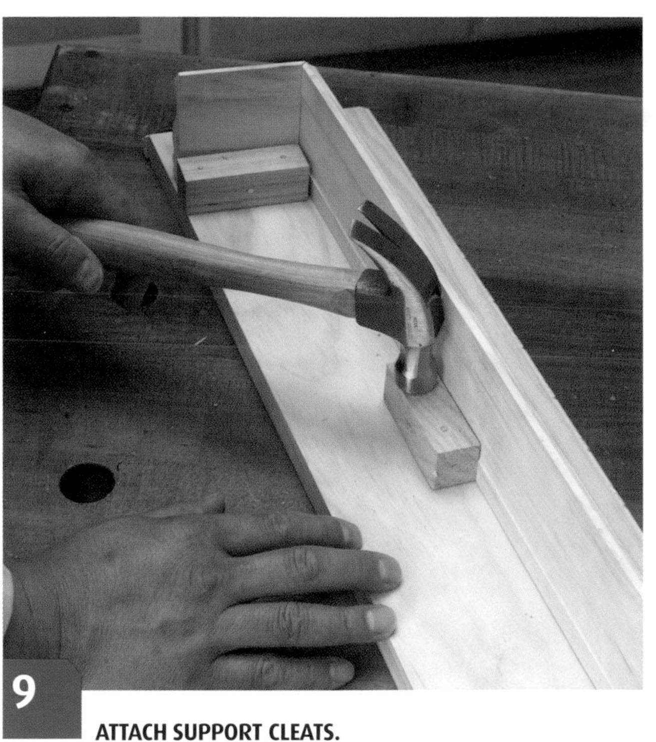

9

ATTACH SUPPORT CLEATS.

Cut three 2-inch lengths of square dowel. For each piece drill a hole in the center. Turn one quarter-turn and drill two holes, one on each side of the center. Use the holes as guides to nail a stabilizer block in the center of the front and one on each side as shown. Nail the pieces in place, using wood glue for additional adherence.

10

MOUNT HANGING HARDWARE.

Screw two shelf hangers onto the back of the shelf, one at each end, positioning the hardware so the hangers cannot be seen at the shelf edges.

11

APPLY FINISH.

Sand the shelf and wipe away the dust using a tack cloth. Apply a coat of wood conditioner and allow to dry. Sand lightly and wipe away dust. Stain the shelf according to the manufacturer's instructions. Allow to dry. Apply a top coat of polyurethane. Allow to dry.

Open shelving

PROJECT DETAILS

SKILLS: Measuring, cutting, basic carpentry skills

TIME TO COMPLETE

EXPERIENCED: 3 hrs.
HANDY: 4 hrs.
NOVICE: 5 hrs.

STUFF YOU'LL NEED

TOOLS: Safety glasses, tape measure, pencil, circular saw, triangular square (12×12×12), clamps, drill, countersink bit, phillips screwdriver bit for drill, chisel, hammer, 150-grit sandpaper, paintbrush, level
MATERIALS: (For each box) One 1×10×5-foot board—cut into two pieces at ¾×9½×18 inches and two pieces at ¾×9½×10½ inches, 1⅝-inch drywall screws, 2-inch drywall screws, two keyhole hangers, paint or stain, two self-drilling anchors

▲ **Open shelving boxes may be arranged in an artful composition suitable to the room and the amount of wall space.**

DESIGNER TIP

FEEL FREE TO EXPERIMENT
The 18-inch boxes, such as the ones shown, are large enough so that there will be at least one stud behind them for hanging. Smaller boxes carrying smaller loads may not need studs behind them. Make the box sizes to suit your needs.

Generic shelving systems work fine for closets or utility areas. But when you want to display something important or just make everyday items—such as bath towels—look a little more special, you're in the market for custom shelves. The display boxes shown are constructed of solid wood, and you need not be a skilled woodworker to put them together. They're made from lengths of standard 1×10 pine. The only cuts necessary are the cross cuts, and if you're not comfortable doing them, you can usually have the cuts made at The Home Depot.

Because the boxes are simple, you can adjust their size to suit the objects to store or display. Each box shown requires one 5-foot length of 1×10 stock. Choose 1×8 or 1×6 for shallower boxes. Finish them to suit your taste and room decor.

Cabinetmaker's secret

To hang the boxes against each other, screw them together first with 1¼-inch drywall screws. It makes hanging—and aligning—much easier.

DESIGNER TIP

CREATE DIFFERENT EDGE STYLES
The square, flat edges of this box are a typical modern treatment. To add decoration rout the edge after you assemble the box. For a simple look choose a round-over bit; for a more intricate look, choose an ogee pattern. Balance the router on the edge of the box and work counterclockwise around it. A smaller laminate-style router works well for this type of cutting; heavier models are harder to control.

1 **LAY OUT AND CUT THE BOARDS TO SIZE.** (A 1×10 is really only $\frac{3}{4}\times9\frac{1}{2}$ inches. 1×10 is the size of the board when it's cut from the tree, before it's planed smooth. This means your boards are already the right width and thickness. All you have to do is cut them to length.) Make the cuts with a circular saw while guiding it with a 12×12×12 square like the one shown here. Make the first cut near the end, cutting off any cracks in the wood. Measure, mark, and cut each piece to length.

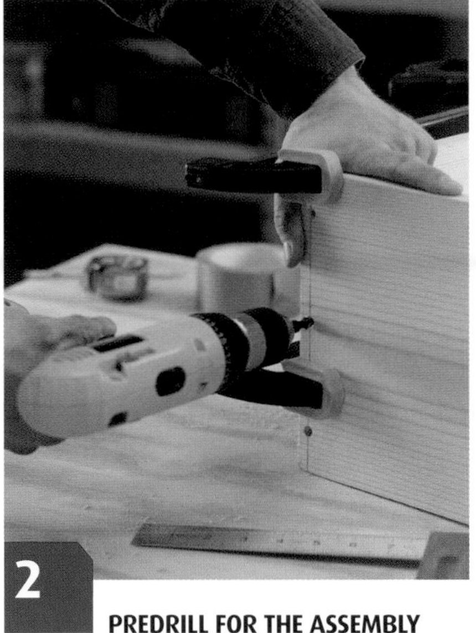

2 **PREDRILL FOR THE ASSEMBLY SCREW.** Put one of the long sides and one of the short sides together to form a corner of the box. Put the long piece so it overlaps the short one and clamp them together. Drill three $\frac{1}{8}$-inch-diameter screw holes through the face of the long side and into the short one. To prevent splitting the wood, keep the holes at least 1 inch in from the sides of the boards. Countersink the holes, as shown, so the screw heads will rest below the surface of the wood.

3 **SCREW THE BOXES TOGETHER.** Drive the $1\frac{5}{8}$-inch screws with an inexpensive bit that fits your drill. Screw two sets of sides together and clamp them together to form a box. Drill and countersink at the corners that need screws and screw the corners together as in step 2.

6 FURNISHINGS

4 **INSTALL HANGERS.** For a clean look the shelves hang using keyhole hangers. In order for the box to sit tightly against the wall, recess the hangers into the back edge of each vertical member. For heavy loads at least one of the keyhole hangers should be on a stud. If you don't want to position the shelves so one of the verticals aligns with a stud, add an angle bracket on the inside top of the box and position it on a stud.

Trace around the hanger with a pencil. Remove most of the waste by drilling a small hole within the lines, making the hole as deep as the hanger is thick. Remove the rest of the waste with a chisel.

Put the hanger in the recess and make sure the narrow slot of the keyhole points toward the top of the box. Screw or nail the hanger in place, depending on the one you buy. (See inset, *above right.*)

5 **PAINT OR STAIN THE SHELVES.** Sand the wood with 150-grit paper and round over the corners and edges slightly so that they feel smooth, and the finish won't rub off with use. The shelves are easiest to handle at this point if you apply finish to the inside first, then to the outside.

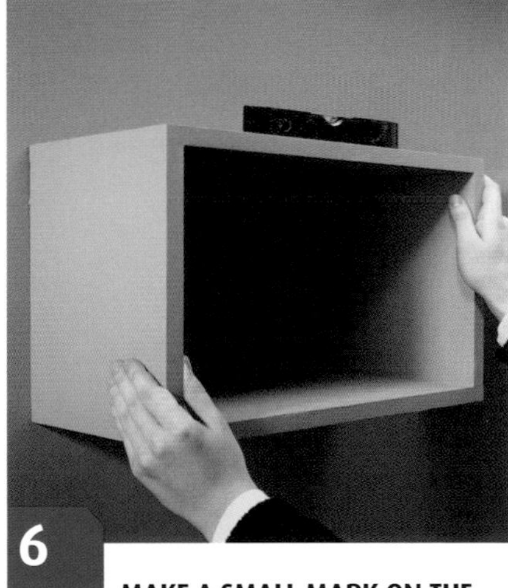

6 **MAKE A SMALL MARK ON THE OUTER SIDES OF THE BOX TO SHOW THE CENTER OF EACH KEYHOLE HANGER.** Position the shelf, make sure it is level, and transfer the marks to the wall. Measure in from the wall marks $\frac{3}{8}$ inch to the center line of the hanger. Drill holes for plastic inserts, tap them into the holes, then drive a 2-inch drywall screw into the slot in the hangers. Position the shelves so the hangers are over the screws in the wall; slide the shelf downward to engage the hangers.

Garden-inspired shelf

PROJECT DETAILS

SKILLS: Filing, spray painting

TIME TO COMPLETE

EXPERIENCED: 1/2 hr.
HANDY: 1 hr.
NOVICE: 2 hrs.

STUFF YOU'LL NEED

TOOLS: Metal file or rasp, drop cloth, brown crafts paper or newspaper, paint respirator and goggles, scrap wood, screwdriver
MATERIALS: 1/2×12×24-inch expanded metal, three 15-inch straight plant brackets, hammered copper spray paint, six 1/2-inch-long brass bolts with nuts

SMART & SAFE

SHARP EDGES
Make sure to smooth the edges using a metal file. You also can dip the rough edges in flexible plastic coating. It goes on as a liquid and dries to a rubberlike coating.

GOOD IDEA

SHELF PLACEMENT
Plant brackets come with predrilled holes for mounting. For flexibility in shelf placement, drill holes anywhere along the straight edge of the plant bracket to mount the expanded-metal shelf.

▲ **Plant hangers support expanded metal in this garden-inspired display shelf.**

This garden-inspired metal shelf is right at home in a sunroom or three-season porch as a whimsical display spot for potted plants and colorful flowers. The support brackets are plant hangers. After you have built the shelf, mount it to a wall with the hardware included with the brackets. Suspend hanging pots from the hangers to fill a room with blooms.

This unit features an expanded-metal shelf because the project was spray painted for a hammered-copper finish. Depending on your furnishings a wooden shelf could be substituted for the expanded metal to coordinate with other wooden items in the room. If a more traditional look suits your decor, see page 162 for a display shelf that is built from decorative molding.

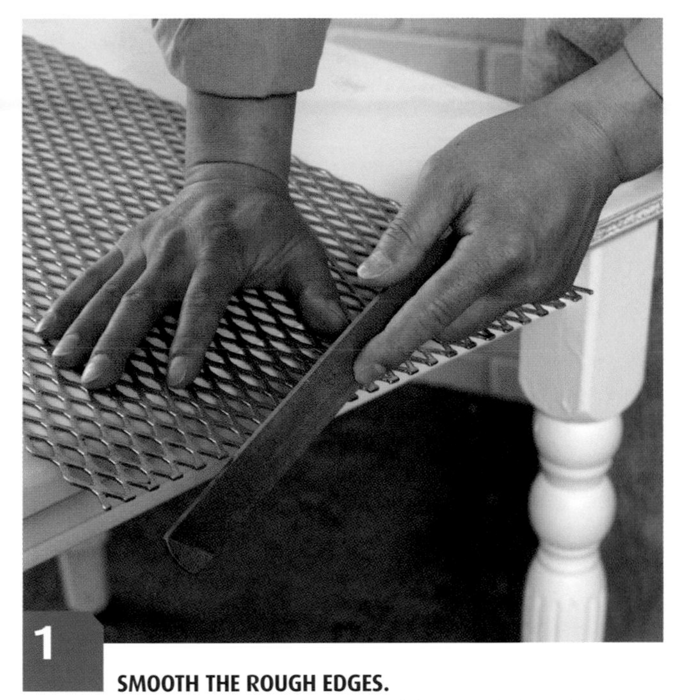

1

SMOOTH THE ROUGH EDGES.
Using a metal file or a rasp, sand the edges of the expanded metal until smooth to the touch. Be cautious as the edges can be quite sharp.

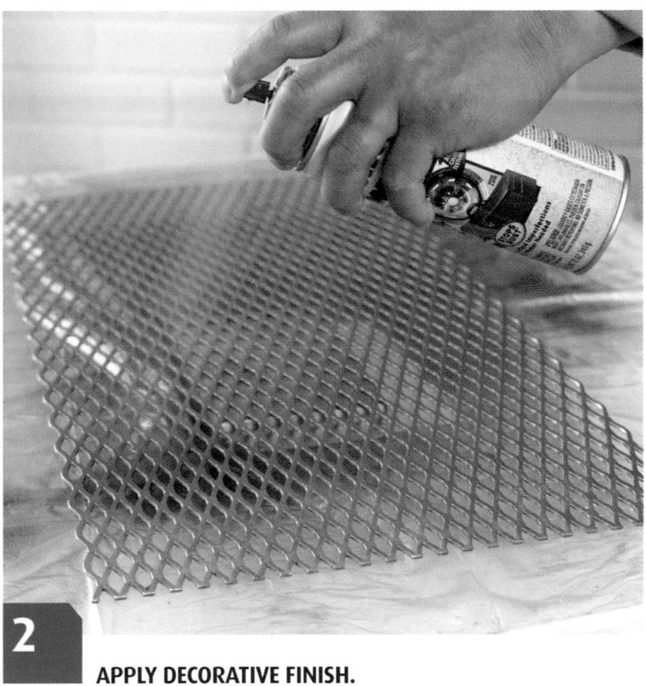

2

APPLY DECORATIVE FINISH.
In a well-ventilated work area, protect the work surface with a drop cloth, brown crafts paper, or newspapers. Wear goggles and a respirator specified for use with spray paints. Place scrap wood under the expanded metal and plant brackets to raise them from the work surface. Spray the surface of the brackets and expanded-metal shelf with hammered copper spray paint for a subtle, textured finish. Allow to dry.

3

PAINT THE OTHER SIDE.
Turn the pieces over, place on scrap wood, and spray the opposite sides of the brackets and expanded metal. Allow to dry. Examine the pieces. Apply a second coat if necessary.

4

ATTACH THE SHELF.
Position a bracket under the center of the expanded metal and screw in place. Place a bracket under each end and screw in place. For a longer shelf or to support heavier items, use additional brackets as needed.

Side table

PROJECT DETAILS

SKILLS: Cutting, sanding, painting, drilling, measuring

TIME TO COMPLETE

EXPERIENCED: 2 hrs.
HANDY: 3 hrs.
NOVICE: 4 hrs.

STUFF YOU'LL NEED

TOOLS: Tape measure, pencil, tablesaw, sander, fine-grit sandpaper, tack cloth, 2-inch high-quality synthetic-bristle paint brush, drill, 13⁄16-inch drill bit, small wire brush, level
MATERIALS: Four pieces of 3⁄4×21×21-inch medium-density fiberboard (MDF), four 24×3⁄4-inch threaded rods, satin water-base polycrylic, thirty-two 3⁄4-inch washers, thirty-two 3⁄4-inch nuts, four 5⁄8-inch rubber chair leg tips

GOOD IDEA

PLAN AHEAD
You can add as many shelves as you need (and that will fit on the threaded rods) to this flexible side table. Before you purchase the fiberboard, decide what you want to store and display on the shelves. Measure the height of the items and calculate how many shelves you need. Purchase enough MDF for all of the shelves.

▲ **Threaded-rod legs contribute an industrial look to this contemporary side table design.**

Add stylish, flexible storage and display space to any room with this contemporary side table. Threaded rods form the legs and support the shelves. Nuts and washers secure the shelves at whatever height you choose. Shelves can be adjusted even after you have completed the project. Just loosen the washers and move the nuts to reposition a shelf. Measure to ensure each shelf is level. Plastic feet slipped on the bottom of the threaded rods prevent flooring from being marred when you move the table.

TIMESAVER

IN-STORE SERVICE
Have the shelves precut to size at The Home Depot. Take precise measurements to the store when you shop for the materials.

1 CUT BOARDS TO SIZE.
Cut four 21×21-inch pieces from ¾-inch medium density fiberboard.

2 SAND BOARDS.
Sand with fine-grit sandpaper as needed to clean and smooth the sides.

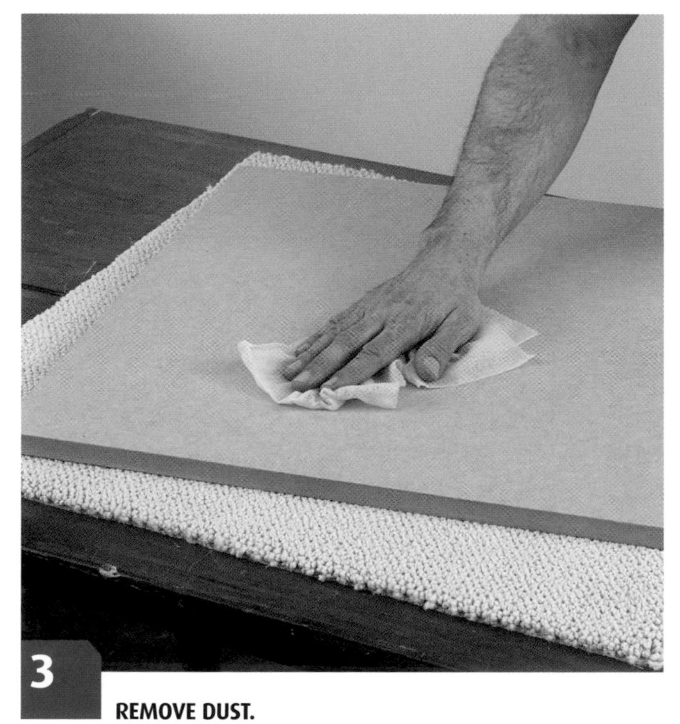

3 REMOVE DUST.
Wipe the surface of each board with a tack cloth to remove debris from sanding and to prepare the surface for the sealer.

4 APPLY SEALER.
Finish with three coats of satin water-base polycrylic, sanding lightly between coats. Allow to dry according to manufacturer's instructions.

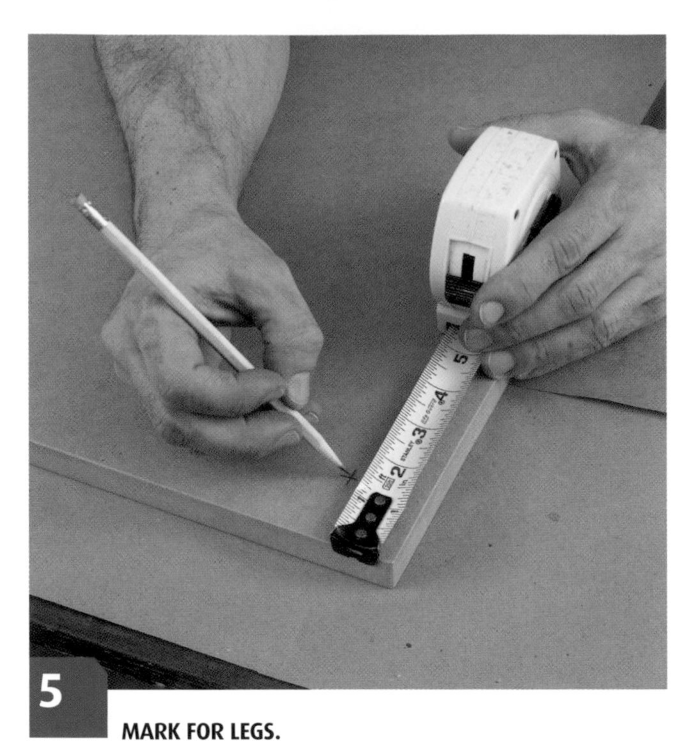

5 **MARK FOR LEGS.**
Mark points 1½ inches from the edges of each corner for the legs of the table.

6 **DRILL HOLES.**
Using a 13/16-inch drill bit, drill holes through the MDF at each of the corner marks. The threaded rods will be inserted in the holes.

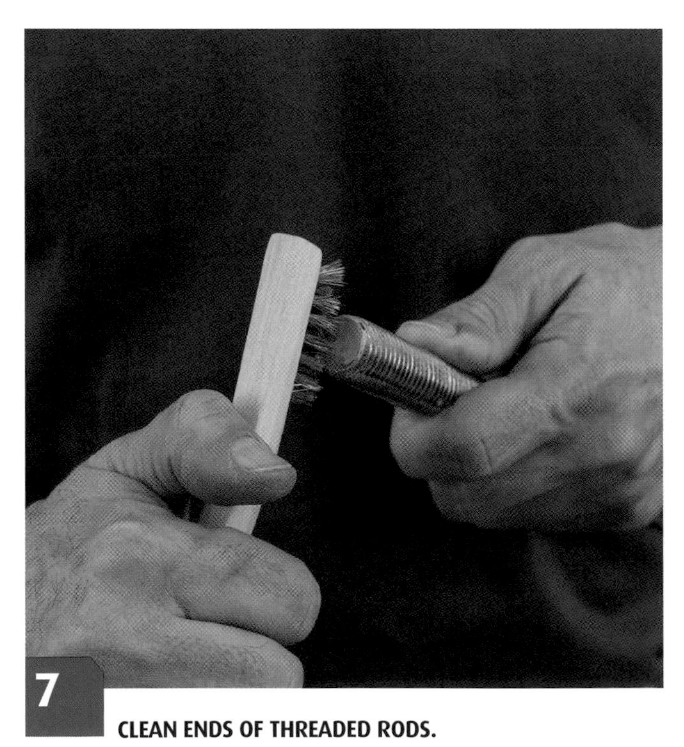

7 **CLEAN ENDS OF THREADED RODS.**
Before assembling the shelves use a wire brush to remove marking paint from the ends of the threaded rods.

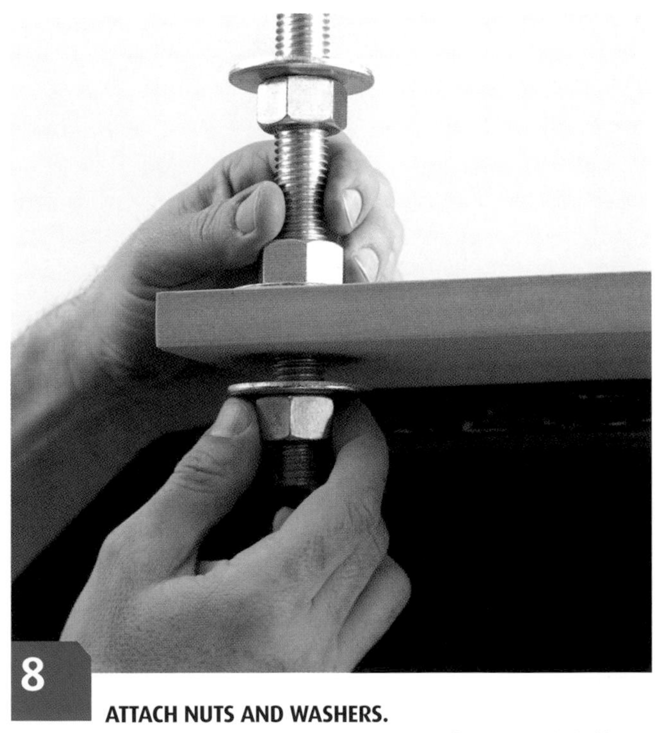

8 **ATTACH NUTS AND WASHERS.**
Place a nut and washer on each of the rods. These will secure each shelf on the table at the desired height. Check that the nuts and washers are at the same height on each leg for level surfaces.

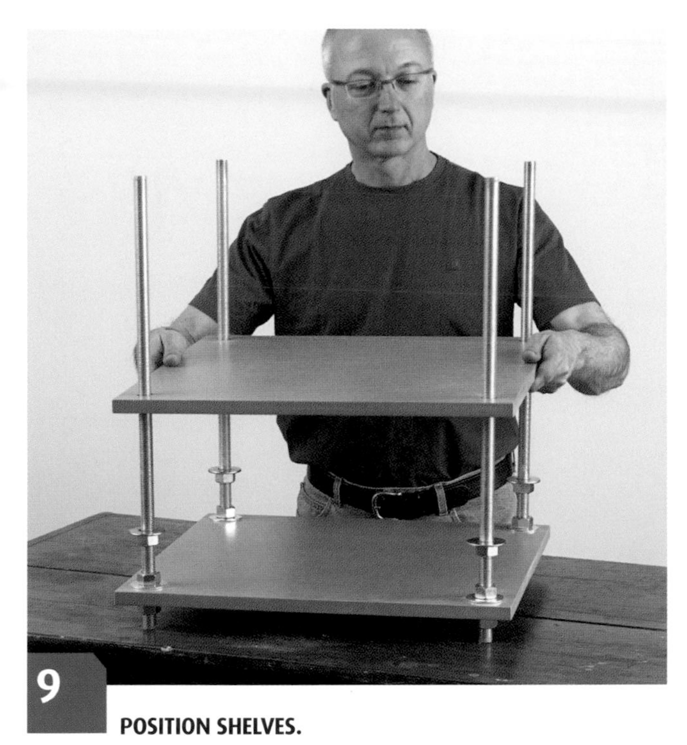

9 POSITION SHELVES.
Position each MDF panel by sliding the holes over the threaded rods. The shelves should fit snugly, so gradually move the shelf down until it rests on the nuts and washers.

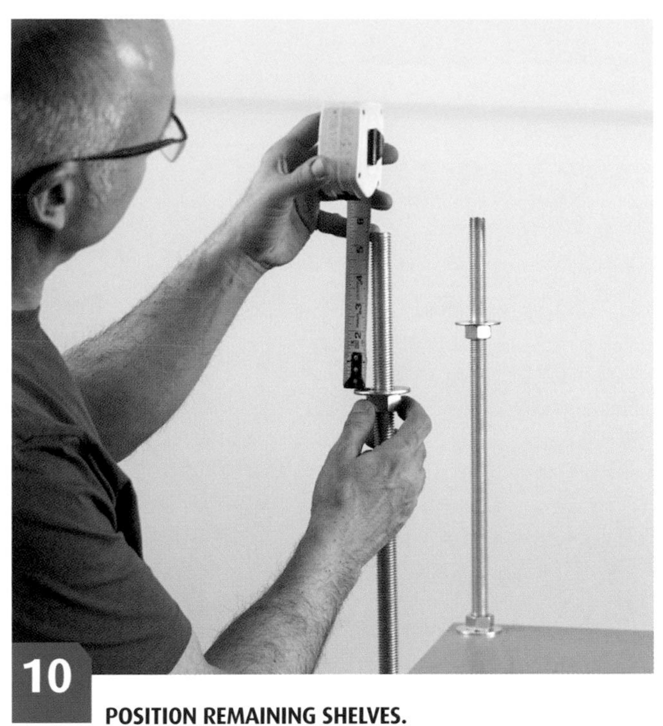

10 POSITION REMAINING SHELVES.
Measure to determine where you want the next shelf. Add another set of washers and nuts. Position the next shelf on the threaded rods. Continue in this fashion until the four shelves are on. Measure each set of rods and washers for level shelves.

11 MAKE ADJUSTMENTS.
Raise or lower the nuts to achieve the desired leveling and placement of the shelves.

12 ADD RUBBER FEET.
Add rubber chair leg tips on the ends of the rods to serve as feet and to protect the floor beneath the side table.

Magazine rack

PROJECT DETAILS

SKILLS: Cutting, sanding, staining, drilling

TIME TO COMPLETE

EXPERIENCED: 1 hr.
HANDY: 2 hrs.
NOVICE: 3 hrs.

STUFF YOU'LL NEED

TOOLS: Tape measure, pencil, tablesaw, sander, fine-grit sandpaper, tack cloth, 2-inch high-quality synthetic bristle paintbrush, scrap wood, drill, $^{11}/_{64}$-inch multipurpose drill bit, blue painter's tape, $^{7}/_{64}$-inch drill bit, screwdriver
MATERIALS: One 1×12×60-inch select white pine board, satin water-base polycrylic, four 10-inch-wide paint bucket roller grids, eight #8×2-inch roundhead slotted wood screws, eight #10 washers, four $1^{1}/_{4}$-inch drywall screws, hole hanger set, four $^{1}/_{2}$-inch wood screws

▲ **Storage becomes stylish and creative with a magazine rack constructed from metal paint bucket roller grids.**

Construct a customized magazine holder with this creative and simple project. Determine how many slots you want based on the number of magazines you typically have piled next to your favorite reading chair. It's easy to add or subtract holders. Simply adjust the length of the pine board to accommodate as many paint bucket roller grids as you need. The grids are reinforced with a wood cleat that also prevents papers from sliding through the bottom.

This design also would make a great addition to a home office as an organizer for paperwork, bills, and reference materials. Make a series of holders and keep specific items in each one. The finished project is practical and trendy, combining metal and natural light wood for a contemporary look.

1 CUT THE WOOD.
Cut one 1×12×60-inch select white pine board to 53 inches. Reserve the remaining piece.

2 CUT THE REMAINING WOOD.
Cut remaining piece of wood into four $1\frac{1}{4} \times 9\frac{3}{4}$-inch pieces. These will serve as supports for each metal holder.

3 SAND THE WOOD PIECES.
Sand the surfaces and edges of the wood pieces with fine-grit sandpaper. Clean and smooth as needed. Wipe with a tack cloth.

Customize your home storage with this sleek and functional magazine rack. Make several to outfit a home office or crafts room.

GOOD IDEA

DRYING TIME
After you sand and apply sealer to the pine board, allow plenty of drying time so you're not trying to work with wood that's tacky. You may mar the smooth finish.

TOOL SAVVY

USING SANDERS
Start and stop an orbital palm sander away from the wood. With an orbital sander you can sand with or across the grain. Let the sander do the work. Pushing down on it will leave marks. If you handsand always work with the grain.

4

APPLY SEALER.

Finish each wood piece with three coats of satin water base sealer, lightly sanding between coats. Allow the sealer to dry according to directions.

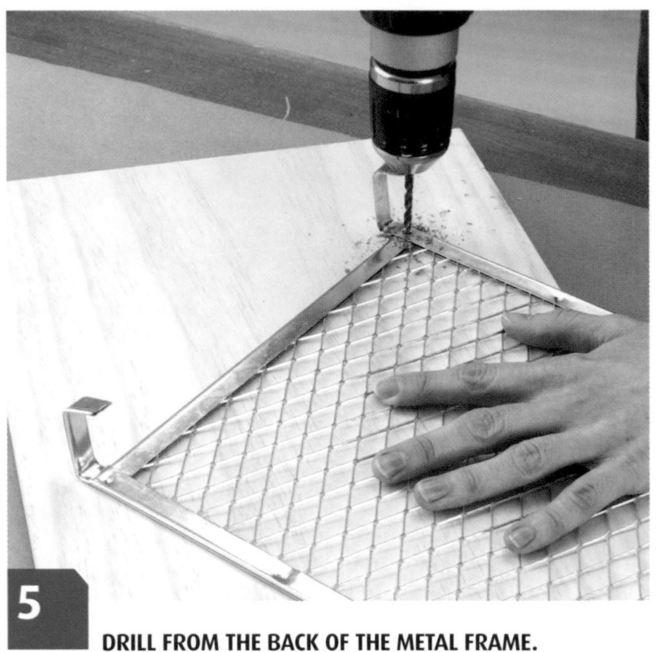

5

DRILL FROM THE BACK OF THE METAL FRAME.

Place scrap wood under the metal frame. Drill two holes from the backside of the metal frame surrounding the paint grid using the $^{11}/_{64}$-inch drill bit. The spots to drill are the dimples in the frame at the corners near the hook end.

6

DRILL FROM THE FRONT OF THE GRID.

With scrap wood still under the metal frame, drill two holes from the front side of the grid using the first two holes as guides. Drill through the end of the hook.

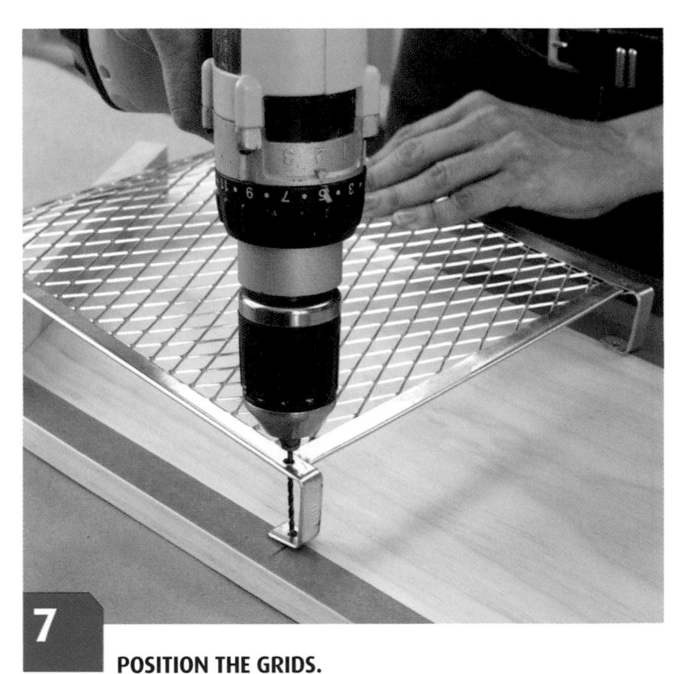

7

POSITION THE GRIDS.

Attach blue painter's tape along the long edges of the face of the board. Mark the tape from the top of the board at 13 inches, 25 ½ inches, 38 inches, and 50 ½ inches. Place the grids on the board one at a time, centered from right to left, positioning the holes over a set of marks on the blue tape. Drill pilot holes into the wood with the $^{7}/_{64}$-inch drill bit using the holes in the grid as a guide. As you drill shim up the end of the grate with one of the smaller pieces of wood.

8 **ATTACH THE GRIDS.**

Remove the blue tape. Attach the grids to the board using #8×2-inch roundhead slotted wood screws and #10 washers.

9 **SECURE A PIECE OF WOOD BETWEEN THE GRID AND BOARD.** Place one 1¼×9¾-inch piece of wood between the grid and the board. Rest the piece of wood on top of the screws holding in the metal to prevent magazines from falling through the bottom of each grid. You may need to loosen the screws slightly to accommodate the wood. Secure the 1¼×9¾-inch piece from the back of the plank with a 1¼-inch drywall screw.

10 **FASTEN HANGERS.**

Attach keyhole hangers to the backside. Note that the screws that come with the hanger probably will be too long. You will need to purchase four shorter screws (½-inch) that won't go through the wood.

Keep magazines neatly corralled in the slim-profile slots of this industrial-look wall organizer.

Two-coat paint finishes

PROJECT DETAILS

SKILLS: Sanding, painting

TIME TO COMPLETE

EXPERIENCED: 1 hr.
HANDY: 2 hrs.
NOVICE: 3 hrs.

STUFF YOU'LL NEED

TOOLS: Sanding block, 80-, 120-, 180-grit sandpaper, natural-bristle paint brush for oil, synthetic-bristle paint brush for latex, tack cloth
MATERIALS: Stain-sealing oil-base primer, latex paint in chosen base color

▲ **Two-coat paint finishes offer versatile decorating options. Similar pieces of furniture take on three distinct looks depending on the painting technique used. From top to bottom: sponging, antiquing, and crackling.**

Refinish antiques or make new pieces look vintage with many techniques and materials available. Sponging, antiquing, and crackling are effective treatments for unfinished pine and other furniture. Invest a few dollars and a little time to create a look to match your style.

Each of these finishes is a two-coat process; each coat is a different color. After the base coat dries, a second (and sometimes a third) color is applied over it.

Like most painting techniques, sponging, antiquing, and crackling began as specialty oil or lacquer finishes. Glazes and crackle mediums are available for easily applied latex-base paints. The finish begins with sanding, cleaning, and applying a base color.

- **Sponging** is the process of painting over the base coat by dabbing on paint with a sea sponge. It creates a multicolor finish without the difficulty of graining or marbling.
- **Antiquing** is the process of applying layers of paint and then hand-sanding through parts of the layers to reveal colors beneath.
- **Crackling** is the process of applying a base coat and covering it with a crackle medium. When you paint on a top coat, the medium causes it to crackle like a coat of old paint, revealing the color beneath.

Preparing for two-coat paint finishes

COMMON STEPS FOR ANTIQUING, SPONGING, AND CRACKLING

1 SAND THE SURFACE. Do not expect paint to hide dents, scratches, or machine marks left from planing at the lumber mill. Unless you want the flaws, and you might (see "Antiquing," page 179), take the time to get the surface exactly how you would like it before painting. Start with 80-grit sandpaper and move to 120-grit. Round over the edges and corners—paint won't stick to sharp edges. The edges should feel smooth to your hand. Finish with 180-grit paper.

Use the primer to help build up the color. Have The Home Depot tint the primer when they tint the paint. By putting about half as much tint in the primer, you can see what has been painted when you apply the top coat. Brush on the primer, let it dry, then sand with 120-grit paper.

APPLY THE BASE COLOR. The base color is the coat of paint that peeks through subsequent colors to create the desired effect. Choose a traditional color scheme or experiment with your own combinations. See page 10 for information about color palettes. Buy the paints for the entire color scheme from the same manufacturer.

3 WIPE OFF THE DUST WITH A DAMP RAG BEFORE PAINTING. Then brush on the base color. If the color looks good when it dries, you may not need to apply a second coat of the base. If primer shows through or if the color isn't as dark as it should be, sand the surface with 180-grit sandpaper and apply a second layer of base color. Once it dries apply the finish.

6 FURNISHINGS

Antiquing

PROJECT DETAILS

SKILLS: Sanding, painting

TIME TO COMPLETE

EXPERIENCED: 3 hrs.
HANDY: 4 hrs.
NOVICE: 5 hrs.

STUFF YOU'LL NEED

TOOLS: Several rings attached to large key ring, 80-, 120-, and 180-grit sandpaper, synthetic-bristle paintbrush, rubber gloves
MATERIALS: Latex paint

In the 19th century many pieces of furniture sported a bright coat of paint to bring color into the home. When its age began to show, the piece would be repainted—often in another color. Continued use caused the original color to wear through in exposed places, and that's what is simulated when you "antique" a piece of furniture. It's easy to do—apply two (or three) coats of paint, distress, and sand the piece to simulate everyday wear and tear. Choose your color scheme; then sand, prime, and apply the base color following the instructions on page 178. Then you're ready to begin antiquing. Dings and chips are common on the surfaces of old furniture so begin by distressing the surface.

GOOD IDEA

PRIME FIRST
Apply a stain-sealing primer. The primer provides a solid base for coats to follow. The stain sealers in the primer lock the resins in the wood to prevent them from bleeding through the paint and ruining your work. (Latex-base sealers sometimes allow the resins around knots to bleed through. Get an oil-base primer; finish coats can be latex.)

1 DISTRESS THE SURFACE.
Put a combination of old and new keys on a large key ring. The variations will help to vary the texture. Holding the keys by the ring, randomly bounce them against the surface to simulate wear. Make a few scratches with a coin or a nail; scrape off some paint by dragging the edge of a knife across a couple of spots. Once the piece is properly distressed, resand to simulate more wear.

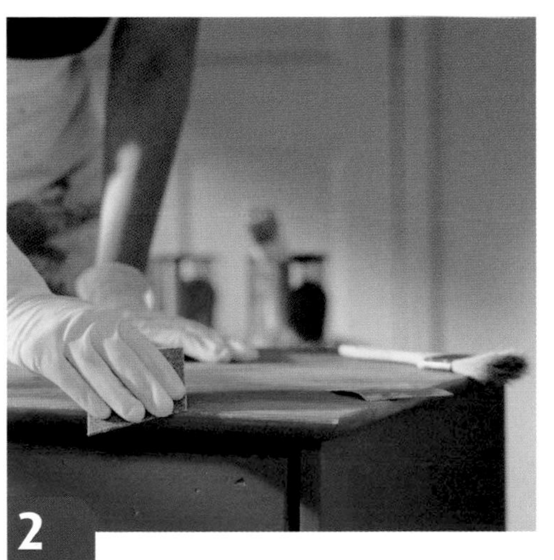

2 APPLY AND THEN DISTRESS THE TOP COAT. The color of the top coat contrasts with the base coat. Brush on the top coat, let it dry, and then distress this coat, using the techniques used previously. In occasional spots that would have received a lot of wear, sand through to the first coat, then sand through part of the first coat to reveal the wood. Elsewhere sand through the paint just enough to reveal the first coat. Repeat, if desired, with a third color and distress it also.

Prep work

As with all painted finishes, thoroughly clean and sand the surface before applying primer and a base coat of paint.

Two-coat paint finishes *(continued)*

Sponging

PROJECT DETAILS

SKILLS: Sponging

TIME TO COMPLETE

EXPERIENCED: 4 hrs.
HANDY: 5 hrs.
NOVICE: 6 hrs.

STUFF YOU'LL NEED

TOOLS: Mixing bucket, paint stir stick, flat container, sea sponge, paper plate or paper towel
MATERIALS: Choice of paint colors, glaze

Finisher's secret

Glaze is basically a neutral, colorless medium that allows you to work with several colors on a surface by extending the working time with the paint. The more glaze to paint in the ratio, the longer you can work the surface before it dries. The standard mix is one part paint to four parts glaze, but you can experiment with different proportions for different results.

Sponge painting, a technique for applying color over a base coat, achieves a multitone finish. A sponge-painted surface has a subtle and natural character that is more interesting than a plain-painted one. It's not used to imitate a particular effect but suggests fabric, stone, leaves, or a cloud-filled patch of sky. Commonly used on walls, sponging also works well on furniture—especially to differentiate one surface from another.

Before you begin, prep the surface according to the directions on page 178. Although you can sponge on a finish with plain paint, it works better when a glazing liquid is mixed with the paint. The glazing liquid has more body than paint and gives the sponged surface more depth and texture. It also makes the mixture workable for a longer time than plain paint. Follow the manufacturer's instructions for mixing the glazing liquid and paint.

A natural sea sponge works best to apply the glaze mix, although a synthetic sponge also may be used. Choose one that fits comfortably in your hand.

1 MIX THE PAINT AND GLAZE.
Glaze may be white or translucent—mix four parts glaze to one part paint. To keep the color constant, mix enough to do the entire job. The directions on the label will give you an idea of how much you need for a specific area. Once you mix the glaze, pour it into a flat container.

2 SPONGE ON THE GLAZE.
Dampen a sponge in water to help it absorb the glaze. Dip the sponge into the glaze and paint mixture and dab it on a paper plate or paper towel to remove the excess. If the paint drips when you apply it, dab more onto the plate. Apply the paint with a light touch. Work in random patterns or in rows and rotate the sponge so that the pattern constantly changes. Cover a 4×4-foot section and do the edges last so that they're wet and blend easily into the next section. After you finish each section, stand back to look at your work. If you see lines or patterns, blot on a little more glaze to break them up. Apply the next section, working from the wet edge.

3 ADD A SECOND COLOR.
If you apply a second color, wait at least 48 hours for the first coat of glaze to dry thoroughly. Sponge on the second color in the same way you applied the first.

Crackle finishing

PROJECT DETAILS

SKILLS: Painting

TIME TO COMPLETE

EXPERIENCED: 4 hrs.
HANDY: 5 hrs.
NOVICE: 6 hrs.

STUFF YOU'LL NEED

TOOLS: Synthetic-bristle paintbrush, pad, or roller
MATERIALS: Crackle medium, choice of latex paints, water-base polyurethane varnish (optional)

Often the top coat of paint on an old piece of furniture crackles with age and allows the previous layer of paint to peek through. Reproduce this look by painting a crackle medium, a technique once used only by professional finishers. First you'll need to prep the surface according to the directions on page 178. Once you have painted a base coat and allowed it to dry, paint the crackle medium on the surface. After this coat has dried, apply a top coat. Buy the same brand of paint and crackle medium because the two usually are formulated to work together.

Alter the effect of the crackle finish by wiping an artist's oil, colored wax, or wood stain into the cracks. Be sure to wipe away the excess and let it dry thoroughly before sealing with a clear top coat.

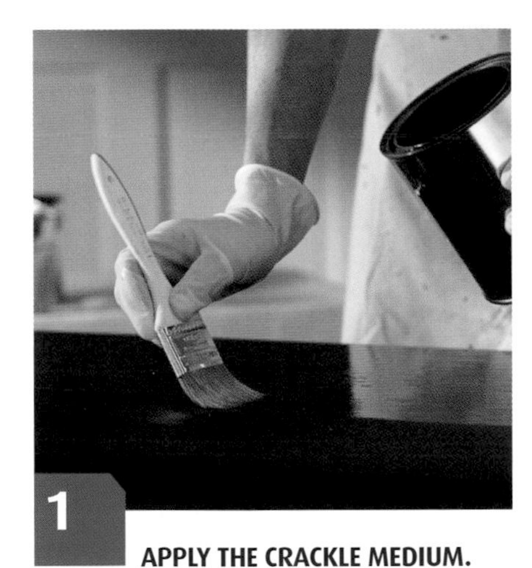

1 APPLY THE CRACKLE MEDIUM.
Once the base coat has dried, paint on the crackle medium with a brush, pad, or roller. Let it dry as recommended, usually 1 to 4 hours.

2 APPLY THE TOP COAT.
Use a matte or satin paint—gloss paints usually crackle poorly. The more paint you apply, the larger the cracks. Control this by the way you apply the paint. Sponging it on tends to apply less paint and results in smaller cracks. Brushing applies more paint, resulting in larger cracks. Whichever method you choose avoid going over the same area twice; it will either fill the cracks or cause the top coat to lift.

3 APPLY A CLEAR SEALER COAT.
A crackle finish may need as much as a month of curing time before it can be subjected to everyday use. If the surface will receive frequent use, especially if it is exposed to spills, protect it with a coat of clear shellac or water-base polyurethane.

Ottoman

PROJECT DETAILS

SKILLS: Cutting, basic carpentry

TIME TO COMPLETE

EXPERIENCED: 3 hrs.
HANDY: 4 hrs.
NOVICE: 5 hrs.

STUFF YOU'LL NEED

TOOLS: Tape measure, pencil, tablesaw, eye protection, four 2-inch spring clamps, needle-nose pliers, hammer, lighter, hot-glue gun, tape, scissors
MATERIALS: One 4-foot piece of 2×2-inch wood cut to four 10¼-inch lengths, two 24-inch-diameter pieces of round particleboard, small box of #18 ⅝-inch wire nails, ⅛-inch tempered hardboard cut to make two 11½×48-inch panels, wood glue, five ball casters, twenty ¾-inch wood screws, 200-foot spool of twisted polypropylene rope

GOOD IDEA

EASY ROLLING
Leave the twisted poly rope on the spool in its box as you work. Set the spool box next to you on the floor. The rope will neatly and easily unwind as you wrap the ottoman.

▲ **This handy ottoman is large enough to double as a coffee table or extra seat.**

This stylish ottoman started as a few boards and a big spool of rope. The polypropylene rope that covers the frame is available in a pleasing camel color that's right at home in a palette of neutral, natural browns and golds. The top and bottom are sturdy pieces of particleboard that you can purchase precut to the right size and shape—no attempting to cut tricky circles for this project. Wrap hardboard around a frame of 2×2 board, and you have a solid foundation for a functional piece. Five ball casters lend stability and make it easy to move the ottoman wherever it is needed. The piece is large enough to double as a coffee table and as an extra seat. Go ahead—sit down and rest your feet when you have finished this project; it's as sturdy as it is stylish.

1 CUT SUPPORTS TO LENGTH.
Using a tablesaw cut four 10¼-inch lengths of 2×2-inch wood pieces. These will connect the top and bottom of the ottoman and provide a framework for the hardboard.

2 BUILD THE FRAMEWORK.
Position the four 10¼×2×2-inch wood pieces upright between the 24-inch rounds. Place them equidistant. Align an edge of each with the edge of the round. Use glue and screws or nails to join the rounds and the 2×2s.

3 RESIZE THE HARDBOARD.
Cut the hardboard to two 11½×48-inch pieces. You'll wrap the frame with these before applying the rope finish.

Polypropylene rope has a smooth finish ideal for this ottoman. The piece may be used for seating as well as putting your feet up. Sisal rope would offer a more rustic look, but it can be scratchy.

WORK SMARTER

FIND A HELPER
It will be easier to work with the hardboard panel if a helper holds the board in place while you attach it to the frame.

TOOL SAVVY

CLAMP IT
Even if you have a helper for this project, use clamps to assist in securing the hardboard around the frame.

4 **MARK THE PANEL.**

Using spring clamps, clamp an 11½-inch end of the panel to the center of one of the 2×2s. Draw a pencil line on the 2×2 to mark where the panel begins. Bend the panel halfway around and mark it so the panel can be cut to end in the center of another 2×2. This measurement will be approximately 37 inches.

5 **ATTACH THE PANEL.**

Remove the panel and cut it to the proper length. Clamp, bend, and mark the second piece of panel. Cut it to the proper length. Clamp a panel in place with spring clamps. Beginning at one end glue and nail it to the 2×2. Continue nailing the edge of the panel to the particleboard, placing nails every 2 inches. Needle-nose pliers can be used to hold the nails if they are too small to handle with your fingers. Finish nailing the other end of the panel to the opposite 2×2.

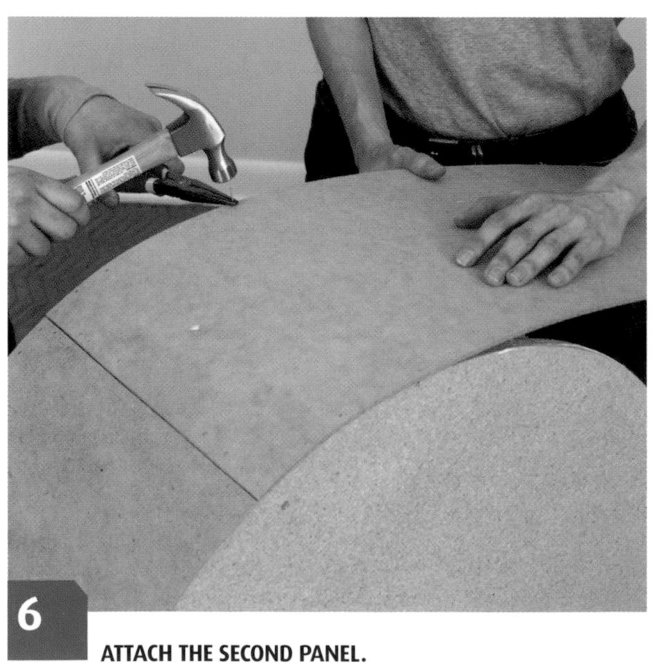

6 **ATTACH THE SECOND PANEL.**

Begin gluing and nailing the end of the second panel to a 2×2 so it forms a seam with the first panel. Have a friend help bend and hold the panel while you glue and nail it in place.

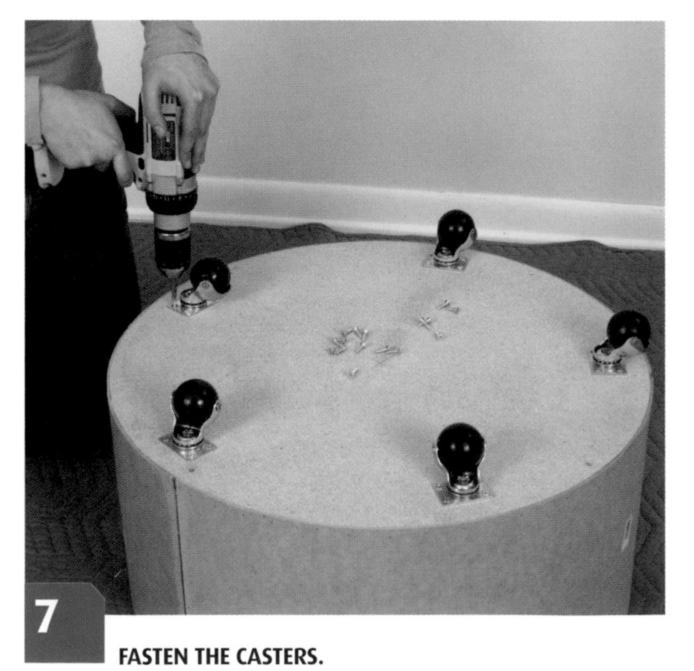

7 **FASTEN THE CASTERS.**

Position the five casters equidistant around the perimeter of the base. Make sure the casters are not positioned too close to the edge. They should not stick out beyond the sides of the ottoman. Attach the five casters to the bottom with ¾-inch wood screws.

8

MELT THE ROPE END.

To prevent the end of the rope from fraying, use a flame to seal the end of it. Use care when working with an open flame.

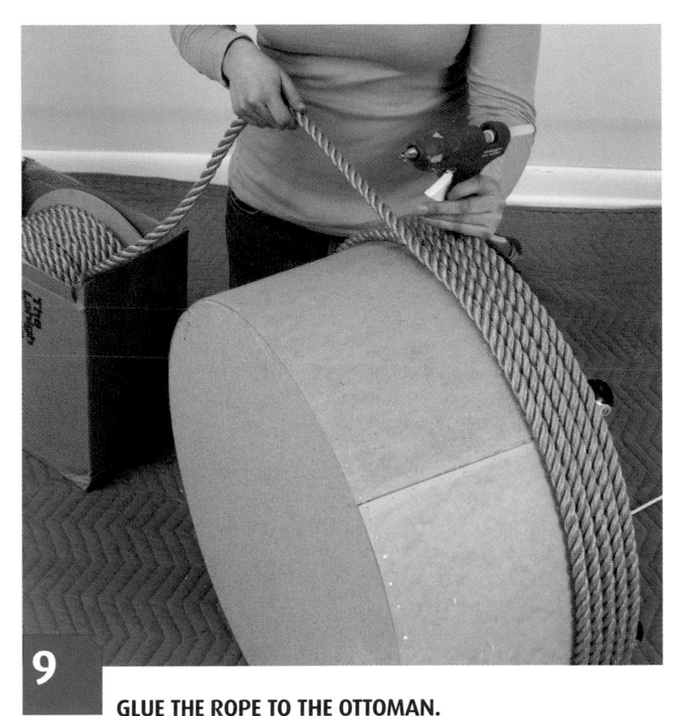

9

GLUE THE ROPE TO THE OTTOMAN.

Beginning at the bottom hot-glue the rope around the side of the frame, continuing to glue and wrap the rope around the ottoman, working your way to the top. Carefully glue at the top edge and continue to wrap the rope around the top, spiraling into the center. Rotate the ottoman on the casters to make wrapping the rope easier.

10

CUT THE ROPE.

When about 1 foot of rope is left before reaching the center, wrap it to the center to determine where it should be cut. Wrap a piece of tape around the rope to the inside of where it will be cut. Use a sharp scissors to cut the rope.

11

SEAL AND GLUE THE ROPE END.

Carefully use a flame to seal the end of the rope to prevent unraveling. Glue the remaining loose rope in place.

RESOURCES

The Home Depot offers products and materials from major manufacturers either in stock or through special order. This extensive inventory offers customers a comprehensive and varied selection that will ensure a home interior that truly reflects their personal style and taste while enabling them to stick to a realistic budget. Each project in this book contains a detailed list of tools and materials. Further information about products and materials can be obtained from Home Depot stores.

Contacting Meredith Corporation
To order this and other Meredith Corporation books call 800/678-8091. For further information about the information contained in this book contact Meredith by e-mail at hi123@mdp.com or by phone at 800/678-2093.

Contacting The Home Depot
For general information about product availability contact your local Home Depot or visit The Home Depot website at www.homedepot.com.

Special thanks to the following organizations and corporations whose products were instrumental in creating this book:

Behr Process Corporation
3400 W. Segerstrom Avenue
Santa Ana, CA 92704
800/854-0133, Ext. 2
www.behrpaint.com

Glidden
800/454-3336

Pier 1 Imports

Ralph Lauren Paint
800/379-7656

World Market

The listings below include the paint manufacturer, the color name, and the manufacturer's color reference number for many of the wall coverings seen in this book.

Page 34—Floor Screen
Wall Color: Ralph Lauren in Faded Seafoam, VM125
Trim Color: Ralph Lauren in Old Violin, VM91

Page 44—No Miter/No Cope Baseboard
Back Wall Color: Behr in Lost Atlantis, 580F-6
Trim Color: Behr in Frost, 1857
Front Wall Color: Behr in Applesauce, 350C-3

Page 47—No Miter/No Cope Baseboard
Trim Color: Behr in Frost, 1857
Front Wall Color: Behr in Applesauce, 350C-3

Page 48—Gallery of Molding Ideas
Lower Wall Color: Behr in Egyptian Nile, 420F-6
Upper Wall Color: Behr in Rejuvenate, 410E-3
Trim Color: Behr in Cottage White, 1813

Page 50—Tin Tile Backsplash
Wall Color: Behr in Sagey, 420F-4

Page 54—Magnetic Chalkboard
Wall Color: Behr in Cafe Pink, 130C-2
Trim Color: Behr in Popped Corn, W-B-200
Alphabet Paint: Rustoleum Chalk Board Paint
Green Table Paint: Glidden in Tart Apple, 420B-4
Blue Chair Legs: Glidden in Ocean Ridge, 580D-5
White Chairs: Behr in Popped Corn, W-B-200

Page 56—Message Center
Wall Color: Ralph Lauren in Burlap, NA11
Desk: Cost Plus World Market
Chair: Cost Plus World Market
File Cabinet: Cost Plus World Market
Waste Basket: Cost Plus World Market

Page 62—Plywood Accent Wall
Wall Color: Behr in Smokey Slate, 460E-3

Page 70—Faux Fireplace
Wall Color: Glidden in Cozy Melon, 70YR 45/261
Mantel Color: Glidden in Bone White, 30YY 72/097

Page 78—Headboard
Wall Color: Ralph Lauren in Pomegranate, VM72
Bedding: Target
Lamp: The Home Depot

Page 82—Medallion Frame
Wall Color: Behr in Boston Brick, 160F-6

Page 84—Etched Mirror
Wall Color: Behr in Rockwood Jade, 440C-3

Page 92—Folding Screen
Wall Color: Ralph Lauren in Faded Seafoam, VM125
Trim Color: Ralph Lauren in Old Violin, VM91

Page 96—Ceiling Fans
Wall Color: Ralph Lauren in Mango Gold, VM34
Trim Color: Ralph Lauren in Evocative Sunlight, VM29

Page 106—Sisal Rug
Wall Color: Behr in Rockwood Jade, 440C-3
Outside Armoire Color: Glidden in Blue Phlox, 58BB 33/270
Inside Armoire Color: Glidden in Spring Fest, 30GY 62/344

Page 116—Carpet Floor Tiles
Main Wall Color: Glidden in Bangor Blue, 50BB 33/164
Map Border Color: Glidden in Woodland Mystery, 90YY 52/138

Page 118
Wall Color: Behr in Boston Brick, 160F-6
Trim Color: Behr in Desert Camel, 320F

Page 120—Roll-Down Shade
Wall Color: Glidden in Mayflower Blue, 70BG 41/201
Trim Color: Glidden in Swiss Coffee, 50YY 83/057

Page 126—Valances
Wall Color: Behr in Boston Brick, 160F-6
Trim Color: Behr in Desert Camel, 320F

Page 132—Door Trim and Molding
Lower Wall Color: Behr in Egyptian Nile, 420F-6
Upper Wall Color: Behr in Rejuvenate, 410E-3
Trim Color: Behr in Cottage White, 1813

Page 134
Wall Color: Ralph Lauren in Tapestry, NA25
Trim Color: Ralph Lauren in White
Bookcase: Cost Plus World Market
Print on Wall: Cost Plus World Market

Page 136—Lighting Plans
Wall Color: Behr in Gallery Red, 150F-6

Page 140—Chandelier Embellishment
Wall Color: Behr in Calm Air, 300E-2

Page 144—Trapeze Lights
Wall Color: Behr in Wine Barrel, 200F-7
Trim Color: Behr in Almond Cream, W-B-710

Page 146—Table Lamp
Wall Color: Ralph Lauren in Tapestry, NA25
Trim Color: Ralph Lauren in White
Bookcase: Cost Plus World Market
Print on Wall: Cost Plus World Market

Page 150
Wall Color: Behr in Eggshell Cream, W-D-300
Colorwash on Wall: Behr in Colorado Springs, 570D-4
Trim Color: Behr in Eggshell Cream, W-D-300

Page 156—Cabinet Door Insert
Wall Color: Behr in Eggshell Cream, W-D-300
Colorwash on Wall: Behr in Colorado Springs, 570D-4
Trim Color: Behr in Eggshell Cream, W-D-300

Page 158—Wood Veneer
Wall Color: Glidden in Jonquil Yellow, 40YY 71/335

Page 160—Toe-Kick Feet
Wall Color: Behr in Sagey, 420F-4

Page 162—Custom Molding Shelf
Wall Color: Glidden in Pacific Pines, 90YY 35/169

Page 168—Garden-Inspired Shelf
Wall Color: Glidden in Cozy Melon, 70YR 45/261

Page 170—Side Table
Wall Color: Ralph Lauren in Faded Seafoam, VM125
Trim Color: Ralph Lauren in Old Violin, VM91

Page 174—Magazine Rack
Wall Color: Ralph Lauren in County Cork, NA06

Page 182—Ottoman
Wall Color: Glidden in Grand Canyon, 20YY 49/271
Chair: Pier 1 Imports
Pendent Light: The Home Depot
Mirror: Pier 1 Imports

INDEX

INDEX

Dale Solomon
San Diego, CA

Debi Peoples
Rancho Cucamonga, CA

Dionne Collins
Woodland Hills, CA

Edna Atkins
Willow Grove, PA

Ed Czyr
Landsdale, PA

Erica Barrett
Downers Grove, IL

Greg Korczak
Lodi, NJ

Jerry Allen
Tustin, CA

Jerry Brennan
Westminister, CA

Jim Pellegrini
Jericho, NY

John Rimar
Parlin, NJ

Joseph Palinsky
S. Plainfield, NJ

Josephine Jackson
Bronx, NY

Many thanks to the employees of The Home Depot® whose "wisdom of the aisles" has made Decorating Projects 1-2-3® **the most useful book of its kind.**

Julie Kay Lenz
Deerfield, IL

Karen Soneson
Aurora, IL

Kelly Banducci
San Leandro, CA

Lonnie Siemons
Crystal Lake, IL

Tom Sattler
Atlanta, GA

Mel Sanders
Totowa, NJ

Mike Alfieri
Temecula, CA

Richard Unnasch
Clifton, NJ

Robert Ferrand
Huntington Beach, CA

Romeo Julian
Chicago, IL

Steve Smith
La Quinta, CA

Terry Clayton
Upland, CA

Terri Sanders
Elgin, IL

Thomas J. Brockett
Darien, IL

Wilfrid Feteau
Evanston, IL

Toolbox essentials: nuts-and-bolts books for do-it-yourself success.

Save money, get great results, and take the guesswork out of home improvement projects with a growing library of step-by-step books from the experts at The Home Depot®.

Packed with lots of projects and practical tips, these books help you design, remodel, decorate, and repair your home or garden. Easy-to-follow, step-by-step instructions and colorful photographs ensure success. Projects even estimate time, skills, materials needed, and tools required.

**You can do it.
We can help.℠**

Look for the books that help you say "I can do that!" at The Home Depot®, www.meredithbooks.com, or wherever quality books are sold.

DPT0173_07